Public Lands in the Western US

Public Lands in the Western US

Place and Politics in the Clash between Public and Private

Edited by
Kathleen M. Sullivan and
James H. McDonald

LEXINGTON BOOKS
Lanham • Boulder • New York • London

Published by Lexington Books
An imprint of The Rowman & Littlefield Publishing Group, Inc.
4501 Forbes Boulevard, Suite 200, Lanham, Maryland 20706
www.rowman.com

6 Tinworth Street, London SE11 5AL, United Kingdom

British Library Cataloguing in Publication Information Available

Library of Congress Cataloging-in-Publication Data

Library of Congress Control Number: 2020944427
ISBN 978-1-7936-3706-2 (cloth)
ISBN 978-1-7936-3707-9 (electronic)

Contents

PART I: OVERVIEW 1

Introduction 3
James H. McDonald and Kathleen M. Sullivan

1 Public Lands through the Prism of Senses of Place 11
Kathleen M. Sullivan and James H. McDonald

PART II: EXPLORING SENSES OF PLACE 33

2 The New Wild West: The Range War as Revitalization Movement 35
James H. McDonald

3 Public Land, Place, and Shadow Displacement in Rural Utah 59
Bruce R. Tebbs and James H. McDonald

4 Claiming the Los Angeles River for "the Public," by Boat and by Permit 67
Sayd Randle

5 Chile and New Mexico: Identity, Difference, and Place 81
David Knowlton

PART III: PRACTICES AND CONTEXTS OF COLLABORATION AND CONFLICT 99

6 A Reckoning of the Nuclear West 101
Jonathan P. Thompson

7 Public Lands Security: The Dispute over Federal versus Local Law Enforcement 115
Jacqueline J. Russell

8 Restoring Wild Bison in the Heart of Cattle Country: Yellowstone's Political Firestorm 133
Scott Turner

9 Through a Forest Wilderness: Native American Environmental Management at Yosemite and Contested Conservation Values in America's National Parks 151
Rochelle Bloom and Douglas Deur

10 Nature's Belonging: Landscape, Conservation, and the Cultural Politics of Place in the Great Basin 175
Paul Berne Burow

Index 199

About the Editors 209

About the Contributors 211

Part I

OVERVIEW

Introduction

James H. McDonald and Kathleen M. Sullivan

Public lands in America have long been a flashpoint for controversy and conflict. These clashes usually fall along the fault lines of federal versus state control, public versus private ownership, environmental conservation versus extractive economies. Of course, these tensions comingle to a considerable degree. At the same time, public lands are increasingly serving as vehicles for coordination and collaboration between state, federal, and tribal governments.

For those not living in or familiar with the western United States, it is hard to imagine its vastness and how much of that land is under public control. The U.S. government owns 47 percent of the land in western states and that figure rises considerably in places such as Utah and Nevada. The vast majority of federal public land is under the stewardship of the Bureau of Land Management (BLM; 41 percent or 247.3 million acres), followed by the U.S. Forest Service (USFS; 32 percent or 192.9 million acres), the U.S. Fish and Wildlife Service (USFWS; 14 percent or 89.1 million acres), and finally the National Park Service (NPS; 13 percent or 79.6 million acres) (Bui and Sanger-Katz 2016). Public lands dominate the landscape and have shaped peoples' lives for generations. Because we are dealing with such a massive resource, it is not surprising that there is conflict over control, ownership, access, exploitation, and conservation.

One might well ask why there is so much public land in the western United States, but not elsewhere in the United States? It is largely a matter of geography, environment, climate, the lure of developing resource extraction economies (mining, ranching, timber, power generation), and social history. Although the federal government was at several points in history keen to settle vast areas of the United States by enticing settlers to create farms and farming towns, especially in woodlands and prairies, much of the land in the western United States is not well-suited to settler society farming practices.

So while a vast amount of federal land was transferred as a private title to homesteader farmers, this did not occur to anywhere near the same extent in the western United States as in the remainder of the country. Indeed, much of the public land in the western states is arid mountainous or desert terrain, and the balance, while suitable for ranching and grazing, did not fit the settler society smallholder model. Settlers, who chose to ranch and graze cattle and sheep, many initially by way of utilizing concessions made by the Spanish Crown, and later through land grants and purchases, ignored carrying capacity, and trampled the soils, freshwater resources, already-established plant communities, and displaced indigenous fauna (Schiffman 2005). However, these lands, plants, fauna, and water resources have been extensively used by many different groups of Native North Americans since time immemorial, including farmers, gatherers, hunters, and sedentary as well as more nomadic societies.

An enduring meta-narrative of the legacy of settler colonialism that has shaped and continues to shape the American West ties the chapters of our volume together. Settler colonialism undergirds the expropriation of Native North Americans' lands and resources, as well as the creation of a reservation system; the formation of the public lands management systems, such as the BLM; the use of large tracts of public lands for various types of polluting, labor-exploitative resource extraction; federal and state laws and policies that shape those lands and the activities undertaken on them or excluded from them; and the complicated relationship between rural, settler communities, and the ranching and mineral economies. The roots of these practices lie in the intersection of contested sovereignties, racial logics, and industrial capital enlightenment ideology. All three logics are embodied in the notion of "manifest destiny"; settler society's westward expansion was inevitable, justified, and necessary. European settler colonialism relies on a cultural logic that entitles its practitioners to remove all obstacles in their way in order to exploit resources that fuel intensive and expansive capitalist growth and expansion.

It is well documented that as European settlers increasingly moved westward in the 1800s, what they saw as the "Indian problem" became one of pacification, removal, containment, and genocide (cf. Hixson 2013). A scant settler population of 1 million in 1815 balloons into 15 million by 1860 (Hixson 2013). Castillo (1978) and Whyte (2018) both argue eloquently about the disruptive dynamics of European settlers on First Peoples' communities and relationships with the environment, particularly given that settler missionizing and settler systems of forced labor were often crucial to maintaining the settler ranching economy being established, and later the mining industry.

The case of the Shoshone-Bannock in Idaho is instructive in this regard. The group was relocated to a reservation near Pocatello in 1868. Farming and hunting on their newly restricted range proved unsustainable and promised government provisions never arrived in sufficient quantities. Shoshone-Bannock hunters would head northeast into the newly established Yellowstone Park (dedicated in 1872) only to find that they were barred from entry (though they kept coming into the 1890s). Burnham (2000) notes that the Anglo-American notion of the wilderness was one of a place that was pristine and devoid of humans. Yellowstone was, thus, founded on a myth that its landscape was so forbidding that Indians avoided it. In contrast, the area had long been used by Shoshone, Bannock, and Crow people. In the Yellowstone Museum at Mammoth, a 1907 Department of Interior notice outlines the "Rules and Regulations of the Yellowstone National Park":

1. No damaging natural resources.
2. No turning livestock loose within park boundaries.
3. No logging or otherwise injuring trees.
4. Fires should be lit only when necessary and fully extinguished.
5. Hunting, killing, wounding, or capturing wild birds or animals are prohibited.
6. Fishing is prohibited.
7. People cannot reside in the park.
8. Persons who render themselves obnoxious or violate park rules will be removed.

These exclusionary policies were mostly about removing and then keeping Native North Americans out. The Shoshone-Bannock even took their case to the courts to argue that their 1868 treaty gave them access to unoccupied land to search for wild game. It was, then, argued that the provisions of the treaty expired when Wyoming became a state in 1890. Ironically, in a recent court case, this was overturned, and Crow and Shoshone-Bannock hunting access was granted (McFarland 2019). The favorable decision for the Crow, as well as the Shoshone-Bannock, suggests that the 1868 treaty remains viable.

When exploring the formation of the nation's largest public lands agencies, we will see in the chapters that follow that the BLM and USFS were formed to manage access to economic resources (grazing, logging, and mineral extraction) at cost rates far below those found in the private sector. This was an arrangement that directly benefited settlers and allowed the formation of their communities and their exploitation of resources in Native North American lands.

The case of the NPS is a different story. The NPS and the national parks and monuments, such as the national wildlife refuges managed by the USFWS, were created to conserve and preserve rather than exploit western lands, but again with settler society as the main beneficiary. As Powell (2016) notes, America's majestic national parks were intended for urban middle- and upper-class white tourists as a way to reinvigorate them after the debilitating experience of city life. Additionally, park landscapes served as a material representation of national grandeur and power (Burnham 2000).

Public lands are sites of resource extraction with mining and drilling being, arguably, some of the most damaging to both humans and the environment. Remarkably, the extraction of hard-rock minerals (e.g., coal, uranium, gold, silver, or copper) is still governed by the antiquated Mining Act of 1872, and its subsequent amendments. Companies can lease public lands and leave behind moonscapes, do not usually pay royalties to the government on profits, and have few safeguards on air, water, or wildlife protection to manage. Palmer and Miller (2019) underscore the breadth of these mining practices, which have polluted 40 percent of the headwaters of western waterways, and left behind 161,000 abandoned mines; all at a cost of $50 billion dollars in cleanup and mitigation. In other words, federal and state governments are regulating mining like it is 1872 and not the early twenty-first century. Arguably, one of the most noteworthy of these mining practices was the extraction of uranium that occurred from World War II to 1971, almost exclusively in the western United States. Native North Americans, and most notably the Diné (Navajos) and Pueblo nations, continue to grapple with the impacts, for they worked in mines and mills. Exposure to uranium dust led to disastrous health outcomes, including high rates of lung cancer and other respiratory diseases (see Brugge and Goble 2002). At present, and in a similar vein, there are increasing numbers of polluting power generation plants being developed on Diné lands.

Throughout the west, but especially the intermountain west, ranching is another ubiquitous feature of the rural economy. Open-range cattle and sheep ranching would be impossible without extensive access to public lands taken from a variety of Native North American groups, and now managed by the BLM and the USFS. Not surprisingly, ranching culture takes on something of a primordial character in many parts of the western United States. Across the western states, annual Western Heritage festivals and rodeos celebrate and defend the hegemony of the settler ranching economy.

Look no further than the Kanab, Utah webpage, which touts the place as "magically unspoiled" (Kanab n.d.). Annually they sponsor a "Western Legends Heritage and Music Festival" that celebrates "our western heritage of old tough and true cowboys, movie history, and the stars that come with it, as well as music old and new that keep our western hearts alive" (Kanab n.d.). Even the event itself is couched in primordial terms: "Previously, Western Legends Roundup has been an event that generations have attended and loved for the last 20 years" (Kanab n.d.). There is also a rodeo, battle of the country bands, and lots of barbeque.

Up the road in Cedar City, Utah, the 2015 Western Freedom Festival was a more political-ideological affair framed by "traditions of freedom, faith, family, and economic prosperity" and the "real harm being done to good people by overbearing and heavy-handed regulatory overreach" (Hyde 2015). Further, "long-held traditions are being regulated out of existence and for the first time in generations, Southern Utahns are in danger of losing touch with their heritage" and "a people who forget where they came from are apt to forget who they are. Those who do not understand their own history become little children who depend upon self-appointed experts to tell them what to think of themselves" (Hyde 2015). Here, again, we see strong appeals to what is characterized as a rapidly disappearing way of life with no mention of the trauma that has been wrought on the Southern Paiute by the federal Indian termination policy of 1953, just one in a series of U.S. federal and state efforts to extinguish Native North American sovereign entities, rights, and Title, and to force assimilation. In the 1980s, the Southern Paiute received federal recognition anew through the Paiute Indian Tribe of Utah Restoration Act of 1980. Native North Americans' struggle to retain autonomy, resources and lands, and federal recognition have taken a steep toll on the cultural and material resources of the tribe, a toll which goes unrecognized and unacknowledged in these local settler society rancher heritage festivals materializing place and identity.

Several recent federal administrations have encouraged more conservation-oriented efforts regarding public lands in western states, as well as insisting on increased coordination and collaboration between tribal governments, state governments, and the federal family of agencies. However, the Trump administration has reversed course, and reduced the size of major monuments, for example, Bears Ears and Grand Staircase-Escalante in Utah, and is working to open those now unprotected lands to mining and drilling for resources ranging from coal to uranium to oil and natural gas (The Guardian 2020). This is very unfortunate, because prior to the Trump administration, Bears Ears National Monument stands as one of the premier examples of a successful collaboration between Native North American tribal governments, state, and federal governments. Meanwhile, the Trump administration is also keen on reducing ocean monuments in the Atlantic and Pacific to allow for increased commercial fishing. Taken together the U.S. ocean monuments exceed the size of California (Milman 2018).

In these divisive times, our volume brings an anthropological, historical, and broad social science perspective to the debates, clashes, and collaborative efforts over public lands, in an especially timely and useful way. This volume emerged out of a 2017 session at the Society for Applied Anthropology entitled, "Public Lands and Seas: What Public? Whose Ownership? Which Experts?" Our approach has been decidedly historical, ethnographic, local, and fine-grained, and our intent is to unpack the stories and complicated dynamics of the myriad struggles and collaborations over public lands. Such an approach underscores the nuances of these clashes and collaborative efforts in terms of cultural logics, ideologies, public policies, and on-the-ground practices. In so doing, our authors reveal how public lands become interpolated with peoples' identities, senses of place, and operate as a central feature to their stories. Rather than presenting readers with broad and sweeping portraits of the political, legal, economic, environmental, historical analyses of public lands, we offer an alternative that better frames and foregrounds the complexities that undergird public lands debates and conflicts.

The volume also comes out of personal experience. I (McDonald) lived and worked in far southwestern Utah in the heart of militia country where the public lands debate was front and center in everyday political discourse and practice. It was a place where major public land managers, the BLM and the USFS, had to put locked doors, metal detectors, and surveillance cameras on their office entries. Public land, its ownership, and its use, was an always-hot topic. It is also important to acknowledge that I lived and worked on occupied land that belongs to the Southern Paiute and who are today recognized as the Paiute Indian Tribe of Utah made up of the Cedar, Indian Peaks, Kanosh, Koosharem, and Shivwits bands. I (Sullivan) grew up in the western states and worked as a Cultural Resource Management (CRM) archaeologist on western public lands for several years after graduating with my BA. I now conduct ethnographic field research into west coast oceans governance issues, coordination efforts between states, tribal, and federal governments, and the social side of oceans, coastal zone estuaries, and freshwater resources. I have spent my life living, working, and playing on the sovereign lands and waters of a number of different First Nations and Native North American nations, and I express my appreciation and gratitude at having been able to do so. We are both concerned with the dynamic tensions between conservation efforts, the growth of polluting industries, increasing commercialization and urbanization, as well as unrecognized and barely recognized time immemorial sovereignties. We feel that our readers will sense the immediacy and urgency of the public lands issues highlighted in this volume, for these concerns are also borne out of personal experiences that have fundamentally shaped both of us as scholars, teachers, citizens, and people.

REFERENCES CITED

Brugge, Doug, and Rob Goble. 2002. The History of Uranium Mining and the Navajo People. *American Journal of Public Health* 92(9):1410–19.

Bui, Quoctrung, and Margot Sanger-Katz. 2016. Why the Government Owns So Much Land in the West. *New York Times*. https://www.nytimes.com/2016/01/06/upshot/why-the-government-owns-so-much-land-in-the-west.html (Accessed March 7, 2020).

Burnham, Philip. 2000. *Indian Country, God's Country: Native Americans and the National Parks*. Washington, DC: Island Press.

Castillo, Edward. 1978. The Impact of Euro-American Exploration and Settlement. In *Handbook of North American Indians*, edited by Robert F. Heizer, vol. 8. Washington, DC: Smithsonian Institute.

The Guardian. 2020. Trump Finalizes Plans to Open Monuments for Mining and Drilling. https://www.theguardian.com/environment/2020/feb/06/trump-utah-national-parks-energy-development-drilling (Accessed March 7, 2020).

Hixson, Walter L. 2013. *American Settler Colonialism: A History*. New York: Palgrave Macmillan.

Hyde, Bryan. 2015. Perspectives: The Western Freedom Festival, Why Heritage Matters. *St. George News*. https://www.stgeorgeutah.com/news/archive/2015/07/20/perspectives-western-freedom-festival-heritage-matters/#.XuaVZ0VKh1t (Accessed June 12, 2020).

Kanab, n.d. Town Webpage. https://visitsouthernutah.com/ (accessed June 12, 2020).

McFarland, Clair. 2019. Shoshones Claim Hunting Rights Under Court Ruling. Northern Wyoming News. https://www.wyodaily.com/story/2019/10/31/news/shoshones-claim-hunting-rights-under-court-ruling/9920.html (Accessed June 13, 2020).

Milman, Oliver. 2018. Trump Plans to Shrink Ocean Monuments Threatens Vital Ecosystems, Experts Warn. *The Guardian*. https://www.theguardian.com/environment/2018/jan/02/us-ocean-monuments-environment-trump (Accessed March 7, 2020).

Palmer, Tim, and Char Miller. 2019. Op-Ed: Why Let Mining Companies Rip Up Public Land Like It's 1872? *Los Angeles Times*. https://www.latimes.com/opinion/op-ed/la-oe-palmer-miller-1872-mining-law-20190412-story.html (Accessed June 12, 2020).

Powell, Miles A. 2016. *Vanishing America: Species Extinction, Racial Peril, and the Origins of Conservation*. Cambridge, MA: Harvard University Press.

Schiffman, Paula M. 2005. The Los Angeles Prairie. In *Land of Sunshine: An Environmental History of Metropolitan*, edited by William Deverell and Greg Hise, pp. 38–51. Pittsburgh, PA: University of Pittsburgh Press.

Whyte, Kyle. 2018. Settler Colonialism, Ecology, and Environmental Justice. *Environment and Society: Advances in Research* 9:125–44.

Chapter 1

Public Lands through the Prism of Senses of Place

Kathleen M. Sullivan and James H. McDonald

This chapter provides a survey of the literature in the form of a critique in order to ground the case-study chapters that follow. Senses of place and public lands are inseparably intertwined and endowed with social meaning. We argue that senses of place underpin practices of access, development, conservation, management, and policing on public lands and at its boundaries, and are the sites of often contentious local, regional, and national placemaking projects that are often dominated by politically and economically powerful groups of people.[1]

During 2016, the United States celebrated in media-saturated style the 100th anniversary of the National Park system, a celebration fostered by the Obama administration, along with Obama's Executive Orders and uses of the 1906 Antiquities Act to further conserve and preserve federal public lands. Meanwhile, the daily news also covered armed grazing stand-offs between ranchers and federal agents in Oregon (Turkewitz and Healy 2016; Turkewitz and Lightblau 2016), and law enforcement agents using tear gas, bean bag guns, and water cannons to prevent the Standing Rock Sioux Nation and their supporters from stopping the Dakota Access pipeline crossing the Standing Rock Sioux Reservation and territory, and endangering freshwater resources (Skalicky and Davey 2016; Upadhye 2016; Upadhye and Healy 2016).

During Trump's 2016–2020 term, his administration has systematically dismantled a broad array of conservation protections on western public lands currently sequestered in national monuments, parks, coastal zones, wildlife refuges, and the outer continental shelf, and has strongly promoted and supported new and expanded uranium mining and production, coal, oil, and gas development, and increased grazing on federal public lands (Turkewitz, Popovich, and McCann 2017; also the publication *High Country News* consistently examines federal administrative and Native North American nations' efforts in western states). The Trump administration's approach echoes and methodically surpasses the efforts of the Reagan administration in the 1980s. Although contradictions, conflicts, and dizzying shifts in the political fields of conservation, preservation, and economic development on rural western federal public lands are not without precedence, the current politically driven re-orientations are occurring even as the world begins to viscerally grapple with the impending effects of climate change.

Public lands are arguably some of the most divisively politicized place-spaces in contemporary America. Much has been written about conflicts over public lands in popular and scholarly venues, some authors focusing more explicitly on legal, economic, environmental, and political relations and histories, some authors focusing on the agencies responsible for public lands management and development, and still fewer authors focusing on Native North Americans' role and sovereign claims on public lands.

In contrast to all but some of the works found in this third cluster of authors, this edited volume starts from an ethnographically driven notion of "senses of place." We argue that by following the rich threads of the many different senses of place that are engendered and entangled with each other around public lands and the boundaries between public and private lands, more nuanced understandings of practices of collaboration and conflict over public lands can be illuminated. This volume examines the role that senses of place play in constellations of performative practices of governance, conservation and preservation, livelihoods, recreation, tourism, and other ways of life dependent on public lands. Arguably shared public natural resources, such as land, soil, forests, grasslands, deserts, air, freshwater, and oceans hold important keys to our capacity to manage the impending results of human-caused changes to our planetary systems, changes expected to greatly impact human societies and all living beings on our planet. More nuanced understandings of the social practices and the cultural logics underpinning human social relations and human socialities are key to improving our efforts to mediate and mitigate some of the effects of climate change.

Senses of place and public lands are inseparably intertwined. Place can be thought of as culturalized space that humans have endowed with meaning. People's sense of what a place is and means specifically to whom, the histories of a place, and the shared cultural logics that define place as a place, as well as its boundaries, are central to the contestations, clashes, and collaborations that emerge in specific public lands. Using the notion of senses of place as a foil, we approach place as a powerful material social imaginary through which moral orders, belief systems, cultural meanings, ideas about social relations, and discursive systems, including legal and economic systems, are expressed and reproduced, often through the stories that people tell, as Basso

(1996a, b) so eloquently demonstrated. We argue that senses of place serve as the cornerstones that underpin short-term and long-term practices of access (or lack thereof), use, development, conservation, management, and policing on public lands and at its boundaries. Boundaries of public lands themselves often become materially important, if fuzzy social fields of great contention. McDonald, Tebbs and McDonald, Thompson, Turner, Bloom and Deur in this volume highlight the significance of boundaries in relation to public lands.

While most groups of people shape their shared social sensibilities of place for themselves, they do not usually do so freely and unfettered. Very often, the local and even regional work of placemaking is undertaken in the context of the placemaking activities and practices of more politically and economically powerful groups of people. Thus, as our chapters explore specific senses of place, they also interrogate more encompassing and influential contextual imaginaries of "the public," "the West," "community," and "jurisdictional authority," all of which influence specific senses of place, and all of which buttress social, legal, political, and economic relations of power that shape whose definition of place proves more influential.

Ethnographers, and others committed to deeply investigative analysis, study peoples' stories in order to understand peoples' meanings and practices. Because places are filled with stories and made through stories, an ethnographic approach is perfectly matched to its subject of study. The goal of this volume is to contribute scholarly research toward developing a critically nuanced understanding of the complex array of socialities, social relations, and cultural logics that comprise public lands in the western United States.

Many interesting and useful discussions about U.S. public lands, public lands agencies, and public lands policies have been posited by historians, environmental studies, policy, legal, and political science scholars, who investigate the way that laws, courts, branches of government, and agencies approach and handle the public lands (Alagona 2013; Appel 2010; Keiter 2005; Klein 2002; Fairfax et al. 1999; Spence 1999; Mansfield 1993; Sax 1993), while another cluster of authors seeks to address agency histories and comparisons of agencies (Glicksman 2014; Zellmer 2014; Clarke and McCool 1996). Discussions of public lands themselves are often framed in the language of rights, specifically states' rights, federal rights, property rights, long-standing use rights, management jurisdictional authority, and limits to each of these categories of rights (Outka 2017; Alagona 2013; Leshy 2001; Fairfax et al. 1999; Babbitt 1982). However, many of these discussions, including those devoted to specific agencies, tend to view the issues from a 10,000-foot altitude, in part because most federal and state public lands laws, policies, and regulations cover vast expanses of territory, and because the government agencies involved often control extensive territories. The upshot is that complex arrays of social actors and socialities tend to get swept into a few oppositional archetypes, and nuanced, complex, ever-changing histories, and social interrelations are often oversimplified.

A third cluster of historians, geographers, journalists, and anthropologists works to illuminate the social histories that challenge hegemonic histories about public lands (parks, forests, seashores) and U.S. settler conservation movements, including Spence (1999), Jacoby (2014[2001]), Thompson (2018), and Leshy (2018) often grounding their analyses in specific cases. A few ethnographically oriented studies exploring a sense of place have also contributed, for example, Brown and Ingram's (1987) study of water in the arid Southwest; Espeland's (1998) close reading of dam builders also in the Southwest; Kosek's (2002) work on socialities in northern New Mexico forests; Whiteley, Ingram, and Perry's (2008) collection, which includes several pieces on the western United States, as well as an introduction on place and water; Watt's (2017) study of ranchers and ranching in Point Reyes National Seashore; Tilly and Cameron-Daum's (2017) work about the social meanings of a heath landscape in southern England; and several texts devoted to Native North Americans' senses of place, including Basso (1996a, b), Nesper (2002), Nadasdy 2005 (First Nations, Canada), Ganapathy (2013), and Thornton (2014, 2015). While not all these authors explicitly refer to a sense of place, their works nevertheless unpack allied and competing cultural logics and moral economies at work in the making of specific places. This volume contributes to filling the still enormous gap. Our chapters demonstrate that a social sense of place underlies the social motivations and social practices of every group of people interacting with each other in the context of public lands. However, and as Brown and Ingram, Kosek, Jacoby, Ganapathy, and Tilly and Cameron-Daum demonstrate, very seldom is a singular sense of place shared among the diverse groups of people focused on one place, and that begins to account for the social fractures arising over public lands.

Usually, scholars and government agencies reserve the terms "public lands" (used interchangeably with "public domain") for federal lands. However, we explore and apply a more expansive notion of "public lands" in this book, applying the social notion of "public lands" to state, county, and municipal lands, as well as federal lands. We use the notion of public lands to cover all of the lands that are held in trust, owned, planned, and managed by governments for tax-paying constituencies, who tend to see government-controlled lands as being their public resources, their public lands. This more inclusive approach also mirrors the ways in which increasingly state, federal, and Native North American representatives and managers are motivated (even when not mandated to do so) to work together, for example, in order to more effectively manage increasing numbers of wildfires or salmon populations. Moreover, the U.S. publics, one might argue, tend to take a more inclusive approach to public lands than do the government agencies, the legal nuances of policy, and legal and political science scholars. The ideas of "a public" and "public lands" are themselves part of a more encompassing modern settler society social imaginary of place and its zeitgeist, in which settler society property laws, economic systems, and political systems are intimately tied to the sensibilities and moral orders of specific groups of people. Because the notion of public lands is firmly situated in a settler legal, economic, and conservation modernity, Native North American modernity, including Native North American sovereign territorial claims and time immemorial rights and Title, is often overridden or at best supposedly confined to reserves established by the settler-colonial state, the upshot of which is discussed below.

By the "West," we mean to address several very different registers of place. We include the geopolitically delineated states west of the eastern borders of Montana, Wyoming, Colorado, New Mexico, and Alaska. These are the states where the majority of U.S. federal public domain lands are situated. Because of historically specific approaches taken by successive federal administrations toward the federal public domain lands in the western states, these federal lands are interspersed with state-owned lands, Native North American nations' territorial lands, as well as their legal take-rights areas that exceed reservation boundaries, county and municipal lands, and privately held lands. Many federal and state government lands do not comprise contiguous land holdings, even though they are often represented in their sum totals of millions of acres in discussions in both popular and scholarly texts and maps (Fairfax et al. 2005; Sax 1976). In the western part of the United States, federal, state, and county public lands, including coastal estuaries, reveal complicated and variegated transactional histories, which make broadly brushed generalizations at best hazardous (Fairfax et al. 2005). The situation is made even more tangled because public lands are generally subject to more than one jurisdictional authority, even when one jurisdictional authority is dominant. All public lands are governed by an impressive array of settler state laws, including, for example, environmental protection laws, water quality laws, air quality laws, habitat and species protection laws, laws governing the commercial and recreational harvesting of various plant and animal species, laws governing ranching, soils, mining and its production stream (milling and smelting), which is part of the reason why so many agencies are involved in any one stretch of public land. Public lands also span a wide variety of categorizations including parks, monuments (for the protection of places of historic and scientific significance), grazing lands, wilderness, potential wilderness, wildlife and bird refuges and sanctuaries, and mining and other subsurface mineral extraction leases, each governed by its own set of laws and policies. Furthermore, some federal and state lands are dominant-use oriented (e.g., designated wilderness areas), while others, including parks, seashores, forests, estuaries, and grazing lands can host a broad range of very different kinds of uses including both recreational uses and industrial uses such as mining and agro-forestry. The boundaries of public lands also present challenges because the effects of some uses of public lands resources, such as mining, logging, oil and gas extraction, pipeline corridors, exceed the boundaries of their leases, affecting water resources, air, soils, and aesthetics. The chapters by McDonald, Tebbs and McDonald, Randle, Thompson, and Turner delve into the material complications and cultural logics of various kinds of boundary excesses.

As suggested above, and integral to this mix is the presence of Native North American sovereign territories. The relationship of Native North American sovereign land claims and settler state sovereign land claims can be thought as "translocal" (Ganapathy 2013), that is as existing in the same space. This translocality, not surprisingly, is coupled with the often fraught relationship between Native North American nations, the settler state (operating through with its various federal and state governments), and private corporations (Powell 2018; Wolfley 2016; Thornton 2014; Stevens 2014; Jacoby 2014 [2001]; Ganapathy 2013; Spence 1999). Although not often given much choice in the matter, Native North American nations do not see their territorial lands as public, but rather as places upon which they may or may not welcome settler society peoples. For example, many Native North Americans, where possible, tend to try to keep culturally significant and sacred places out of the settler society circuits of tourism, development, and resource exploitation, while increasingly working to create their own resource and habitat management infrastructure, including planning, scientific, and cultural knowledge gathering, regulatory frameworks and enforcement, as well as working to form collaborative governance relations with federal and state agencies. A large part of the history of Western lands is one in which federal, state, and tribal lands interweave one another in complex patterns of contested, and sometimes collaborative jurisdictional authority, territorial claims, and boundaries. The creation of Bears Ears National Monument under the Obama administration was particularly historical because five Native North American nations were integral to its creation, and this was the first-ever collaboration between Native North American nations and the U.S. federal government on this scale. Unfortunately, the Trump administration has worked relentlessly to undo that momentous effort, as well as other previous administrations' efforts to protect other national monuments from extractive industrial development. Chapters in this volume by Burow, and Bloom and Deur provide insight into the forms such interwoven relations with public lands take.

The authors in this volume work to interrogate "the West" as a settler society's social imaginary that is itself rooted in and is emblematic of a peculiarly U.S. national social sense of place, one that originates in the founding myths of the United States as a settler nation. Interestingly, the sensibilities of place and performances of place that we seek to unpack generally belong to a particularly western conversation, although this conversation is not limited to groups of people in those states where the large tracts of public lands are sitting, and where consumptive uses (e.g., mining, drilling, logging, ranching, fishing, hunting) and nonconsumptive uses (e.g., conservation, preservation, camping, hiking, rafting) occur in often vociferously debated circumstances. Those who feel marginalized from the local and regional conversations and decisions, as well as those who seek to drive local and regional conversations and decisions, have often sought the help of senators, representatives, presidents, and the agencies of the executive branch, bringing decisions made in state capitals and Washington D.C. to bear heavily on the rural regions of the western United States in materially significant ways. These groups have long utilized social media (before that term came to exclusively refer to electronic mediums) including large letter writing, petition signing, and phone calling campaigns, advertisements, and more recently, email and electronic social media campaigns to organize support for their projects and positions. They work to enlist citizens who are not from the region and who may never visit the region under the banners of the nation, national resources and treasures, and the public understood as a national public (cf. Sullivan 2019)—just the sort of actively imagined and performative-based social formation of nation that Benedict Anderson (1998) sought to understand. Salient examples of this process of successfully enlisting people from outside the region to create pressure on government include the wilderness and national seashore protection movements in the early 1960s, and systematic efforts to convince federal agencies to deregulate and expand oil and gas development, and uranium and coal mining on federal lands in the western states in 2017. These often deeply opposed efforts, are built on and in turn contribute to the reinforcement of shared senses of place, shared identity, and shared sensibilities that can be highly localized or nationalized, and sometimes both in contradictory and in contested ways.

The chapters in this volume explore the ways in which shared identities are forged through cultural logics pertaining to public lands. We have divided the remainder of our volume into two parts. Part II, the next part of the volume, explores senses of place in depth as these are evinced by various social groups associated with particular places, ranging from clearly delineated working groups of ranchers (chapters by McDonald; Tebbs and McDonald), recreation and conservation groups utilizing the Los Angeles River (chapter by Randle), to the more broadly situated New Mexico state-based identity used to entice and captivate tourists (chapter by Knowlton). Part III of this volume pushes the notion of senses of place further, focusing on the relationship between particular senses of place, on the one hand, and laws and jurisdictional authorities, on the other hand. These chapters explore the social relations that bind often disparate groups together in practices of conflict or collaboration, as well as issues concerning legal boundaries between public, sovereign, and private lands (Thompson; Turner; Bloom and Deur), law enforcement on federal lands (Russell), and settler state conservation practices (Thompson; Turner; Bloom and Deur; Burow).

The following section of this introduction discusses the ways in which senses of place ground and bind together groups of people. The section after discusses the way in which performatives of practice rely on, even as they reinforce, senses of place, particularly in the context of legal and policy regimes.

GROUNDED IN SENSES OF PLACE

Anthropologist Keith Basso (1996a, b) took seriously the idea that sociocultural senses of place are shared and maintained through storytelling about often elaborate and highly socially contextualized understandings and knowledge about specific places, as well as through the social practices of inhabiting and using specific places. In other words, social senses of place contribute to and help maintain place-based socialities and identities. Native North American groups construct their own complex social senses of place, as Basso (1996a, b) and Thornton (2014, 2015) have documented. While each Native North American nation fosters and maintains its own unique approach to a sense of place, the legal and historical notion of time immemorial occupation is a sense of place that is shared across Native North American nations and First Nations in the settler states of the United States and Canada. Time immemorial provides legal foundation for asserting sovereign claims and for contesting the contemporary internal colonial occupation of Native North American territories by settler society. Time immemorial, however, does not mean that contemporary Native North American Peoples are somehow frozen in time and place, rather it means that they hold sovereign claims, rights, and titles that were in place before the claims asserted by settler society governments and members. Similarly, the term consultation as asserted by Native North American nations in conjunction with place-based activities in their territories entails more than a right to be notified of an impending change to place-based activities and practices, consultation means that Native North American nations have a fully functioning, legally enforceable right to review, to refuse, or to give permission for place-based activities and practices (such as building pipelines, creating no-take reserves, mining, tourism, pot hunting, etc.) and to shape resource and habitat management regimes in their territories. However, and as Wolfley (2016:68) points out, asserting a right to be consulted is often a challenge for Native North American nations because tribal and nation resources, including legal and administrative staff are often minimal. Native North American nations assert their territorial claims only over their own specific (and forcibly truncated) territories and over their use rights, which may exceed their settler society assigned reserves (cf. Nesper 2002), carefully not speaking for each other, allotting to each nation its own unique sense of place.

Settler society is not homogeneous, and its various groups of citizens craft very different senses of place, and these can be quite at odds with the senses of place that organize and inform the work of settler society government agencies, as the chapters by McDonald, Tebbs and McDonald, and Turner suggest, is the case for ranching families, and, as Randle suggests, is the case for the public waterways of the Los Angeles River. Knowlton, Thompson, Russell, Burow, and Bloom and Deur highlight the contradictions arising from the frictions between different senses of place operating at different scales.

On the other hand, there circulates a widespread nationally hegemonic social imaginary of the West as a place built from the pioneering spirit of U.S. settler society members, who covet independence from government control, prize hard work, and value economic and social self-sufficiency. Spence (1999) argues that after the Civil War, these national myths also came to revolve around notions that the West comprises open spaces conveniently and largely devoid of any long-term pre-settler human inhabitants and their occupations and their societies. This particular social imaginary continues to take on fresh iterations in popular novels, popular films, and television shows, and in the retold founding myths used to sustain the system of national parks, monuments, and wilderness areas, manifesting itself in what are referred to as sagebrush rebellions, and ever renewed campaigns emanating from some coalitions in western states to encourage the federal government to turn its lands over to the states (see discussions of sagebrush rebellions in Cawley 1993; Graf 1990; Babbitt 1982; Leshy 1980). McDonald, in this volume, explores these manifestations in relation to religious discourses that anchor and bolster a place-based ranching identity.

In a related vein, not all of the different groups of settler society people who perceive themselves as having a legitimate interest in public lands and as caring about either a specific public land or public lands in general, are local to the specific place or even the region where the public land is physically located. For example, the National Park Service has long worked to cultivate a broadly shared, national sense of place concerning the National Park System. Elite white and then their middle-class American counterparts were enticed through campaigns aiming to get these people to visit, or at least imagine themselves visiting their national parks (M. Powell 2016). The National Park Service and its supporters work to foster a shared sense of place among people who will never live near the parks, who may never even visit any or may visit just a few of the parks.[2] While operative even at the outset of the creation of the National Park System, including the creations of Yosemite National Park and Yellowstone National Park, this spatial disjuncture between local, regional, and national registers of senses of place has only grown deeper through time as more nongovernmental organizations of conservationists, preservationists, and environmentalists have coalesced and worked to broaden public political support for the expansion of state and federal park and wilderness systems, sometimes in the face of vociferous local opposition.

Arguably, cultivating national and statewide bases of support, as opposed to relying solely on local support has proved crucial for the creation and maintenance of state and national parks, wilderness areas, and systems of bird, wildlife, and fisheries reserves, sanctuaries, and refuges, and in order to make space available for many forms of nonconsumptive development such as tourism, ecotourism, scientific, and preservation activities.[3] Importantly, this practice of discursively building place-based political support, which is integrally tied to senses of place, has been important for a varied group of parties with an interest in federal and state public lands, and not just for the National Park Service and environmentalists. According to Cowart and Fairfax (1988), the fostering of a nationally powerful political base of support for western ranching interests has played a key role in keeping much of the publicly held grazing land in western states available as low-cost leaseholds for ranchers and herders. Deploying similar strategies aimed at cultivating and shaping national interests, the Trump administration is currently working to unwind conservation and preservation efforts by using social media, executive privilege, and powerful political allies to generate support for expanding the consumptive development of mineral, oil, and gas reserves on western federal lands, touting the economic contributions, including job growth, that such development will purportedly engender.

Nationally shared senses of place can contribute to the actual or perceived sense of displacement experienced by groups of people who physically use and/or inhabit particular places. This locational disjuncture has always been a characteristic of federal public domain lands, given that only some of the governing politicians and bureaucrats making overarching law and policy decisions for western states live near the public lands that they govern. However, this process of displacement can also occur at the regional level in the disjuncture between urban and rural centers of control, and between very different local and regional notions about how places should be treated and used.

On a new front, human-induced changes to the large and fluid systems of oceans and the atmosphere, are precipitating not national senses of place, but global senses of place, making already-existing tensions and layers of hierarchical relations that inform senses of place more significant, particularly as emerging senses of place are likely to replicate and buttress existing relations of power in the absence of sensitive understandings of the role played by senses of place in the governing, developing, and conserving of lands, resources, and habitats. At this juncture, analytically sensitive analyses highlighting the nuanced layers of senses of place that come into play and change, especially as people grapple with changing circumstances, are both relevant and timely.

PERFORMATIVES OF COLLABORATION AND CONFLICT

Senses of place are an integral part of configuring places as sites of cultural significance, work, governance, home, economic activity, and belonging. Access, use, and management practices foreground mutually exclusive as well as mutually conducive uses, take versus no-take uses, management regimes, conservation, and development practices, all of which are situated in an already-hierarchized social order. Intersections between place and law take many forms, including sagebrush rebellions, collaborative planning exercises where a constellation of different governments with jurisdictional authority come together to consider options for uses and management regimes, and stakeholder planning exercises where governments and their constituencies work together. The chapters in Part III of this volume examine the practices and roles of Native North American nations (Bloom and Deur; Burow), scientific and technical experts (Turner; Burow), law enforcement (Russell), and environmentalists, corporations, and uranium mining practices (Thompson). The following discussion, resonating with Part III of our volume, explores the ways in which jurisdictional authority, legal, policy, and management contexts saturate social sensibilities of place in efforts to access, use, and manage living landscapes in concrete ways.

The work of governing constitutes a significant dimension of public lands, both in the sense of forming a context in which senses of place and other practices must operate, and in the sense of actively shaping what practices that can and cannot be undertaken in a specific place. Sarat, Douglas, and Umphrey (2003) assert that place is determined by a combination of specific territory, specific jurisdictions, and specific boundaries, all of which can be fluid over time, and (following Ford 1999) more vague in definition than the concrete lines drawn on maps suggest. Fairfax et al. (2005:8–11, 15–18) use the term "mosaics" to capture this fluidity, and to underscore the complications of intertwined jurisdictional authorities, and layers of ownerships that have arisen since property rights came to be treated as divisible bundles of rights and claims after the Civil War. As Fairfax et al. (2005) point out, there has been much to-ing and fro-ing in lands transactions since the 1700s, exchanges of many kinds (leasing, selling, exchanging, gifting), and of many different bundles of rights (e.g., surface rights, water rights, subsurface mineral rights) delineated and exchanged between various federal, state, and private entities. Stevens (2014), Thornton (2014), Wolfley (2016) point out that until recently Native North American nations, in spite of original and continuous occupation, have been largely excluded from these processes or brought in late in the game. Chapters by Turner, Burow, and Bloom and Deur explore the contemporary ramifications and changing aspects of relations between Native North American nations and settler governments regarding management of land, plant and animal populations, habitats, and wild fires.

Anthropologists, cultural geographers, legal and policy theorists (for excellent examples, see Brown and Ingram 1987; Harris 2003; Thornton 2015) have approached place as resulting from performativity, that is from the perspective that practices themselves create places and boundaries. Ford (1999) argues that jurisdiction and especially its boundaries are always performatives, while Blomley (2002) focuses on property and land as performative verbs, and Sullivan (2006) explores performatives of sovereignty. J. L. Austin (1975 [1962]) suggests that performatives are more than just performances and distinguishes performatives from mere performances—such as making descriptive statements, asking questions, and giving commands. Rather, Austin argues, performatives are discursive acts that materially change a state of being, such as his example of the role of the mutual saying of "I do" in a marriage ceremony, language that is both a ritual spectacle and a legal reconfiguration of the status of the persons marrying each other, or the point at which the judge formally calls court into session, thereby reconfiguring herself and the courtroom into material manifestations of state for the duration of the court session. All of these authors highlight the integral linkages between discursive acts and other forms of practice, such as physically surveying a boundary, installing fencing, regulating harvesting, mining for uranium, drilling for oil, or cordoning off a specific place and designating it a wilderness. Blomley (2002) emphasizes the importance of storytelling, narrative-making in legal performatives of land and property. Those stories, which he deftly examines in order to call attention to the fundamentally social nature of property and land, all articulate their own senses of place, even as they also relate place-based practices to senses of place.

The authors above also highlight the contingent nature of property, jurisdictional authority, jurisdictional boundaries, sovereignty, and, as Blomley suggests, land itself. Contingency is an important aspect of place in that it opens the possibilities that conflicts can transform into collaborations, and alliances can be made, broken, and remade over time, particularly as the conditions in which the socialities and social relations that make performatives possible, change. Contingency suggests that senses of place can change with changing circumstances or newly formed perceptions of existing social relations and sociality.

In 1982, Bruce Babbitt, attorney general and then governor of Arizona 1978–1987, and later Secretary of the Interior under Clinton, in commenting on the sagebrush rebellion of that period, argued that the real issue between federal and state jurisdictions was one of distinctly separate federal and state management authorities that were not responsive to each other, and that the issue was not one of ownership. He continued by asserting that the Federal Lands Policy and Management Act 1976 (FLPMA), along with several more specifically targeted federal Acts that immediately preceded it, and several more that followed FLPMA in the 1970s and then into the early 1980s, provided a number of avenues for establishing more cooperative and collaborative management relations between states and federal entities regarding western public lands (Babbitt 1982:853–857, 859). Keiter (2005) argues that the 1964 Wilderness Act, 1969 National Environmental Policy Act, the 1973 Endangered Species Act, and the 1976 National Forest Management Act were also key pieces of public lands legislation during this time period, laying the groundwork for decades of changes. Wolfley (2016:62–67) asserts that the 1960s also launched a significant shift in federal government's approach to its relationship with Native North American nations, including an emphasis on respecting Native North Americans' self-determination and rights, an approach, which, she argues, the Clinton and later the Obama administrations strengthened. Since then, collaborative arrangements have emerged on a number of fronts regarding managing and maintaining public lands—everything from managing fires, harvests and harvest limits, to controlling erosion, as well as managing for an ever-increasing number of settler society stakeholder groups and sub-constituencies asserting that public lands should be used for this or that purpose.

Federal, state, and Native North American governmental entities have turned to sharing jurisdictional authority, to collaborating in more effective ways. While Bloom and Deur in this volume highlight one such successful undertaking, Thompson, Turner, and Burow underscore intrinsic limitations to these efforts, including limitations arising from the legal and policy constraints on the settler state government agencies. Until recently, Native North Americans' sovereign rights, Title claims, and positions regarding their territories, resources, and habitats have only infrequently been recognized in the creation of settler society visions of conservation, preservation, and development on both federal and state public lands and on private lands. Events like those that occurred on Standing Rock Sioux territory in 2016 attest that there is still much ground to be covered. Native North American nations that have recently achieved some degree of recognition and control in government-to-government negotiations and relations concerning access, use, development, management, and conservation practices in their territories, have accomplished this mainly because of their own persistence. Federal recognition of some but not all nations has also hindered increased government-to-government collaborative efforts. Now that such collaborations have begun to emerge, they are slowly, if imperfectly spreading and deepening through quotidian governance exercises and practices, as Thornton (2014), Wolfley (2016), the establishment of Bears Ears National Monument in Utah in 2016 with the significant help of five Native North American nations (Turkewitz 2017; Healy 2016), attest.

Not only have settler society ideas about property changed from the notion of property as an undifferentiated block to the notion of property as a bundle of ever more dividable bundles of rights (Fairfax et al. 2005:15–18), so too have settler society ideas about boundaries changed, along with ideas about the ways that lands and water resources can be configured for use. Increasingly, the documenting of many kinds of effects of industrial production activities (e.g., water usages, uranium and coal mining, oil and gas extraction, commercial logging, overgrazing) has shown that the effects of production are not, and often cannot be confined solely to the particular space (or time period) allotted to the operators, thus jeopardizing the notion of a legal boundary as a fixed line of confinement and restraint (Sax 1976; Thompson in this volume; Turner in this volume). In part, this shift has arisen because of more scientifically and statistically accurate ways of measuring the impacts and externalities of industrial forms of production on water, air, soils, and human health. The shift can also be attributed to changes in environmental law that Lazarus (2004) documents as starting in the 1960s and 1970s and gaining momentum over time. Lazarus shows how environmental law came increasingly to be reconfigured around notions of torts, personal injury, and harm, particularly in relation to issues of pollution and health, beginning in the 1960s. Arguably, this kind of a shift in legal emphasis not only provides ways to prosecute polluting practices, but it also encourages increased documentation of impacts from industrial production for future prosecutions, and as a means to regulate production practices.

Another major change, which can be traced to the 1960s and 1970s, is the introduction and application of laws directing government agencies to categorize all unreserved public lands according to their suitability for various activities ranging from preservation to industrial development, while at the same time, and often the same laws encouraged some agencies, for example, the Forest Service and the Bureau of Land Management, to work to accommodate multiple uses on a single parcel of land (Babbitt 1982:850 for a definition of multiple uses), even as the National Park Service and the Fish and Wildlife Service remain predominantly single-use agencies (Zellmer 2014).

Since the 1960s, increasing numbers of constituent groups, often with competing interests, have formed, all of whom want to use public lands to what they feel are the best social ends.

The governing entities, laws, and policies involved in holding, managing, and policing public lands evince complex interrelations, even as these interrelations also posit the conditions for both acting upon senses of place and for managing and using public lands. Here again, an ethnographic approach is well-suited to capturing and analyzing the relationship between senses of place and the role and effects of law, jurisdictional authority, territory, and boundaries, particularly as more nuanced understandings of the socialities of place will be increasingly needed in the face of managing and mitigating the effects of human-induced changes to our planetary freshwater, oceanic, atmospheric, and terrestrial systems.

PLAN OF THE BOOK

We have organized our volume into three parts. Part I introduces our readers to our subject of inquiry, and includes a review of relevant work on the topic. Part II delves into senses of place and the identities that arise from senses of place. Part III follows the rich currents of senses of place and identities into the realm of public lands laws and policies, jurisdictional authority, and state-based land management. Most of the senses of place found in the western United States entail some interaction with law, policy, and jurisdictional authorities.

In Part II, the conflicts that structure ranching life and identity that James H. McDonald, and Bruce Tebbs and James H. McDonald portray have developed in conjunction with a long history of state leasing policies and practices, which while changing with different administrations and policy approaches to public lands, have generally supported ranching families. Over time, the grazing leases have become necessary for maintaining family ranching operations because private holdings are either broken up by public holdings or are simply inadequate in size to maintain the herds. McDonald explores the ways in which the ensuing notions of ranchers' rights, that is rights arising out of past relations with government agencies' public lands leasing practices, and the ranchers' shared senses of place have become imbricated with religious and revitalization discourses, which, in turn, lend increased authority among the ranchers for their own rights claims. The kayaking and environmental identities and senses of place portrayed by Sayd Randle have been forged in long-term relationships to various contested legal prohibitions on access to the public waters of the Los Angeles River, as well as fostering challenges to dominant policy regimes regarding consumptive uses of that water. David

Knowlton's chapter on the statewide enchanted/enchanting identity anchored in ethnicized tourist and military-industrial relations of power in New Mexico shows how this place-based identity draws on and reproduces historic and extant colonial social relations and legalities. Even as these authors acknowledge and take into account these larger legal and political contexts, they do so from the perspective of the ways in which socially shared sense of place ground and reproduce socialities.

While the authors in Part II acknowledge the legal and policy contexts in which senses of place are steeped, the authors in Part III launch their analyses from a priority focus on the legal, policy, and state managerial contexts in which senses of place are constrained and fostered. Part III opens with a chapter by Jonathan P. Thompson in which he explores the role of pervasive uranium mining in shaping place in the western United States, including the intertwined legal and economic contexts which have fostered this industry. He highlights the senses of place that accompany uranium development, ranging from corporations seeking to make money in the sacrifice zones of the West, to those of the local denizens, environmentalists, and Native North Americans living in these zones. Then, Jacqueline Russell addresses the fraught role and constraints on law enforcement agents, funding, and policies from the perspective of resource conservation law enforcement. The next three chapters all focus on concrete public lands management situations that involve settler state agencies and Native North American governments. Scott Turner examines the management, economic, environmental, and social complexities that have arisen around "The Interagency Bison Management Plan" in Yellowstone National Park. When the wild park bison forage outside of the park boundaries, they carry the risk of infecting domesticated cattle, located on park-adjacent grazing leases, with brucellosis. One answer has been to enact management policies for culling the bison herds, policies that in turn are not ubiquitously favored as a methodology for keeping the Yellowstone bison herds in ecological balance with the park boundaries. Native North American tribes, settler government agencies, ranchers, and environmentalists all evince very different senses of place as they try, with much contention, to manage wild bison herds for the future. Rochelle Bloom and Douglas Deur examine the history of the role of the Native North American plant gathering and plant population maintenance in Yosemite National Park, including the systematic exclusion of Native North Americans by the National Park Service, and subsequent Native North American efforts to maintain their ties with the plants and habitats through traditional plant management and harvesting practices. Bloom and Deur's chapter highlights the importance of Native North Americans' ongoing efforts to be recognized and included as government-to-government partners in the recent emergence of collaborative governance initiatives. In our final chapter, Paul Burow examines the human-nonhuman boundary through the lens of commodification. Taking into account the social history of mining, ranching, and urban development, Burow delves into settler state-led management regimes for sage grouse and their habitats, a potentially endangered species in the Great Basin. As do Knowlton, Thompson, Turner, and Bloom and Deur, Burow takes account of the material, social, management, and sovereignty ramifications of settler colonialism in the struggles over public lands in the western United States, and more importantly, efforts by Native North American nations to protect and foster these same lands through traditional practices.

Taken as an integrated piece, this volume sheds light on the way on which very different, and often contentious, senses of place are key to understanding the clashes over public lands, as well as emerging collaborative efforts.

NOTES

1. Kate Sullivan thanks Jim McDonald for all of his generosity, open-minded curiosity, sense of fun, and unflagging support as a collaborator on this volume. We both thank our editor, Kasey Beduhn, at Lexington Press for her encouragement and patience.

2. The extensive effort by the National Park Service was captured in a recent two-part exhibition of historic National Park Service flyers, advertisements, posters, and related publications and artworks on display at Geographies of Wonder: Origin Stories of Americas National Parks 1872–1933, May14, 2016, to September 5, 2016, and Geographies of Wonder: The Evolution of the National Park Idea 1933–2016 Part 2, October 22, 2016, to February 13, 2017, at the Huntington Gardens, Los Angeles, celebrating the anniversary of the National Park System.

3. The notion of "nonconsumptive development" requires additional interrogation. National Parks actively barred Native North American groups from foraging and hunting within park boundaries even though they had done so for millennia, relying on those resources for survival. Indeed, references to Native North Americans who once occupied the lands that are now National Parks is largely nonexistent in park histories and museums. The National Park Service museum at Mammoth in Yellowstone is an exemplar of this practice of erasure (M. Powell 2016).

REFERENCES CITED

Alagona, Peter S. 2013. *After the Grizzly: Endangered Species and the Politics of Place in California*. Berkeley, CA: University of California Press.

Anderson, Benedict. 1998. *Imagined Communities: Reflections on Origins and Spread of Nationalism*. New York: Verso Press.

Appel, Peter A. 2010. Wilderness and the Courts. *Stanford Environmental Law Journal* 29:62–129.

Austin, J. L. 1975[1962]. *How to Do Things with Words*. Cambridge, MA: Harvard University Press.

Babbitt, Bruce. 1982. Federalism and the Environment: And Intergovernmental Perspective of the Sagebrush Rebellion. Symposium: Federalism and Environment. *Environmental Law* 12:847–861.

Basso, Keith H. 1996a. *Wisdom Sits in Places: Landscape and Language among the Western Apache*. Albuquerque, NM: University of New Mexico Press.

Basso, Keith H. 1996b. Wisdom Sits in Places: Notes on a Western Apache Landscape. In *Senses of Place*, edited by Steven Feld and Keith H. Basso, pp. 53–90. Santa Fe, NM: School of American Research Press.

Blomley, Nicholas. 2002. Mud for the Land. *Public Culture* 14(3):557–582.

Brown, F. Lee, and Helen Ingram. 1987. *Water and Poverty in the Southwest*. Tucson, AZ: University of Arizona Press.

Cawley, R. McGreggor. 1993. *Federal Lands, Western Anger: The Sagebrush Rebellion and Environmental Politics*. Lawrence, KS: University of Kansas Press.

Clarke, Jeanne Nienaber, and Daniel C. McCool. 1996. *Staking Out the Terrain: Power and Performance among Natural Resource Agencies*, 2nd edition. Albany, NY: State University of New York Press.

Cowart, Richard H., and Sally K. Fairfax. 1988. Public Lands Federalism: Judicial Theory and Administrative Reality. *Ecological Quarterly* 15(3):375–476.

Espeland, Wendy Nelson. 1998. *The Struggle for Water: Politics, rationality, and Identity in the American Southwest*. Chicago, IL: The University of Chicago Press.

Fairfax, Sally K., Laurin Gwin, Mary Ann King, Leigh Raymond, and Laura A. Watt. 2005. *Buying Nature: The Limits of Land Acquisitions as Conservation Strategy, 1780-2004*. Cambridge, MA: MIT Press.

Fairfax, Sally K., Louise P. Fortmann, Ann Hawkins, Lynn Huntsinger, Nancy Lee Peluso, and Steven A. Wolf. 1999. The Federal Forests Are Not What They Seem: Formal and Informal Claims to Federal Lands. *Ecological Law Quarterly* 25(4):630–646.

Ford, Richard T. 1999. Law's Territory (A History of Jurisdiction). *Michigan Law Review* 97(4):843–930.

Ganapathy, Sandhya. 2013. Imagining Alaska: Local and Translocal Engagements with Place. *American Anthropologist* 115(1):96–111.

Glicksman, Robert L. 2014. Wilderness Management by the Multiple Use Agencies: What Makes the Forest Service and the Bureau of Land Management Different? *Environmental Law* 44:447–495.

Graf, William T. 1990. *Wilderness Preservation and the Sagebrush Rebellions*. Lanham, MD: Rowman and Littlefield Publishers.

Harris, Cole. 2003. *Making Native Space: Colonialism, Resistance, and Reserves in British Columbia*. Vancouver, BC: University of British Columbia Press.

Healy, Jack. 2016. Remote Utah Enclave Becomes New Battleground Overreach of U.S. Control. *New York Times*. URL:https://www.google.com/search?q=new+yo

rk+times&rlz=1C1CHZL_enUS725US725&oq=&aqs=chrome.2.69i58j0i66l3j5i66l2.559191553j0j4&sourceid=chrome&ie=UTF-8 (January 13, 2018).

High Country News. https://www.hcn.org/ (January 17, 2020).

Jacoby, Karl. 2014[2001]. *Crimes Against Nature: Squatters, Poachers, Thieves, and the Hidden History of American Conservation*. Berkeley, CA: University of California Press.

Keiter, Robert B. 2005. Public Lands and Law Reform. *Utah Law Review* 4:1127–1226, University of Utah Legal Studies Paper No. 06–02.

Klein, Christine A. 2002. Preserving Monumental Landscapes under the Antiquities Act. *Cornell Law Review* 87:1333–1404.

Kosek, Jake. 2002. *Understories: The Political Life of Forests in Northern New Mexico*. Durham, NC: Duke University Press.

Lazarus, Richard J. 2004. *The Making of Environmental Law*. Chicago, IL: The University of Chicago Press.

Leshy, John D. 1980–1981. Unravelling the Sagebrush Rebellion: Law, Politics and Federal Lands. *University of California Davis Law Review* 14:317–355.

———. 2001 Shaping the Modern West: The Role of the Executive Branch. *Colorado Law Review* 72(2):287–310.

———. 2018 *Debunking Creation Myths about America's Public Lands: The 2018 Wallace Stegner Lecture*. Salt Lake City, UT: The University of Utah Press.

Mansfield, Marla E. 1993. A Primer of Public Land Law. *Washington Law Review* 68:801–857.

Nadasdy, Paul. 2005. *Hunters and Bureaucrats: Power, Knowledge, and Aboriginal-State Relations in Southwest Yukon*, revised edition. Vancouver, BC: University of British Columbia Press.

Nesper, Larry. 2002. *The Walleye War: The Struggle for Ojibwe Spearfishing and Treaty Rights*. Lincoln, NE: University of Nebraska Press.

Outka, Uma. 2017. State Lands in Modern Public Land Law. *Stanford Environmental Law Journal* 36:147–217.

Powell, Dana. 2018. *Landscapes of Power: Politics of Energy in the Navajo Nation*. Durham, NC: Duke University Press.

Powell, Miles A. 2016. *Vanishing America: Species Extinction, Racial Peril, and the Origins of Conservation*. Cambridge, MA: Harvard University Press.

Sarat, Austin, Lawrence Douglas, and Martha Merrill Umphrey. 2003. Where (or What) Is the Place of Law? An Introduction. *In The Place of Law*, edited by Austin Sarat, Lawrence Douglas, and Martha Merrill Umphrey, pp. 1–20. Ann Arbor, MI: University of Michigan Press.

Sax, Joseph L. 1976. Helpless Giants: The National Parks and the Regulation of Private Lands. *Michigan Law Review* 75(2):239–274.

———. 1993 Property Rights and the Economy of Nature: Understanding Lucas v. South Carolina Coastal Council. *Stanford Law Review* 45(5):1433–1455.

Skalicky, Sue, and Monica Davey. 2016. Tension between Police and Standing Rock Protesters Reaches Boiling Point. *New York Times*. URL: https://www.nytimes.com/2016/10/29/us/dakota-access-pipeline-protest.html (January 13, 2018).

Spence, Mark David. 1999. *Dispossessing Wilderness: Indian Removal and the Making of the National Parks*. Oxford, UK: Oxford University Press.

Stevens, Stan. 2014. Indigenous Peoples, Biocultural Diversity, and Protected Areas. In *Indigenous Peoples, National Parks and Protected Areas: A New Paradigm Linking Conservation, Culture and Rights*, edited by Stan Stevens, pp. 15–46. Tucson, AZ: University of Arizona Press.

Sullivan, Kathleen M. 2006. (Re)Landscaping Sovereignty in British Columbia, Canada. *PoLAR Political and Legal Anthropology Review* 29(1):44–65.

———. 2019. Troubled Currents and the Contentious Moral Orderings of Drakes Estero. In *Everyday Justice: Law, Ethnography, Injustice*, edited by Sandra Brunnegger, pp. 135–160. Cambridge, UK: Cambridge University Press.

Thompson, Jonathan P. 2018. *River of Lost Souls: The Science, Politics, and Greed Behind the Gold King Mine Disaster*. Salt Lake City, UT: Torrey House Press.

Thornton, Thomas F. 2014. A Tale of Three Parks: Tlingit Conservation, Representation, and Repatriation in Southeastern Alaska's National Parks. In *Indigenous Peoples, National Parks and Protected Areas: a New Paradigm Linking Conservation, Culture and Rights*, edited by Stan Stevens, pp. 108–129. Tucson, Az: The University of Arizona Press.

———. 2015. *Being and Place among the Tlingit*. Seattle: University of Washington Press and Sealaska Heritage Institute.

Tilly, Christopher, and Kate Cameron-Daum. 2017. *Anthropology of Landscape: The Extraordinary in the Ordinary*. London: UCL Press.

Turkewitz, Julie. 2017. Trump Slashes Size of Bears Ears and Grand Staircase Monuments. *New York Times*. URL: https://www.nytimes.com/2017/12/04/us/trump-bears-ears.html?action=click&contentCollection=Climate&module=RelatedCoverage&region=Marginalia&pgtype=article (January 13, 2018).

Turkewitz, Julie, and Eric Lightblau. 2016. Police Shooting of Oregon Occupier Declared Justified, but F.B.I. Faces Inquiry. *New York Times*. URL: https://www.nytimes.com/2016/03/09/us/oregon-lavoy-finicum-shooting.html?action=click&contentCollection=U.S.&module=RelatedCoverage&region=Marginalia&pgtype=article (January 13, 2018).

Turkewitz, Julie, and Jack Healy. 2016. LaVoy Finicum: "I Would Rather Die Than Be Caged." *New York Times*. URL: https://www.nytimes.com/2016/01/28/us/lavoy-finicum-protester-killed-in-oregon.html?action=click&contentCollection=U.S.&module=RelatedCoverage&region=Marginalia&pgtype=article (January 13, 2018).

Turkewitz, Julie, Nadja Popovich, and Matt McCann. 2017. Here Are the Ten National Monuments the Interior Department Wants to Shrink or Modify. *New York Times*. https://www.nytimes.com/interactive/2017/09/18/climate/bears-ears-changes-monuments.html?action=click&contentCollection=U.S.&module=RelatedCoverage&region=Marginalia&pgtype=article (January 13, 2018).

Upadhye, Neeti. 2016. Dakota Pipeline Protests: American Indians vs. Dakota Pipeline. *New York Times*. https://www.nytimes.com/video/us/100000004607887/american-indians-vs-dakota-pipeline.html (January 13, 2018).

Upadhye, Neeti, and Jack Healy. 2016. Dakota Pipeline Protest: A Timeline from Standing Rock. *New York Times*. https://www.nytimes.com/video/us/100000004805966/a-timeline-from-standing-rock.html (January 13, 2018).

Watt, Laura Alice. 2017. *The Paradox of Preservation: Wilderness and Working Landscapes in Point Reyes National Seashore*. Berkeley, CA: University of California Press.

Whiteley, John M., Helen Ingram, Richard Warren Perry. 2008. *Water, Place, and Equity*. Cambridge, MA: The MIT Press.

Wolfley, Jeannette. 2016. Reclaiming a Presence in Ancestral Lands: The Return of Native Peoples to National Parks. *Natural Resources Journal* 56:55–80.

Zellmer, Sandra B. 2014. Wilderness Management in National Parks and National Wildlife Refuges *Environmental Law* 47:497–547.

Part II

EXPLORING SENSES OF PLACE

Chapter 2

The New Wild West

The Range War as Revitalization Movement

James H. McDonald

The Western United States is a public land–dominated landscape that becomes especially interesting at the intersection of ranching, religion, public lands, the Constitution, and libertarian politics that together have spawned the region's new range wars. Range warriors are hanging onto a dying and unsustainable cattle ranching industry. Recent dramatic and sometimes quite violent standoffs and occupations can be understood as a type of revitalization movement in the face of an incrementally growing existential threat to livelihood and culture.[1]

To say that Western ranchers value their autonomy and independence would be in, some instances, a gross understatement. Take, for example, observations from one of the best-known rancher-activists, Cliven Bundy of Bunkerville, Nevada: "I'm not being regulated to death anymore" (Sottile 2017) and "The Lord told me . . . if [the local sheriff doesn't] take away these arms from federal agents, we the people will have to face these arms in a civil war" (Politico 2014).

Living in the public land–dominated Western United States is an ongoing adventure, especially at the intersection of ranching, religion, public lands, the Constitution, and libertarian politics that have spawned the new range war led by smallholder, independent cattle ranchers. Range wars have been historically catalyzed over access to public land for grazing and water. Conflict over access escalates dramatically in the late 1800s as improved transportation coupled with booming markets for beef made ranching a lucrative business. Disputes rise and fall across the arc of the twentieth century, and have remerged in the twenty-first century.

Today, western cattle ranchers are hanging onto a dying and unsustainable industry. On the one hand, they are plagued by low cattle prices, a declining market, increasing production costs, foreign competition, and a surge of boutique, hobby ranchers. On the other hand, they face marked degradation of public rangeland and uncertainty over government regulation and management of those public land resources that might prove more sustainable while limiting rancher access (Freilich et al. 2003; Ward 1998; Klockenbrink 1991). It is impossible to find an economic indicator in their favor. It is not surprising that ranchers feel as though they are under siege.

This dynamic has materialized into recent dramatic and sometimes quite violent standoffs and occupations at Bunkerville, Nevada (spring 2014) and the Malheur National Wildlife Refuge, Oregon (winter 2016) that underscore the tensions between ranchers and the federal government. It is useful, at this point, to make a distinction between the different groups of players who coalesce around range war events: ranchers, militia, and followers of various sorts. All take a strongly libertarian, anti-federal government stance that emphasizes states' rights and rejects federal ownership of public land and its right to manage and regulate those lands.

The Cliven Bundy Ranch in Bunkerville serves as the epicenter for the new range wars, for it is the site of the first violent confrontation between federal agents, ranchers, militia, and all manner of hangers-on. Bundy and sons Ammon and Ryan figure prominently in this range war fluorescence. Others are also noteworthy including rancher LaVoy Finicum from the desolate Arizona Strip north of Flagstaff and militia leader, Ryan Payne.

Over the course of the events detailed in this chapter, I had a front-row seat living and working in Cedar City, Utah, nestled in the far southwestern corner of the state. Bunkerville was a mere 100 miles south—a straight shot down I-15 toward Las Vegas. I frequently drove past the Bundy Ranch that marks the start of militant opposition to the federal government and its agencies that manage public lands: The Bureau of Land Management (BLM) and the U.S. Forest Service (USFS). Over the course of the past five years, he rose from being a "crotchety old rancher" (to quote a friend from Bunkerville) to a folk hero to the anti-federal alt-right. Bundy and his sons, most notably Ammon and Ryan, perform the part always appearing in public decked out in full cowboy gear with a pocket-sized Constitution always present. In his day job, Ammon works in Phoenix as a valet car fleet manager. Ryan owns a construction company in Cedar City, and made a failed attempt to run for Governor in Nevada in 2018 as an independent.

The range war came very close to home. The rancher militia was considering moving from Malheur to Cedar City where there was a highly sympathetic county commissioner. That move was short-circuited by the death of a range-warrior leader, Finicum, on a rural Oregon highway—shot by an FBI agent a short while after meeting with the commissioner and ranchers to exhort them to support the rancher militia and renounce their grazing contracts for public lands access (Maffly 2016; Scott 2016a, b).

I have laid this out, not just in the interest of full disclosure, but to underscore the kinds of tensions that swirl around public land in the Western United States. It is hard for people who have never lived there for significant amounts of time to understand the depth of hatred and disdain that rural people have for the federal government and its ownership of public land. Often the federal government presence is understood as a colonial occupying force imposing rules and regulations that impedes people's lives and livelihoods. In the states discussed in this chapter, it is useful to recall that in Utah 65 percent of the land is public; in Nevada that number is a whopping 85 percent; and in Oregon it stands at 53 percent. In the three places I have lived over my academic career, in contrast, that figure is 2.6 percent (Alabama); 1.8 percent (Texas); and 10 percent (Michigan) (cf. Ballotpedia n.d.; BLM 2017). In the West, public land dominates the landscape, and its management is a constant on rural peoples' radars whether it is about public land grazing, mining, or recreational access and use.

The chapter begins by outlining the history of range wars in the West and then segues into brief vignettes of the new and violent range war. Next, it examines the ideological foundation upon which the current range war is anchored, as well as issues of western rancher identity. Finally, it will be argued that these contemporary dynamics can be understood as a type of revitalization movement in the face of an incrementally growing existential threat to rural rancher lives and livelihoods (Wallace 1956).

A BRIEF HISTORY OF AMERICA'S WESTERN RANGE WARS AND SAGEBRUSH REBELLIONS

Range wars are nothing new to the western United States and can be traced back to the mid-1800s. It is useful to make a distinction between range wars that are violent clashes (late 1800s, 2014–present) versus sagebrush rebellions (1920s into the 1940s; 1970s) that are typically conducted through legal actions and political channels. This is to say that today's conflict between western ranchers and the federal government is very much of the range war variety characterized by armed clashes.

Together, they center on access to open range on public land and the water on it by ranchers. The 1934 Taylor Grazing Act sought to regulate the use of public land for grazing in a manner that would better steward rangeland and guard against rampant overgrazing. Access is granted through a renewable permit process to approximately 285 million acres across the United States in the lower forty-eight states.

In the late 1800s, the cattle industry boomed as demand coupled with improved transportation allowed for operations to open up in the American West, newly devoid of Indians and bison. As Merrill (2002:25) observes:

> As more ranchers vied for a diminishing piece of the range, they became involved in volatile disputes about controlling land use, particularly as sheep growers began very successfully to occupy the public domain. . . . Range wars were the most notorious events, crystalizing the deepest conflicts over Western range use and signaling the need for closer policing of public lands.

The classic pattern in these range wars was one of internal conflicts due to overstocked, overgrazed lands; larger versus smaller cattle operations; illegal fencing; accusations of rustling against smaller ranchers; all of which was exacerbated by the encroachment of sheep ranching. Indeed, the first legislated action to regulate public lands was the 1885 Unlawful Enclosures Act that outlawed illegal fencing, though the ability to enforce the act was limited. The key here is that the early range wars were local struggles between ranchers over access and control of public domain resources.

World War I dramatically altered the political-economic dynamics of public lands cattle ranching. Because the federal government was strongly encouraging increases in beef production, it is the relationship between federal agencies and ranchers that became foundational to understanding the politics of public lands and ranching. Note that this was not, largely, a legal relationship fought out in the courts. Rather, as we shall see, federal agencies increasingly take on range management power, and their relationship with the ranching community is negotiated politically.

Previously, cattle ranchers and the USFS had been an allied force against homesteaders, which both entities understood as a threat to public grazing lands. Post–World War I, however, homesteading was no longer a policy priority for the federal government. As Merrill (2002:68) smartly notes, "What was left was simply the relationship itself, a relationship structured around the public property of the national forests." Thus, ranchers and the USFS were now pitted against one another in a clash over the interpretation of property relations and the extent of federal control exerted over public lands.

In order to diminish the power of the USFS, ranchers (and most importantly cattlemen's associations representing them) increasingly embraced a states' rights position that staked out the claim that the federal government should cede land in the public domain to individual states. This debate became supercharged in the 1920s over the payment of grazing fees to the USFS to gain public lands access. This was not solely a reaction to the imposition of what was effectively a tax. Additionally, it was about federal public land ownership and the extent of range management control (Merrill 2002:103). Their argument was greatly aided by President Herbert Hoover (1929–1933) who adopted a fairly radical states' rights position on public lands in support of their return to states in the west. The onset of the Great Depression unspools

Hoover's efforts, but the state's rights and the challenge to federal authority form the core ideological features for public lands ranchers moving forward.

Tensions, again, resurface in the 1940s. Recall that the 1934 Taylor Grazing Act imposed a new fee structure, required permits, and generally institutionalized the governance presence of the USFS over western public grazing lands. It also unambiguously establishes the federal government as property owner of public lands. The Act is a reaction to the Dust Bowl tragedy of the 1930s when unsustainable farming methods destroyed agriculture in the Midwestern Plains, and recognized that western public grazing lands were overstocked and overgrazed, thus leading to significant problems with erosion and other forms of environmental degradation.

Fast forward to the 1970s Sagebrush Rebellion, and yet another assertion of states' rights over public lands. This time, there is a new element added to the rancher-state-federal trilogy, namely the environmental movement. The passage of the 1970 National Environmental Policy Act required federal public lands agencies to file environmental impact statements assessing activity on public lands. Those reports became the basis for lawsuits by environmental groups against the federal government, especially concerning the impact of grazing (Merrill 2002:206).[2] The environmental movement has also been successful in lobbying the federal government to expand wilderness areas, national parks and monuments, and other forms protected public land.

The catalyst for the late 1970s rebellion was the 1976 Federal Land Policy and Management Act. This act ended homesteading and further centered control of public lands with the federal government. Through the act, the BLM was instructed to continue its work collaborating with ranchers and the mining industry. Critically, it also charged the BLM with developing formal strategies to shield fragile public land from damage caused by grazing and mining.

Underscoring that the rebellion was a political rather than legal fight, Ronald Reagan famously signed on during his 1980 presidential campaign at a rally in Salt Lake City: "I happen to be one who cheers and supports the Sagebrush Rebellion. Count me in as a rebel" (Coates 1986). Under pressure from ranchers and the oil industry, Utah senator Orrin Hatch (1977–2019) introduced a land-transfer bill designed to return public lands back to states with the exception of national parks and monuments. Ultimately, the effort failed and rebellion again receded, which brings us to its most recent reincarnation in Nevada, Oregon, and Utah, which will be detailed later in the chapter. It is important to emphasize that with the exception of the late 1800s, rural western militancy and unrest has largely been conducted through political channels. The latest example is one of armed insurgency making it a noteworthy departure from previous iterations, though founded on the same states' rights platform.

The states' rights position is, further, informed by a particular reading of the Constitution's 10th Amendment where it is asserted that only states have political authority over the disposition of land within their borders. It is further contended that, as a sovereign nation, the United States could not own land on which private economic activity occurred. Such action would deepen the federal government's presence in people's daily economic lives, thus depressing economic development and individual's pursuit of their livelihoods (Merrill 2002:126). It is an interesting argument, for at its base it contends that there is structural inequality baked into public lands pie in the Western United States because the federal government controls the majority of land there (Merrill 2002:126).

Merrill (2002:104) rejects the states' rights position as a simple outgrowth of western libertarian individualism in reaction to an increased federal presence. Rather, she argues that this was driven more by notions of rightful ownership of property and the relationship of states with the federal government.[3] However, she does note that states' rights do serve as a discursive proxy for individual rights and their fate in the face of an expanding federal bureaucracy (Merrill 2002:124). We will return to this notion of western traditionalism and heritage for it has been grafted onto the states' rights position adopted by many ranchers as an unassailable and essentialized source of legitimacy.

BUNKERVILLE, MALHEUR, AND CEDAR CITY

Bunkerville

On April 5, 2014, BLM staff along with federal agents and private contractors began herding and confiscating cattle that belonged to rancher Cliven Bundy. They grazed on public land south of Bunkerville, Nevada in the Gold Butte region (now Gold Butte National Monument of approximately 500,000 acres). Authorities arrested 380 of his cows and planned to auction them off later in the year to partially offset the twenty-one years that Bundy had failed to pay grazing fees then totaling in the neighborhood of $1.2 million dollars. On April 6, Bundy posted a message on the ranch web page: "They have my cattle and now they have one of my boys. Range War begins tomorrow" (Prokop 2015).

It is worth recalling that Gold Butte is home to the endangered desert tortoise, and thus the area had been subject to increasing management and regulation. It is further worth recalling that Nevada is home to over twenty anti-federal government organizations and militias (e.g., Oath Keepers, The Nevada Light Foot Militia, and the Three Percenters) (Parsons, Magnus, and Jones 2016). Cows, militia, ranchers, and tortoises all convened in Bunkerville. Over 1,000 people responded to Bundy's call to arms. Early on, one of Bundy's sons, Dave, was arrested for failing to depart temporarily closed government land; another son, Ammon, was tasered and arrested after he kicked a government dog; on April 12, armed Bundy supporters took up sniper positions against federal agents on I-15, protected by concrete barriers. At this point, the BLM called off the operation, released the cattle, and diffused the situation. Cliven Bundy claimed victory against "overwhelming tactical superiority" (Parsons, Magnus, and Jones 2016:12).

Malheur

In early December 2015, Ammon Bundy and well-known militia member, Ryan Payne, took up residence in Burns, Oregon in rural, southeastern Oregon near the Malheur Wildlife Refuge. On December 30, the staff at Malheur were dismissed early because of rising tensions between militia and local residents in Burns. A 41-day occupation of Malheur by militia and their supporters ensued in what is commonly seen as a sequel to the Bunkerville standoff.

On January 2, 2016, a group of self-proclaimed militia led by Ammon Bundy occupied the Malheur refuge. They took over buildings, established defensive positions, and constructed a roadblock into the refuge. They were protesting the jailing of two area ranchers, Steven and Dwight Hammond. The Hammonds had initially been at odds with the federal government over unpaid grazing fees. They were arrested and jailed in 2012 for arson and served abbreviated terms. Subsequently, they were resentenced in late 2015 to five years in prison and then pardoned by President Donald Trump in July 2018.

The occupiers may have had a protracted occupation, but they were effectively surrounded by federal and local authorities during the dead of winter. Along the way, one of the leaders, LaVoy Finicum, was killed by state troopers at a roadblock outside the refuge on January 26, when he appeared to be reaching for a weapon, which was, indeed under his coat.

While occupiers had gradually left the Wildlife Refuge, and many of the militia turned themselves into the FBI. The final four militia holdouts abandoned Malhuer on February 11.

Cedar City

In Cedar City, Utah you must pass through a metal detector and get buzzed into the local USFS field office. It is an uncanny experience in what appears to be a laid back, intermountain west town. All is not what it appears, though.

Pivot from Malheur to Cedar City where Malheur occupiers met with a powerful county commissioner and sympathetic local ranchers.

LaVoy Finicum showed up with one of the Bundy sons, Ryan. Finicum described the trip as designed to meet with county officials interested in supporting "a similar standoff with federal authorities over public lands ownership" (Zinda 2016; also see REAL 2016). The meeting was confirmed by the county commissioner as taking place on January 13 (Scott 2016a). Finicum additionally made an appearance on a local afternoon talk radio program. Local activist, Chris Zinda blogged, "Rancher LaVoy Finicum and militia organizer Cope Reynolds were recently recruiting support among southern Utah ranchers to stop paying their grazing fees and to create a local militia so that national militias can come and protect them from the consequences of their actions" (REAL 2016; also see Gettys 2016; Scott 2016c).[4]

On January 23, Cedar City hosted the Western Rangelands Property Rights workshop at the town's Heritage Center. The event was headed up by Bundy lawyer, Todd McFarlane, with approximately 100 ranchers in attendance. The goal: get ranchers to renounce federal grazing permits but continue grazing. According to McFarland, "We are looking for the next wave. The early adopters, the legitimizers, those people who are ready to step up and help shape grazing and land policy in the West for the foreseeable future. If we don't then the federal government is going to do it" (Scott 2016b). McFarlane continued, "This is an act of civil disobedience in response to a long trail of abuses. They aren't going to go out and plunder that land and the resources. They are saying, 'We are exercising our liberty to exercise personal choice for our ranch and do it responsibly'" (Maffly 2016). Eight ranchers pledged to stop paying their grazing fees and decline the contracts that regulate access to public land grazing allotments (Maffly 2016).

On March 25, a sympathetic county commissioner abruptly resigned his position in order to pursue new opportunities in Alaska.

CATTLE GRAZING AND THE RANCHERS' BEEF WITH THE FEDERAL GOVERNMENT

Clearly, there are deep and enduring tensions between western ranchers, grazing access, and, what those ranchers would see as their federal overlords. Again, for those not living the western United States, with all its vastness, it is hard to comprehend the scale of public land use.

First, it is useful to put the scale and impact of cattle grazing on federal public land into perspective. Two major public lands agencies administer grazing rights to ranchers. The BLM administers 18,000 licenses and permits for ranchers who graze on 21,000 allotments totaling 155 million acres (63 percent is open to grazing; BLM 2016). The USFS administers 8,455 allotments covering just under 90 million acres (47 percent is open to grazing) (GAO 1993). The cost of grazing was $1.35 per head per month in 2014, largely unchanged from 1978 (Clarke 2014). Public lands agencies could hardly be accused of holding back land or over charging for access. However, they might be accused of less than stellar management of those lands when one-third are deemed in satisfactory condition with the remaining two-thirds as unsatisfactory (Muir 2012).

Range and farmland have become rapidly desertified with as much as 85 percent of America's vast 685 million acres suffering from marked environmental degradation (Klockenbrink 1991). Seventy-five percent of land that is publicly grazed is overstocked with no management plan to reduce those numbers, and 13 million acres of which are degraded beyond recovery (Klockenbrink 1991). Much of this problem stems from the federal government's inability to monitor and regulate herd sizes. Minimal grazing fees cannot support the cost of the much-needed federal supervision and management. It is a tragedy of the commons scenario whereby self-interested resource users deplete a common resource against the overall common good (cf. Hardin 1968).

In sum, western public land gets grazed on the cheap with considerable environmental impact but with little cost transferred to those doing the impacting. The hidden cost, or externality as economists would say, of cheap beef is the environment. One might, then, credibly ask what is the western rancher's beef with the federal government?

At base is the notion that public land is an open-access, free resource per a particular reading of Article 10 of the Constitution—free for the taking as either open range or privatized land. Public land under the stewardship and authority of the federal government never existed from this perspective.

Bartrum (2018) applies a particularly fine-grained legal analysis to range warrior claims that the federal government cannot own and manage property within states. He begins by exploring commonplace "disclaimer clauses"[5] in western states' statehood acts that cede public land to the federal government as a condition of statehood. Range warriors have made the claim that they settled land and improved it before statehood (and in some cases before the land became U.S. territory). Basically, they argue that they have a preemptive claim to the land (a sort of squatters' rights) (Bartum 2018:71). They also make a constitutional argument that the federal government cannot own land within a state based on Article 10 of the Constitution. Further, they contend that there is a binding "equal-footing" doctrine in the Constitution that ensures that new states entering the nation do so on an equal-footing with all others, especially the original thirteen states. Large tracts of federally owned public land hinder the state's economic development and growth so the argument goes. Therefore, all public land should have transferred to the state upon statehood, rather than to the federal government. Consequently, if anyone regulates the use of public lands for grazing and other activities, it should fall to the state (Bartrum 2018:72). As a legal matter, Bartrum (2018:89) concludes, there is little, if any, support for the claims of states' rights arguments concerning public land.

There are, however, two paths to making a successful claim to public land as private property. First, early settlers could have recorded title to surveyed public land with their appropriate land district to establish a preemptive claim per the 1841 Preemption Act. Second, settlers could have formally homesteaded a tract of surveyed public land per the 1862 Homestead Act, again vesting title through proper, recorded title. It is also important to note that the maximum size of these allotments was 640 acres (Bartrum 2018:73–74). While Cliven Bundy may claim deep historical connections to Bunkerville dating to 1847, there is no hard evidence of this in the form of an application for title. Indeed, Bundy's father purchased the ranch he now owns in 1948 (Bartum 2018:75).

Blumm and Jamin (2017) conduct an equally detailed legal analysis of the so-called "property clause" (Clause 2) of the Constitution. It invests Congress with the power to transfer, privatize, swap, or otherwise divest itself of public land holdings. They, too, note that the federal ownership is clearly stated, thus divestiture of those lands is a political and not a legal issue. Hence, standoffs, occupations, and other range war tactics gain little traction in a legal environment. Rather, efforts among sympathetic federal legislators form the only means by which there could be a legal transfer of federal public land back to states. In addition to noting the equal-footing argument, they go on to explore other rancher challenges. Two of the more interesting ones focus on water and grass since these are critical means of production for the cattle industry.

The water rights challenge contends that there are implied easements to graze on public land so that cattle can gain access to water. In other words, how can you stop cattle from having a quick snack on the way to the watering hole as a right set out under state law.[6] Courts have consistently rejected this because the 1934 Taylor Grazing Act preempts any state law (Blumm and Jamin 2017:811–812).

Blumm and Jamin (2017:812) refer, somewhat tongue in cheek, to a range-warrior "labor theory of grass." That is, grass belongs to cows (and their owners) because they have historically eaten it. A long history of grazing a particular tract of public land equates, in this form of logic, to ownership of the resource. Again, this is short-circuited by the Taylor Act, as well as the terms of their grazing permits, which expressly denies ranchers any land rights. Those ranchers might argue (for there is no court case on these grounds) that they have enhanced those grasslands and therefore have an entitlement to the value of that enhanced grassland. It is not hard to envision the federal government sending them a bill for the environmental degradation that has occurred on those same rangelands.

As Cliven Bundy puts it, when his kin's cattle first set foot on the land that his cattle still grazes today and took that first drink of water or a bite of grass, it was a "beneficial use" of a renewable resource (Quammen 2016).

> That's how our rights are created. So now we have created them and we use them, make beneficial use of them, and then we protect them. And that's sort of a natural law, and that's what the rancher has done. That how he has his rights. And that's what the range war, the Bundy war, is all about right now, it's protecting these three things: our life, liberty, and our property. (Cliven Bundy quoted in Quammen 2016)

To truly appreciate range-warrior political-legal arguments, it is imperative to explore them in religious context, which figures profoundly in many ranchers' worldviews.

GOD, THE NAY BOOK, AND THE CONSTITUTION

Among a subset of range warriors, there is a strong religious thread that weaves together their politics and ideology. As Sottile (2018) observes, "Ryan Bundy is saying that he found permission from God to disregard the government altogether" (in the LDS 12th Article of Faith).

There is a homespun book put together by ranchers Keith Nay and Cliven Bundy, neighbors in Bunkerville. Both are devout members of the Church of Jesus Christ of Latter-day Saints (LDS, or more colloquially Mormon). They compiled it in the mid- to late 1990s out of frustration with perceived federal regulatory encroachment on their livelihoods. The book purports to provide religious justification and legitimacy to anti-federal government ideas and actions. Hence, it is foundational to rejection of and resistance to federal public land ownership and management.

The book is a collection of letters, LDS scripture, and writings of LDS leadership—words of the prophets. It critically views the Constitution as a document written by God that had to be defended at all cost. LDS founder, Joseph Smith, saw the Constitution (with particular focus on the First Amendment) as a divine document from the hand of God for it protected religious freedom and agency to live as you saw fit. It is also a document that supports the idea of small, non-interventive government, personal and religious freedom and liberty, and local control of everything. As Sottile (2018) astutely points out, the key to the Nay Book is the LDS 12th Article of Faith, which focuses on the role of government. The 12th Article of Faith reads, “We believe in being subject to kings, presidents, rulers, and magistrates, in obeying, honoring, and sustaining the law” (quoted in Sottile 2018). One reading of that article is that LDS members submit to the rule of land. As noted in the quote that opened this section, an alternative reading suggests voluntary submission predicated on rulers upholding the ideal of “obeying, honoring, and sustaining the law.” So, perceptions that those rulers are violating peoples’ rights, imply that their rule is illegitimate (Sottile 2018). It is important to note that this is a radical reading of 12th Article of Faith, and certainly not one advocated by the mainstream LDS Church.

Drawing together the threads of range-warrior logic that focus on key pieces of the Constitution and articles of LDS faith is useful at this juncture. Critical elements include Article 4 of the Constitution (equal-footing, property clause); 10th Amendment of the Constitution (state’s rights); Preemptive Act/Homestead Act (settler rights prior to statehood); and 12th Article of Faith (small government, religious freedom, personal agency, local control). To this, it is important to note that the Bundy’s reading of the Constitution is heavily influenced by the W. Cleon Skousen[7] (1913–2006) annotated version of that document, which is common reading fare among the far right. At Malheur, for example, it was a prominent feature among militia and ranchers alike (Duara 2016).

Especially among LDS ranchers, the Bible and the Constitution are understood as divinely inspired texts. Add to this mix a strong libertarian, anti-federal government ethos that lines up with and goes well beyond the states’ rights movement, and you have the broad outlines of the dynamic of contemporary rural western range war ideology. The Bundys and other range warriors, simply put, do not recognize the federal government or its authority as defined by their celestial imperative.

Quammen (2016) observes that founder Joseph Smith forewarned the LDS faithful that

> this Nation will be on the very verge of crumbling to pieces and tumbling to the ground when the Constitution is upon the brink of ruin; this people will be the Staff upon which the Nation shall lean and they shall bear the Constitution away from the very verge of destruction.

One can only imagine that the Bundy’s and other range warriors perceive themselves as that very staff driven by an urgency to act in the face of tyrannical federal forces whose very existence and actions are, by their definition, unconstitutional.

The idea of a divine Constitution near ruin is key to the following analysis, for it suggests a kind of cultural chaos reminiscent of the conditions that undergird revitalization movements, which seek to banish the wicked and return the world to a bygone era of cultural stability and plenty.

IDENTITY, HERITAGE, AND A NOSTALGIC IMAGINED PAST

Building upon the discussion of LDS rancher culture and identity, it will be useful to examine broader identity construction as it plays out in ritual. In Cedar City, this was performed in three different rituals during my time there. The first two are Pioneer Day and the Cedar City Livestock and Heritage Festival. A third is the Western Heritage Freedom Festival. That "heritage" is in the title of two of those events should draw our attention. On the surface of it, it is all seemingly benign enough.

Pioneer Day and the Cedar City Livestock and Heritage Festival are very similar in content and performance—one celebrates the founding of the state by white LDS settlers in 1847, the other celebrates the founding of Cedar City in 1851. Here, I will conflate the two and their use of heritage as a dominant trope.

On the benign side, heritage is a great excuse for a parade with marching bands, old ranchers on their antique tractors, cowboys in full regalia, the tank from the local National Guard armory, and stupendous amounts of candy. But the main attraction is multiple herds of sheep heading down Main Street that periodically break into intricate maneuvers under the watchful eye, nip, nudge, and bark of very-well-trained cow dogs. Multigenerational ranch families feel nostalgia that is deeply tied to place and their family's role in carving out a living against desperate odds (see Tebbs and McDonald, this volume). As one newspaper op-ed writer summed it up:

> The Pioneer Day Holiday honors the values, courage, and unfailing determination by our ancestors. It is the recognition that the foundations for the beauty, peace, and prosperity that we currently enjoy were laid by those who came before us. Their efforts included deep personal sacrifices and a willingness to think and plan beyond the present. Even today, modern motorcycle riders still appreciate the wide old streets . . . that were built wide enough to turn a team of horses and wagon. (Hyde 2015)

On the less benign side, the festival becomes a symbolic crucible for and celebration of male whiteness, power, and control. There is a primordial element along with notions of common history and experience, shared norms and values, and the like. It is a ritual of imperialist nostalgia (Rosaldo 1989: Chapter 3). It is a yearning for that which has been destroyed and irrevocably lost. The days of sheep drives and living for long, isolated stretches of time in sheep camps is long gone.[8] Today sheep move from lowland to highland settings in tractor-trailer trucks. The cowboys watching the sheep are as likely to be on an all-terrain vehicle as they are on a horse. Those cowboys are also most often indigenous Peruvians from the Andes Mountains who are well versed in working with ruminants at high altitudes and isolated settings. But none of that is to be found in the festival, nor are local Paiute bands included as part of the heritage. Certain elements, then, are foregrounded: rugged white male cowboys, productivity, taming of the land (and the other), foresight, and "American" values.

The Western Freedom Festival was a far more controversial event in which county taxpayer dollars funded what many saw as a thinly veiled political rally for far right-wing ideals and policies. The festival was an amalgam of speakers and performances supporting an anti-federal states' rights platform. Again, the op-ed writer captures the overall essence:

> Long-held traditions are being regulated out of existence and for the first time in many generations, Southern Utahns are in danger of losing touch with their heritage. [The Western Freedom Festival] is intended to be a rallying point for those who still cherish the core values of freedom, family, responsible stewardship, economic prosperity, and other traits that made Southern Utah . . . . A people who do not remember where they came from are apt to forget who they are. Those who do not understand their own history become like children who depend on self-appointed experts to tell them what to think of themselves. An effort to reprogram the thinking of Americans by attempting to cut them off from their history is already underway in many parts of the nation. (Hyde 2015)

Historical social memory is, in this light, an interesting mix of relatively enduring traditions coupled with contemporary agency, creativity, and strategic social action. That is, the past gets selectively used and recast toward contemporary ends. Stories about heritage and how they are told serve as a reference point for contemporary identity.

All this came into sharp focus in a conversation with the sympathetic county commissioner at a local Rotary Club meeting. He asked if I still taught classes as a university administrator. Yes, indeed, and I was currently teaching a course on "Language, Thought, and Culture." He said that he was deeply interested in language and would love to talk to me about it in much greater depth. But did I not agree that everyone in American should speak English and embrace American values? I suggested that we take that statement and turn it on its head by assuming that diversity is the dominant reality. The critical job, then, is to find ways to bridge across languages and cultures, and understand and appreciate the power of those diverse perspectives.

Conversation over. As he was pivoting away in haste, I handed him my card and said we should get together to chat more about language and culture. I still await his phone call.

Terrance Turner (1993) has done a deep analysis of anthropology's dis-ease with the multicultural concept and movement in America (also see Shweder, Minow, and Markus 2004 for an equally critical analysis). He notes that one dominant strain within that movement treats diversity as essentialized difference—closed, bounded, homogeneous, overdetermined. The commissioner is, no doubt, not a fan of multiculturalism. It occurred to me, though, as he was talking about English and American values that he was, ironically, making the same essentialized argument—American values are rural, white, male, conservative, LDS values. Pioneer Day, the Cedar City Livestock and Heritage Festival, and the Western Freedom Festival all champion that essentialized history and identity.

RANGE WAR AS REVITALIZATION MOVEMENT

Journalists, activists, and scholars who have explored the new range war have done so in a mostly descriptive mode. Their goal has been to sort out the timeline and what happened. Analysis deepens when there is a turn toward understanding the motivations that undergird this phenomenon. Sottile (2017) and Quammen (2016), for example, do an excellent job of mining the "Bundy War," carefully tracing out the linkages between religious ideology, politics, and the Constitution. Bartum (2018) and Blumm and Jamin (2017) provide a fine-grained analysis of legal issues surrounding the new range war from a Constitutional-legal perspective.

What is missing is an analysis out of the social sciences that could draw all this description into a more holistic analytical frame that helps explain this new range war phenomenon as more than a series of conflicts, but rather as part of a sustained and enduring social movement. Indeed, the new range war has all the trappings of a revitalization movement that connects faith, ritual, and a return to a bygone past.

Work by Wallace (1956) is the most common starting place for a consideration of revitalization movements. It is a notion that seeks to understand culture change under conditions of stress and decline in which an old cultural system is under siege and dissembling. A new system must be discovered and replace it for shear survival. In this scenario, a visionary receives a divine message to resist oppressors through a variety of incantations and rituals. If the specified incantations and rituals are correctly produced and repeated enough times, the desired transformation will occur. It is a concept born most commonly out of the colonial experience as a form of resistance.[9]

Revitalization seems particularly apt as a theoretical approach. In Harkins's (2004:xxii) terms, every case has a prototype (range war), a script (rise up against illegitimate federal government that seeks to destroy local life and livelihood), and has recurrent metaphors (life, liberty, agency, God, the Constitution). As Harkins (2004:xxii) notes, "This helps us to understand why the actors in these dramas seem to the remote observer really to be following a predetermined script, much more so than in non-revivalistic encounters between colonizer and colonized."

Under Siege on the Ecological Margins

Whatever the stresses of being on the ecological margins might have brought to ranchers in the region, much of the rural west lived under conditions of relative isolation until the mid-twentieth century with the construction of two-lane roads connecting major cities. As the region became increasingly integrated into the larger United States, stress builds as lifeways are challenged building to a cultural distortion that foreshadows the end of a viable ranching economy. In this context, the groundswell of "standoffs" and "occupations" in the west might well be seen as examples of secular ritual designed to chase off the federal government and reestablish the old order of open lands and unfettered, free access. Indeed, from Cliven Bundy's perspective, the initial use of a natural resource establishes open, free access as "natural law" (Quammen 2016).

It is clear that scratching out a living cattle ranching on the desert margins is a hard way to make a living. As Ward (1998) underscores, most ranchers do not run their operations in particularly cost-effective ways. Like most smallholders, they have no leverage in the market so their costs of production are high compared to their corporate counterparts. They are also poor range managers in his view. We know that public lands are chronically overgrazed, in some instances leading to wholesale desertification (Klockenbrink 1991). Ward (1998) advocates a rotational grazing system carried out by shifting access to water while also keeping herds 30–40 percent below carrying capacity. He goes on to further outline sound herd management techniques coupled with operations diversification. Additionally, he contends that many ranchers are not good financial managers. Taken as a whole, he paints a picture of ranching operations that are not sustainable environmentally or as a business proposition (also see, Freilich et al. 2003).

Focusing on the dynamic tension between cattle ranching and conservation efforts, Fletcher (2013) frames Costa Rican ranching operations as, provocatively, an extractive resource because of its negative environmental impacts. In the United States, the tension between environmental interests and those of cattle ranching on public lands first fired up in the 1970s. While policies have evolved in terms of environmental protection, federal management has not—the BLM and Forest Service are simply not funded to undertake those large-scale activities. Nevertheless, in the range war the federal government and environmental groups are often bundled together as an enemy of rural life and livelihood.

In sum, rural western ranchers are under considerable stress in a hostile economic environment. Qualman (2018) succinctly outlines how, for Canada, 1989 marked a watershed year in the beef industry. Since that year, beef price levels that marked the bottom of the market pivoted to mark the top. What happened? Major global corporate players aggressively consolidated the market. Packing plants became larger but less numerous, thus dampening competitiveness (i.e., if you are the only game in town, you can set the price). Major international trade deals were also beginning to lock into place, including the precursor of the North American Free Trade Agreement, which encouraged corporate meat-packer consolidation in the industry. Finally, corporate meat packers established their own feedlots as a hedge against rising market prices that also dampened demand for rancher's cattle as well as price. Similar processes are afoot in the United States that will continue to push small, independent operations to the brink. And it is the brink that catalyzes revitalization movements.

Mapping Revitalization onto the Range War/Bundy War

Wallace (1956:267) lays out a number of variations of revitalization movements, none of which is mutually exclusive: nativistic; revivalistic; cargo cults; vitalistic; messianic; and millenarian. The case of the modern range war has nativistic, revivalistic, and millenarian strains running through it. Nativism focuses on eradicating the outside other and their materials and cultural trappings. Revivalism emphasizes the renewal of traditional cultural and materials elements from generations past, which have eroded or fallen away. The messianic dimension heralds the participation of a divine savior in human form who will chart the path to salvation.

The expulsion of the federal government control and authority from the western United States is a key goal of the range war movement, and underscores its nativistic dimension. States' rights serve as a core tenant of the range war. The Bundys and others refuse to recognize the federal government as a legitimate authority that is entrusted with the stewardship of public lands. As Cliven Bundy notes, "They [federal authorities] are acting—I don't know—acting like an army coming against we, the people" (quoted in Quammen 2017:1). Bundy invokes, "We, The People" regularly in his Manichean world that pits hard-scrabble ranchers against the evil federal empire.

Cliven Bundy links his ranch historically to ancestor-pioneers who settled in the Bunkerville vicinity in 1847 when the area was still part of Mexico.

The explicit connection between the past and the present in a kinship idiom adds a revivalistic dimension to revitalization. Recall that part of the Bundy land-claim narrative is that those ancestors put the land and water to beneficial use. Thus, he argues that he has "ancestral rights" to water, grazing, and the land because of property improvements (Bartrum 2018; Quammen 2017). He further argues that he has the inalienable right to live on that land and use it as he sees fit (a variation on Plato's "good life"). This fits squarely with LDS historical-cultural conservatism, traditional values, and ancestor worship.

Elsewhere in this volume (Tebbs and McDonald), I have made the argument that LDS ranchers have a deep connection to place and landscape. In the analytical frame of philosopher Edgar Casey (1996), people become existentially habituated to places that are filled with objects, histories, discourses, activities, and relationships. The only thing that makes sense to humans is an embodied culturalized space that is endowed with meaning (i.e., place). Quammen (2017:123) argues that because of the struggle to carve out a livelihood in a hostile environment, improvements and alterations to that landscape "were symbols of intrepidness that their ancestors carved into stretches of impenetrable country."

It is also important to note that the standard LDS understanding of the environment is a place that provided them with the means of production (Quammen 2017:137). Quammen (2017:140) further notes that the modification and engineering of land, what she terms its "ordering," renders it sacred. In working the land, LDS ranchers infuse it with divinely ordained crafting. In other words, working the land is pursuing God's will and creating Zion on Earth. This puts Cliven Bundy's argument about making "beneficial use" of land and water in context. This was appropriately modifying the land to productive ends. God had given the faithful the land, not the federal government.[10]

Range war as revitalization movement also has strongly divine element to it giving it a dash of messianic quality. Cliven Bundy and his followers see themselves as defending the Constitution as a sacred document pitted against the evil and illegitimate forces bent on destroying it. And the Bundy bunch hear from God and see themselves as divinely authorized to defend the Constitution as they read and understand it.

Cliven Bundy and his kin, then, are the charismatic evangelists carrying the message of God, liberty, freedom, and the Constitution. Indeed Bundy conflates the "Range War" with the "Bundy war" (Quammen 2016). He also "equat[es] himself with the national spirit, saying he represents millions of Americans" (Carroll 2015).

> Cliven Bundy and his sons Ammon and Ryan believe themselves to be the staff [divinely chosen] and have been dangerously empowered through Mormon prophecy to wage war against American federal law. (Quammen 2017:22)

Cliven Bundy has said that he was instructed by God to engage the BLM at Bunkerville and more broadly disarm federal security agencies in a religious battle of good against evil (Canham 2014). Ammon Bundy heard the word of God tell him to defend the Hammonds in Oregon and mount the occupation at the Malheur Wildlife Refuge (Frontline 2017).

> If I broke some laws, why don't they come and arrest me? If I'm breaking the laws, why did several hundred, maybe thousands, of people feel inspiration to stand with me? If I am breaking the laws of the land, then I would think the Lord wouldn't be with us for one thing. (Cliven Bundy quoted in Canham 2014)

CONCLUSION

Cliven Bundy and his kin were, in fact, arrested and numerous trials ensued. The first one ended in broad acquittals of the Bundys and the militia who were directly involved in the Malheur takeover, as well as other assorted followers who showed up. In a second trial, prosecutors were able to convict four of the occupiers and get another fourteen plea deals. A third trial focused on militia who crossed state lines to get to Bunkerville expressly to block federal agents from doing their jobs—that one ended in a hung jury. A fourth trial in Nevada also centered on armed militants and ended with no convictions. And finally, the high-profile trial of Cliven Bundy and his sons in Nevada was dismissed by the judge because of flagrant misconduct on the part of the prosecution team.

Speaking of the final trial dismissal in Nevada, Cliven Bundy state, "I'm not used to being free. I have been a political prisoner for more than 700 days" (Anglen 2018). At one of the Oregon trials, an occupier stated, "It didn't bother me to be arrested because I'm where I want to be right now. Like the Bundys, I've been called by a higher power . . . we all know this is what God called us to do." Yet another said, "God said we weren't guilty. We weren't guilty of anything" (Irish Times 2016).

To adopt the role of aggrieved political prisoner who clearly has God on his side was a seemingly unlikely outcome, especially when you consider the number of botched trials in the wake of the Bunkerville standoff and the Malheur occupation. Cliven Bundy was acquitted in 2018 and the new range war seems quiet for now.

It is often assumed that revitalization movements have an expiration date. They can only sustain themselves for so long before followers peel away having done all the right rituals without banishing the oppressors with the return to better times. Importantly, the Bundys and the new range war movement have had some significant victories against their perceived oppressors.

Federal agents withdrew from the Bunkerville standoff and improbably five federal trials failed to convict the Bundys and many other followers of any wrongdoing. It would only be a logical conclusion to assume that people with anti-federal agendas would feel emboldened. Yet as a legal issue, as we have seen, the states' rights argument for the return of public lands has no footing. As a political issue, there are pockets of support, most notably in the State of Utah, but broad support is doubtful. Utah legislators' attempts at pushing legislation through Congress for the return of public lands to states have always fallen decidedly flat.

It is useful to turn to other long-lived revitalization movements. They serve as a useful reminder that even when the rituals do not result in the desired transformation, the movement can carry on for a noteworthy amount of time. Take, for example, the Lakota Sioux version of revitalization as embodied in the Ghost Dance that started in the late 1800s. The means were militant, and the end goal was apocalyptic—American oppressors would be eradicated, and there would be a return of old resources (e.g., bison), venerated ancestors, and a lost precolonial culture and society. It is worth remembering that the Lakota Ghost Dance continued on the Plains into the 1920s and 1930s (Daniel Gelo, personal communication).

The looming end of an economic lifestyle and livelihood is not going out quietly. This amazing fantasy ideology of the range warriors goes far beyond the state's rights movement.[11] It has a kinship with Scott's (2009) notion of "reactive or stateless foragers"—self-governing, kin-based groups that have actively fled the state and its depredations, while at the same time strategically using the state's presence for raiding or trading. How land would miraculously revert to a supposed original condition of open, free access is baffling. Even more mystifying is an alternative reading that calls for public lands to be privatized and, apparently, given to the range warriors—a new *latifundia*[12] (Clarke 2016). In either case, there is a clear need for divine intervention in order to return the world to its supposed true and correct condition.

NOTES

1. James H. McDonald thanks Kate Sullivan for being a patient, thoughtful, wise, and a good-humored collaborator on this volume, as well as for catching the vision for where this work might take us. He also thanks Bruce Tebbs and Jacqueline Russell for generously sharing their insights into the complicated dynamics of the Intermountain West.

2. Also see, Freilich et al. 2003 on ranching's environmental impact. Ward (1998) provides an interesting take on the environmental issue from a rancher's perspective. He notes that "considering all the money that federal and state governments have spent on range research and management, I've always found it amazing that most ranchers

have so little knowledge of the subject" (Ward 1998:33). Ward further critiques common ranch management along a series of dimensions from their inability to leverage the market through economies of scale similar to dairy cooperatives; diversification of operations; and sound financial management. Taken together, he argues that modern ranching could be far more economically and environmentally sound and sustainable.

3. Interestingly, she notes that by the 1930s Wyoming and Nevada ranchers form the most radical faction of states' rights advocates in the West. Recall that the new western sagebrush rebellion occurred in southwest Nevada in Bunkerville.

4. It is worth noting that not all militia presence has gone uncontested in the rural west. In Arivaca, Arizona, a group of community members has systematically worked to block the militia presence in their small town (Wiles 2019).

5. A provision of statehood transferred the right and title to unappropriated public land to the federal government.

6. This is fascinating because if that property were private there would certainly be no easement.

7. Skousen was a far-right conspiracy theorist and publisher of a variety of anti-communist and religious books.

8. Sheep camps were small caravans with enough room for one or two people to live in. Initially, they would have been pulled up the mountain by horses and later pick-up trucks.

9. Though Wallace (1956) and others would be quick to point out that these types of movements can also be found in noncolonial settings.

10. Indeed, this also helps illuminate the anathema that LDS ranchers feel toward environmentalists where nonhuman species (read here, nonproductive) take precedence over productive labor in the form of resource extraction: grazing, minerals, lumber.

11. At least in Utah, it would appear that the idea of public land transfer, as exemplified in the 2012 Utah Transfer of Public Lands Act, centers on economic development, increased access fees, and decreased oversight—a revenue generator rather than a free resource.

12. A term used in colonial and postcolonial Latin America for a private landed estate.

REFERENCES CITED

Anglen, Robert. 2018. Cliven Bundy Walks Free as Federal Judge Dismisses Bundy Ranch Standoff Case. *Arizona Republic*. https://www.azcentral.com/story/news/local/arizona-investigations/2018/01/08/cliven-bundy-ranch-standoff-case-retried-federal-court-ruling/1008051001/ (Accessed May 6, 2019).

Ballotpedia. n.d. Federal Land Ownership by State. https://ballotpedia.org/Federal_land_ownership_by_state (Accessed May 3, 2019).

Bartrum, Ian. 2018. Searching for Cliven Bundy: The Constitution and Public Land. *Nevada Law Journal Forum* 2:67–90.

Blumm, Michael C., and Olivier Jamin. 2017. The Property Clause and Its Discontents: Lessons from the Malheur Occupation. *Ecological Law Quarterly* 43(4):781–826.

Bureau of Land Management (BLM). 2016. Fact Sheet on the BLM's Management of Livestock Grazing. http://www.blm.gov/wo/st/en/prog/grazing.print.html (Accessed February 25, 2016).

———. 2017. Public Land Statistics 2016. https://www.blm.gov/sites/blm.gov/files/PublicLandStatistics2016.pdf (Accessed May 3, 2019).

Canham, Matt. 2014. Mormon Cliven Bundy Says God Showed Him Path to Avoid Civil War. *Salt Lake Tribune*. https://archive.sltrib.com/article.php?id=58267899&itype=cmsid (Accessed May 6, 2019).

Carroll, Rory. 2015. A Year after Armed Standoff, Cliven Bundy Still Star of His Own Tea Party-tinged Western. *The Guardian*. http://www.theguardian.com/us-news/2015/jun/01/cliven-bundy-standoff-grazing-rights-nevada-ranch (Accessed February 25, 2016).

Casey, Edgar S. 1996. How to Get from Space to Place in a Fairly Short Stretch of Time: Phenomenological Prolegomena. In *Senses of Place*, edited by Steven Feld and Keith H. Basso, pp. 12–52. Santa Fe, N.M.: School for American Research Press.

Clarke, Chris. 2014. This Year's Public Land Grazing Fee a Bargain, Continuing at 30 Year Trend. *KCET ReWild*. http://www.kcet.org/news/redefine/rewild/commentary/2014-public-land-grazing-fee-the-same-as-2013-and-2012-and-2011.html (Accessed February 26, 2016).

———. 2016. The Bundys Have a Vision for the West, and You Aren't Included. *KCET ReWild*. http://www.kcet.org/news/redefine/rewild/commentary/malheur-commentary.html (Accessed February 26, 2019).

Duara, Nigel. 2016. Oregon Armed Protesters Invoke the Constitution—Annotated by a Conspiracy Theorist. *Los Angeles Times*. https://www.latimes.com/nation/la-na-ff-oregon-standoff-constitution-20160121-story.html (Accessed May 4, 2019).

Fletcher, Robert. 2014. Between the Cattle and the Deep Blue Sea: The Janus Face of the Ecotourism-Extraction Nexus in Costa Rica. In *The Ecotourism-Extraction Nexus: Political Economies and Rural Realities of (Un)Comfortable Bedfellows*, edited by Bram Büscher and Veronica Davidov, pp. 69–87. New York: Routledge.

Freilich, Jerome E., John M. Emlen, Jeffrey J. Duda, D. Carl Freeman, and Philip J. Cafaro. 2003. Ecological Effects of Ranching: A Six-Point Critique. *BioScience* 53(8):759–65.

Frontline. 2017. American Patriot: Inside the Armed Uprising Against the Federal Government. https://www.pbs.org/wgbh/frontline/film/american-patriot-inside-the-armed-uprising-against-the-federal-government/ (Accessed May 6, 2019).

General Accounting Office (GAO). 1993. Rangeland Management: Profile of the Forest Service's Grazing Allotments and Permittees. http://www.gao.gov/products/GAO/RCED-93-141FS (Accessed February 24, 2016).

Gettys, Travis. 2016. Oregon Militants LaVoy Finicum and Ryan Bundy Travel to Utah to Plot Another Armed Showdown. *Raw Story*. https://www.rawstory.com/

2016/01/oregon-militants-lavoy-finicum-and-ryan-bundy-travel-to-utah-to-plot-another-armed-showdown/ (Accessed May 3, 2019).

Hardin, Garrett. 1968. The Tragedy of the Commons. *Science* 162(3859):1243–48.

Harkin, Michael E. 2004. Introduction: Revitalization as History and Theory. In *Reassessing Revitalization Movements: Perspectives from North America and the Pacific Islands*, edited by Michael E. Harkin, pp. xv-xxxvi. Lincoln, NE: University of Nebraska Press.

Hyde, Bryan. 2015. Perspectives: The Western Freedom Festival, Why Heritage Matters. *St. George News.* https://www.stgeorgeutah.com/news/archive/2015/07/20/perspectives-western-freedom-festival-heritage-matters/#.XNQ6-RRKhQI (Accessed May 8, 2019).

Irish Times. 2016. Oregon Militants Acquitted: "God Said We Weren't Guilty." https://www.irishtimes.com/news/world/us/oregon-militants-acquitted-god-said-we-weren-t-guilty-1.2846775 (Accessed May 6, 2019).

Klockenbrink, Myra. 1991. The New Range War Has the Desert as Foe. *New York Times.* https://nyti.ms.29nuzed (Accessed May 1, 2019).

Maffly, Brian. 2016. Utah Ranchers Renounce Federal Control of Their Lands at Gathering with Ties to Oregon Occupation. *Salt Lake Tribune.* https://archive.sltrib.com/article.php?id=3467639&itype=CMSID

Merrill, Karen R. 2002. *Public Lands and Political Meaning: Ranchers, the Government, and the Property Between Them.* Berkeley, CA: University of California Press.

Muir, Patricia. 2012. Western Public Lands as an Example. http://people.oregonstate.edu/~muirp/wpubland.htm (Accessed February 24, 2019).

Parsons, Chelsea, Annette Magnus, and Jordan Jones. 2016. Violent Words, Violent Crimes: Anti-Government Extremism and Gun Violence in Nevada. Center for American Progress. https://cdn.americanprogress.org/wp-content/uploads/2016/09/21083723/NevadaViolentExtremism-reportINTRO.pdf (Accessed May 2, 2019).

Politico. 2014. Cliven Bundy: God Was On Our Side. https://www.politico.com/story/2014/08/cliven-bundy-109681 (Accessed May 9, 2019).

Prokop, Andrew. 2015. The 2014 Controversy Over Nevada Rancher Cliven Bundy, Explained. *Vox.* https://www.vox.com/2014/8/14/18080508/nevada-rancher-cliven-bundy-explained (Accessed May 3, 2019).

Qualman, Darrin. 2018. The Cattle Crisis: 100 Years of Canadian Cattle Prices. https://www.darrinqualman.com/canadian-cattle-prices/ (Accessed May 6, 2019).

Quammen, Betsy Gaines. 2016. The War for the West Rages On. *New York Times.* https://www.nytimes.com/2016/01/30/opinion/the-war-for-the-west-rages-on.html (Accessed May 3, 2019).

———. 2017 American Zion: Mormon Perspectives on Landscape from Zion National Park to the Bundy Family War. Ph.D. dissertation, Montana State University.

Responsible for Equality and Liberty (REAL). 2018. USA: "Sovereign Citizen" Bundy Terrorist Group Plans for Utah Insurrection, Possible Additional Takeover. https://realcourage.org/2016/01/bundy-terrorist-plans-utah-attack/ (Accessed May 3, 2019).

Rosaldo, Renato. 1989. *Culture & Truth: The Remaking of Social Analysis*. Boston, MA: Beacon Press.

Scott, Haven. 2016a. Finicum, Bundy in Iron County Before Deadly Encounter. *The Spectrum*. https://www.thespectrum.com/story/news/local/cedar-city/2016/01/29/finicum-bundy-iron-county-before-deadly-encounter/79541424/ (Accessed May 1, 2019).

———. 2016b. More Rangeland Discussion in Cedar City. *The Spectrum*. https://www.thespectrum.com/story/news/local/cedar-city/2016/01/23/more-rangeland-discussion-cedar-city/79243986/

———. 2016c. Utah Ranchers Gather in Vigil for Oregon Protester Killed in FBI Crackdown. *USA Today*. https://www.usatoday.com/story/news/nation-now/2016/01/28/utah-ranchers-gather-vigil-ore-protester/79445274/ (Accessed May 1, 2019).

Scott, James C. 2009. *The Art of Not Being Governed: An Anarchist History of Upland Southeast Asia*. New Haven, CT: Yale University Press.

Sottile, Leah. 2017. Cliven Bundy's Fight against the Feds Has Roots in "Radical" Interpretation of Mormon Scripture. *Salt Lake Tribune*. https://www.sltrib.com/news/nation-world/2017/12/10/cliven-bundys-fight-against-the-feds-has-roots-in-radical-interpretation-of-mormon-scripture/ (Accessed May 3, 2019).

———. 2018. Bundyville Chapter 4: The Gospel of Bundy. *Longreads*. https://longreads.com/2018/05/18/bundyville-chapter-four-the-gospel-of-bundy/ (Accessed May 3, 2019).

Shweder, Richard, Martha Minow, and Hazel Rose Markus. 2004. *Engaging Cultural Differences: The Multicultural Challenge in Liberal Democracies*. New York: Russell Sage Foundation.

Turner, Terence. 1993. Anthropology and Multiculturalism: What is Anthropology That Multiculturalists Should Be Mindful of It? *Cultural Anthropology* 8(4):411–29.

Wallace, Anthony F. C. 1956. Revitalization Movements. *American Anthropologist* 58(2):264–81.

Ward, Nol. 1998. Sustainable Ranching: A Rancher's Perspective. *Rangelands* 20(3):33–37.

Wiles, Tay. 2019. Public Pushback: Arivaca, Arizona, Became a Magnet for Anti-immigrant Activists. Locals Wouldn't Have It. *High Country News* 27: 12–17.

Zinda, Chris. 2016. FBI to Malheur Militia: You're Free to Travel. *Counterpunch*. https://www.counterpunch.org/2016/01/14/fbi-to-malheur-militia-youre-free-to-travel/ (Accessed May 3, 2019).

Chapter 3

Public Land, Place, and Shadow Displacement in Rural Utah

Bruce R. Tebbs and James H. McDonald

The relationship between private and public land has increasingly become a contentious one for ranchers in the western U.S. Federal policy, and practice has increasingly disrupted deeply embodied senses of place, access, and protection of privately held land. Rural Utah is often characterized by kin groups that have five or six generations of depth in small rural communities. The ultimate effect is a shadow displacement of rural ranching families and culture.

This chapter explores public-private land tensions through a personal-narrative case study in which a multigenerational ranching family working a private landholding has found itself at complete odds with the federal government and its public lands agencies. The property in question is part of a family-owned ranch with over 100 years of time depth. It is a high-mountain operation located near the small town of Panguitch, Utah on the eastern flank of Cedar Mountain in the Dixie National Forest.

This is a story of a once-thriving smallholder operation that is now a private island surrounded by public land.[1] It is told through an ongoing discussion with a former university colleague and rancher, Bruce Tebbs whose family's earliest ranch holdings date to the late 1800s. For relatively untethered urbanites, it is often hard to grasp deep attachment to place, and the chapter concludes with a discussion of ranching and sense of place in the rural West.

MYERS VALLEY: A PRIVATE ISLAND IN A PUBLIC LAND SEA

Bruce's grandfather, Delbert "Ray" Tebbs purchased their family's 400-acre Myer's Valley property in 1932 when he was twenty-two years old. He had been studying economics at Utah State University when the Great Depression hit. His father asked him to come back and help on the family farm. After his return, he cashed out a whole life insurance policy for $700 and made the land purchase for $500 from his aunt, Lois Tebbs (who had had a falling out with her son who would have been the inheritor). To round out his holdings there, he also had forest permits around that private land. Additionally, his father had a nearby ranch house and another 640 acres of ranchland. The land was initially settled by the Butler Brothers who had squatter's rights but abandoned the property. It was shortly thereafter homesteaded by the Dodds family in the late 1800s or early 1900s. The ranch purchase was for $10,000 in 1926. Aside from grazing, the ranch eventually had a cheese factory, a shingle shop, and a blacksmith operation.

The Myers Valley property is an island in many ways. Its centerpiece is a valley cove with a large high-mountain meadow and dotted with numerous springs—perfect for grazing sheep, which was its primary initial usage. Three roads tie three forests together and those intersect on their ranch property. Bruce's grandfather was heavily involved in constructing those roads to provide access to the property.

Today, their private land is challenged by those who seek public access for their ATVs and four-wheel drive trucks, as well as hunters. Those off-roaders often get rather drunkenly stuck in ponds on the property, and they have to pull them out. Trophy hunters kill elk and deer and cut through the fences to drag the animals off the property. This leads directly to the first challenge between public and private stewardship—who has access to public and private land and why?

Issue #1: Private Ranching and the Federal Government

Initially, private ranchers were in partnership with the federal government and the agencies that would become the Bureau of Land Management (BLM) and the U.S. Forest Service (USFS). The federal government focus was on developing and supporting the agricultural industry.

Today, Bruce sees this as having changed markedly into one where public interests aggressively challenge the right of private ownership. The ATV and four-wheeler trespass problem serves as an interesting case in this regard for it underscores numerous tensions between public and private interests.

After numerous problems with trespassing off-roaders, the Tebbs put locks on the gates that lead into their property with the idea of securing them every five years as a reminder to the public about the private status of their land. The last time they locked the gates they were torn down by "drunken and dangerous" off-roaders and received physical threats when manning the gates in person, advising hunters of alternate routes to their destination.

A County Commissioner (a relative) threatened legal action over the locked gates arguing that the roads that cut through their property were historic "scenic routes." His evidence was a diner placemat from the 1960s that had photos for tourists on scenic byways in the region. As historic routes, gates and locks could not prevent access. They were removed, cattle guards were installed that resulted in the death of one of their cows whose leg got jammed in the grate.

As a response, the Tebbs family worked for five years to develop a plan, an alternative road that would skirt their property so that public off-roaders could still access the forest without going through the Tebbs property.

This project, which included numerous public hearings along with close work with the USFS, was blocked one day before country equipment was scheduled to start on the project. An interim regional director blocked the project and offered an alternative. He proposed a single access road into their property, which they would have to maintain. "They locked us out," noted Bruce.

Bruce felt the interim director wanted the public/county closed out of the area, underscoring the tensions between federal and country government. The Tebbs's Myers Valley property was being leveraged by the interim director toward that end to lock the county out. When Bruce made it clear that the Tebbs's intention was not to exclude the public from overall access to the area, just to their private property, the conversation shifted. The interim director then argued that the USFS did not have enough funding to undertake a $50,000 project. Bruce objected by noting that the county would supply all equipment and materials to allow for continued public access and that the USFS only needed to approve and permit the project. The interim director, then, took another tack by arguing that the original approvals and permitting by the USFS was done by a USFS employee who did not have the proper level of authority. The road re-route project was dead—the interim director had shut out the Tebbs from their property and the public from surrounding USFS lands. The interim director, who was on a two-month contract, told Bruce directly that "My 60 days is to kill this project." In the end, the attempted lockout of both the country/public and the Tebbs family failed—it's back to ground zero after five years of attempted negotiation as that solution was undone.

Issue #2: Fence Lines, Property Boundaries, and Physical Barriers

When the Myers Valley ranch was established, Ray Tebbs walked the property with the Forest Ranger, surveying the property boundary with a handheld compass. It was a common procedure to step fences back from property lines and then only fence those areas where sheep or cows were likely to wander onto public forest. Bruce pointed out that in establishing the fence line, the two sought advantages to utilize existing drift fence and steep surrounding mountains that formed a natural barrier. Elk and deer cross over them but not domesticated animals that will stick with their meadow forage and good water sources. Fencing followed natural contours where it made sense topographically, and, thus, saving money and materials.

In the 1960s, ranchers also did numerous land swaps with public lands agencies to best organize and make use of the natural resources and manage the varied topography that didn't always coincide with a standard grid. The Tebbs family swapped for two public lands plots that cut into their Myers Valley property. Later, the USFS changed its policy but granted them an on/off permit for five animal unit months for cattle, effectively letting them use those plots of land so they did not have to add an additional fence. This permit has continued to be used and is still in effect to date.

Fencing, topography, and boundaries became an acute and ongoing issue in summer 2009 when a forest fire moved through Myers Valley and destroyed timber, equipment, fencing, and a cabin while also heavily impacting the local ecosystem. Because of the loss of tree cover, erosion from rains quickly damaged meadows, roads, and ponds by clogging them with soot and other debris.

The fire started naturally through a lightning strike and the USFS used it as an opportunity to manipulate it as a "managed" fire to avoid doing a controlled burn in the area. The local USFS office assured the Tebbs that the fire would not come close to their property. Wind conditions changed, and it swept through destroying 90 percent of the timber. To put this in perspective, ranchers often obtain operating capital through timber sales. In this instance, the property was logged in 1992 generating $300,000. The Tebbs family was just about to log it again after a seventeen-year hiatus—making that timber revenue a critical loss.

As Bruce underscored, "That year they burned us out." And, as noted above, he continued, "The next year they locked us out." (Bruce would later add that by this he meant eliminating access.)

Numerous claims to the federal government about the loss of timber and damage to equipment and land have been denied. Initially, this was explained as a standard operating procedure to deny all claims as a method to winnow out frivolous cases. After five years, the claim has now risen to the level of the Department of Justice (DOJ). The DOJ has recently ruled that the fire was an "Act of God," and therefore dismissed the claim. Bruce notes this is simply not practical. "They want it to cost you or for you to give up."

To re-fence the property would cost $100,000, along with a permit from the USFS to do so. As a requirement, the USFS is demanding that the fencing go up into the mountains rather than along the old fence line. The cost is expensive though not impossible, but there are more practical ways to undertake the operation than fencing on the exact property line, which does not follow natural contours. As Bruce would say, "it zigs and zags." Thus, there would be extra and, from a pragmatic and practical point of view, unnecessary fencing added.

The anti-public lands Utah delegation in Washington, DC frame this case as a public versus private land clash with the federal government strategically making it so hard to access and use land like the Myers Valley property that the Tebbs family will simply give up and abandon it.

Bruce ends with a parable: "Tell me where it makes sense in New York City or any other urban place for this to happen. A city hasn't maintained their park for 30 years. It's a mess with massive undergrowth. Their management plan is to burn it down. A private residence backs up to the park, but was not involved in the decision to manage the burn. In the process of the city managing the fire for their resource benefit, control is lost and the private residence is destroyed. Early in the aftermath, the city threatens to eliminate access through the park for the private residence unless the owners of the residence submit to a leveed fee to access their property. Who can do that? But it's happening. Where does that happen? How is this the United States? How is this our government?" He continued, "This isn't about a permit on [public] land. It's about private property with 100 years of improvements and investments." The USFS has not tended to and has neglected its public lands, which engulf a small island of private land that is collateral damage with no compensation, help, or support from those who did the damage.

DISCUSSION AND CONCLUSION: RANCHING AND PLACE IN RURAL UTAH

As Keith Basso (1996) long-ago well understood, "Knowledge of place is closely linked to knowledge of self, to grasping one's position in the larger scheme of things, including one's own community and securing a confident sense of who one is as a person." This chapter is as much about place as it is about the political economy and public policy of ranching in the rural West. In America, where many are tied more closely to job moves than place, it is easy to ethnocentrically ignore the power of place for people anchored to a locale over multiple generations. Casey (1996:15–16; also see McDonald 2015) argues convincingly that humans are, first and foremost, "placelings," that is, place is a priori to space. We cannot know a space and what fills it without making it a meaningful, culturalized space that we would refer to as place. Our bodies become habituated to place—place is a sensory, embodied experience. Places have both depth and a horizon. Places are also populated with things: objects, histories, discourses, activities, and relationships. Places are also like schema. They are filled with contrastive but related elements. Thus, we have a kind of embodied cultural knowledge within place. We know place by means of the body, its senses, and how we operate physically within it.

Basso (1996) further reminds us that places are also filled with stories that carry morals, lessons, ancestral tales, and spiritual connections. They allow us to understand the past and situate ourselves in the present. Place, thus, becomes a memory device. The collusion of people and place creates wisdom that is deep human knowledge of place as told through stories. And those stories have the ability to not just speak to us, but to accompany us. They tell us how to live as correct, moral human beings.

As underscored by the Basso quote that opens this section, place shapes self and personhood. Places are filled with names that are like cognitive placeholders. They help us index a story or stories related to that place. Those stories are often infused with moral content. Names and physical place shape memory and our social identities. Thus physical space, place names, stories, memory all link together to situate us. The mind is, in a certain sense, extended into environment, landscape, and society.

In sum, place can be a powerful force for highly contextualized people. For people who are deeply anchored to place, the horizon can be very near, indeed, and its transgression highly decentering (cf. McDonald 2016).

The story of the Tebbs family and Myers Valley is one of anchoring to place in which USFS policy and practice disrupt place. Bruce's many attempts to get restitution from the federal government and maintain access to the ranch is only partially about money and restitution. It is also about maintaining identity that is situated in place. As but one window onto the anguish experienced by the Tebbs, Bruce told the following story:

> My own government? My grandpa bought this in 1932. Middle of the depression. Not easy to do. While he was fencing the property with a double-bladed ax [approximately 1941], he lived in a sheep camp[2] with his wife and four children all under the age of seven. My aunt was the oldest who looked out over the split door and did a painting of that memory years later. She remembers how it looked as a child, to spend the summer with her dad as he labored for their future. It matters. Yeah, it matters.

NOTES

1. It is the opposite of what has happened in Wyoming and elsewhere in the West where private landholdings block access public lands—an odd variation on enclosure. In fact, a new class of billionaires is buying up vast tracts of private land, which is supercharging this problem. In some cases, not only are gated fences erected but also armed guards are put to use to ensure that there is no trespassing (Peterson 2019; Turkewitz 2019; Randall 2019). Indeed, Turkewitz (2019) notes that across the United States, 100 families own 42 million acres or 65,000 square miles, and the amount of land tied up by that small number of families has jumped 50 percent since 2007.

2. A sheep camp is a small caravan or trailer home that can house one or two people. They would have been hauled up to mountain pastures by horse or, later, by pickup truck.

REFERENCES CITED

Basso, Keith H. 1996. *Wisdom Sits in Places: Landscape and Language among the Western Apache*. Albuquerque, NM: University of New Mexico Press.

Casey, Edgar S. 1996. How to Get from Space to Place in a Fairly Short Stretch of Time: Phenomenological Prolegomena. In *Senses of Place*, edited by Steven Feld and Keith H. Basso, pp. 12–52. Santa Fe, NM: School for American Research Press.

McDonald, James H. 2015. The Situated University: Political-Cultural Context, Organizational Culture, and Leadership. In *Navigating the Volatility of Higher Education: Anthropological and Policy Perspectives*, edited by Brian L. Foster, Steven W. Graham, and Joe F. Donaldson, pp. 91–119. Charlotte, NC: Information Age Publishing.

———. 2016. Review of "Happy Anyway: A Flint Anthology." *New York Journal of Books*. https://www.nyjournalofbooks.com/book-review/happy-anyway (Accessed March 1, 2016).

Peterson, Christine. 2019. Shut Out: How Wyoming Ended Up With a Third of the West's Landlocked Public Land. *High Country News* 4:8–9.

Randall, Cassidy. 2019. Sportsmen Flex Their Political Muscles: In the Midterms, Public Land Access Issues Helped Several Candidates Grab Governorships. *High Country News* 21:10–11.

Turkewitz, Julie. 2019. Who Gets to Own the West?: A New Group of Billionaires is Shaking Up the Landscape. *New York Times*. https://www.nytimes.com/2019/06/22/us/wilks-brothers-fracking-business.html (Accessed July 3, 2019).

Chapter 4

Claiming the Los Angeles River for "the Public," by Boat and by Permit

Sayd Randle

"Raise your hand if you've been to the Los Angeles River before," Ellen[1] instructs the twenty college students sprawled by her feet on a patchy expanse of grass. A single palm creeps into the air. Some members of the assembled group chuckle uneasily, seemingly embarrassed at their collective unfamiliarity with the waterway flowing a few yards away. Shaking her head and laughing quietly, Ellen directs the students to take advantage of being so close and go explore the riverbed. Following some cautious glances at their professor, who nods his assent, the class stumbles down the riverbank to climb boulders and attempt to grab stray pieces of garbage strewn within the channel.

An hour later, as Ellen drives me back from the river to the office of the environmental NGO that she runs, I ask her if she was surprised at the students' lack of familiarity with the waterway and she shakes her head. Though instructors from local universities ask her to guest lecture about the river's history and ecology with some frequency, she's never encountered a class where even half of the students say they've spent time along its banks. She's quick to point out the irony that, as a result of the design of the LA freeway system, many of the same students have ridden over or alongside the river hundreds of times—yet seemingly never noticed their proximity to the city's eponymous stream. Encased in concrete for most of its fifty-one-mile path to the Pacific, the LA River strikes many LA residents as easy to overlook.

As her feet-first approach to teaching students about the river suggests, Ellen is passionate about building appreciation for the waterway as a place to be known and experienced directly, and considers spending time within the channel to be a valuable tactic to further this goal. This way of thinking got a substantial boost in 2010, when, following a protracted review, the U.S. Environmental Protection Agency (EPA) changed the river's classification from a federally managed flood control channel to "traditional navigable waterway of the United States," as defined by the federal Clean Water Act (CWA). Southern California's environmentalist community celebrated this legal shift, which placed the river squarely in the public—and publicly accessible—domain, and secured its protection under the CWA. Several new riverside parks, bikeways, and art installations have opened in the years since, and a handful of LA River kayaking companies have launched to lead guided paddling trips within the waterway. Substantial federal funding is even slated to flow toward the channel's partial restoration in the coming years, removing sections of the concrete that contains its flow. In short, the LA River's status as a place to spend time is decidedly on the rise.

But this tidy narrative—at the behest of united environmentalists, a city rediscovers and then moves to restore the river it once transformed into an unlovely storm drain—is far simpler than the reality in the U.S. west's most populous city. Back at Ellen's NGO office, where a clipped magazine photo of her kayaking down the LA River is displayed prominently, much of the day-to-day work goes into advocating for changes to LA's water supply mix. Supporting the city's plans to recycle wastewater and capture stormwater for incorporation into LA's potable supply mix, Ellen, like most of her environmentalist colleagues, seeks to repurpose the river's primary water sources for use as public water supply. While she sees the river as a place that Angelenos should know and visit, she also understands its flows as a potentially crucial water resource for a growing city in a semiarid region.

As Ellen's example suggests, among local environmentalist actors, ascribing a stable "sense of place" to the LA River is complicated by its dual character as both a watery landscape and a vessel containing the flow of water. Residents of the city value both water for their taps and local spaces to experience nonhuman nature. The waterway has the potential to provide both, thus serving the public as two very different kinds of natural resources. These are not necessarily mutually exclusive uses, and individuals or organizations can certainly support both aims. But they do entail competing (and at times, conflictual) interpretations of the stream's primary role within the cityscape. As such, the two understandings of the river frequently complicate the politics of its management. The work necessary to make the river an accessible public natural space is not always the work required to transform its flows into a water source for the city.

This chapter explores the tensions and overlaps between such senses of the LA River, focusing particularly on how they animate practice within the city's environmentalist community. I draw on long-term participant observation among NGO workers, activists, and water managers, as well as readings of histories, journalistic reporting, legal documents, and documentary films about the river to show how contrasting interpretations of the waterway's nature and purpose can create conflict among its ostensible "green" allies.

The chapter proceeds in four sections. First, I introduce the significance and history of the LA River, focusing on how its waters were largely understood and managed as hazards throughout the twentieth century. The next two sections contrast this approach with contemporary views that interpret the river as two distinct sorts of resources, a water supply resource and a space of nature for the public. Analysis in these two sections is grounded in assessments of recent efforts to exercise water rights claims on the river's flows and to boat in the waterway and efforts. I conclude with a brief consideration of how these "senses" of the river hold the potential to produce clashes, rooted in the multiple understandings of the riverscape and scales of environmental benefit at stake in its management.

A HAZARD

Though nonexistent on the mental maps of many present-day Angelenos, LA River is frequently cited by historians as the reason for the settler city's siting. The earliest evidence of colonizer enthusiasm for the waterway comes from the diary of Father Juan Crespi, a Spanish priest and member Captain Gaspar de Portola's 1769 expedition from San Diego to San Francisco. The group entered present-day LA County in late July, where they found a "good sized, full flowing river . . . with very good water, pure and fresh" (Crespi 1769 in Gumprecht 2001:37). Crespi also wrote favorably of the verdant lands surrounding the river, terming the area "a very lush and pleasing spot, in every respect" (Crespi 1769 in Gumprecht 2001:38). The new settlement established along the river, which grew slowly through periods of Spanish, Mexican, and American rule in the early to mid-nineteenth century, relied on the river's flows and local groundwater for all of its water needs.

While the river was essential to the development of early LA, it was not always gentle to its new residents. The waterway's course shifted dramatically due to storm flows in 1815, 1825, and 1889 (see Gumprecht 2001:140 for a map depicting these shifts). The stream's peripatetic nature is largely the result of the region's climatological, meteorological, and hydrological patterns. Southern California's characteristic rainfall rhythm, which is seasonal, inconsistent, flashy when it does come, and especially intense in the mountain ranges that ring much of LA County, can create massive water and debris flows throughout the geological basin. However, the same regional patterns leave the streambeds dry and the sun in the sky for the vast majority of the year. A river changing its course three times within a century sounds like a pattern to an observer a century removed. But it is easy to see how in a migrant-dominated, settler-colonial landscape like nineteenth-century LA, these events likely seemed isolated, if catastrophic. Ideas about the river that people knew most days were thus cordoned off from the occasional storm-swollen flows and the destruction they wrought, a pattern immediately apparent when one considers nineteenth- and twentieth-century settlement history along the river.

The jumble of material and perceptual factors detailed above contributed to the dense pattern of permanent floodplain development that took hold as the nineteenth century lurched into the twentieth and early agricultural and pastoral land uses gave way to more concentrated, urban and industrial forms. Consequently, when the river flooded in 1914 (an event carrying far less water than the deluges of 1862 and 1889), the loss of life and valuation of the destroyed property exceeded those caused by earlier inundations, when there was far fewer buildings for the floodwaters to damage. This dramatic event spurred the establishment of the LA County Flood Control District and set the region on a path to remaking the river from something easily recognized as "natural."

The events of January 1, 1934, played a key role in furthering this transformation. LA received 7.4 inches of rain in 24 hours, and the limited flood control infrastructure developed since that last big deluge could not contain the storm's runoff. Hundreds of homes were destroyed, and dozens of people were killed as stormwater and debris filled the floodplain. The Flood Control District's two decades of work toward containing the waters were widely deemed a failure, and the widespread destruction undermined faith in the agency's ability to ever properly manage the flows.

Folk singer Woody Guthrie's "Los Angeles New Year's Flood" captures the widespread interpretation of the flood as an example of nature's power and capriciousness. Through his lyrics, he also depicts the sense of jarring, punctuated time associated with the deluge, emphasizing the calm before and devastation immediately following the storm. Guthrie's presentation of the flood's suddenness is impossible to miss. The cloudburst hits, and in the very next line, the homes have been swept away. The violent deluge is something utterly unpredictable: "You could not see it coming/till through our town it rolled." This heightened sense of danger associated with the river and its flashy, sometimes violent, and somewhat unpredictable flows shaped the approaches to watercourse management that followed.

Following the flood, LA politicians and engineers implored the federal government to underwrite a more thorough taming of their river. With the passage of the 1936 Flood Federal Control Act, Washington was able to offer money and expertise via the Army Corps of Engineers. However, the Corps had barely begun to sink its $70 million allocation into LA's waterscape when a week of rain overfilled the region's streams once again. The March 1938 floods caused more than $78 million in damage and took forty-five lives. The destruction helped legitimize an idea for a whole new scale of flood control along the river, including lining the vast majority of the channel in concrete. Over the course of the next two decades, Congress would authorize more than $400 million beyond the initial 1936 allocation completing this "water freeway" through the heart of the city and paving the vast majority of its tributaries. The legacy of the Corps' work is an immensely efficient network of single-purpose flood control infrastructure, built on the principle of moving stormwater to sea as quickly as possible.

The dominant organizing concept for river management within this regime was very simple: keep the river's storm flows away from the people and the private property, and move the water out to the ocean as quickly as possible. This is also the view recounted mainstream histories of the LA River (e.g., Gumprecht 2001; Orsi 2004), as well as the histories recounted among my environmental activist interlocutors in the field. A favorite story invoked to illustrate the state's understanding of local waterscape goes like this: Back in the 1990s, the late Lewis MacAdams, founder of the group Friends of the Los Angeles River (FoLAR), attended a meeting with some engineers from various water agencies. Throughout the conversation, the engineers would refer to the LA River as the city's "flood control channel." Every time they did so, MacAdams would interject: "You mean river!" These interruptions escalated until MacAdams and an engineer were shouting at each other and pounding the table. If nothing else, the engineer's flaring temper suggests considerable bureaucratic investment in emphasizing the flood risk carried by the river's storm-time swells, and that these concerns have shaped the long-term work of managing those flows.

This "hazard" view of the LA River persists within the local context. Indeed, many of my environmentalist interlocutors express active concern that administrative tools like the Federal Emergency Management Agency's official flood maps vastly underestimate the potential for flooding from the even stronger storm systems that climate change will likely bring to the region (see Berg and Hall 2015). However, as others have detailed, recent decades have seen the rise of new, more hybrid paradigms of urban stormwater management in the U.S. west, approaches that seek to prioritize multiple forms of environmental benefit alongside a desire for public safety (Orsi 2004; Karvoven 2011; Cousins 2017). The sections below detail how these new paradigms have intersected with and at times, complicated long-established forms of riparian politics in twenty-first-century LA.

A WATER RESOURCE

Entering the Metabolic Studio's just-south-of-downtown warehouse headquarters on the banks of the LA River, I was struck by just how much that space felt like, if not a proper playground, the world's best cabinet of curiosities. Walls were covered with screen printed exhortations to value nature, love water, and take down Donald Trump. Rows upon rows of large glass jars full of honeycombs sat on wooden shelves. "ARTISTS NEED TO CREATE ON THE SAME SCALE THAT SOCIETY HAS THE CAPACITY TO DESTROY" read a wall-mounted neon sign behind a jumble of musical instruments. As I waited for our facility tour, organized by a professional association of landscape architects, to begin, I reflected on my surprise that this was the aesthetic favored by the organization that mobilized the legal savvy to make the first-ever private claim on the water of the LA River.

On October 24, 2013, the California State Water Resources Control Board granted artist and Annenberg heiress Lauren Bon, the founder and leader of the Metabolic Studio, the right to divert 106 acre-feet of water from the LA River on an annual basis. Permit 21342, the document granting that claim, succinctly outlines Metabolic Studio's plan for capturing that water: the construction of an inflatable rubber dam within the river channel. Not mentioned in the permit is the water wheel that will raise the water from the river channel, the artificial treatment wetland that will cleanse it to the standards required for non-potable use, or the irrigation system that will distribute those flows to the landscaping of public parks on either side of the river channel (Christensen 2015). Those extraordinary prospective infrastructures were to be the focus of our tour that day in June 2018.

Our tour guide Sean, a slightly disheveled white, male Metabolic Studio employee, walked us through the project's history and the Metabolic Studio facility, pausing to focus on the scale-model of the water wheel. Such wheels, he explained, were common sights along the river during its early years as a Spanish *pueblo* (a claim that historical writing and photos alike confirm). Part of the point of the new wheel, Sean told the group, is to educate Angelenos on the history of how humans have used the river from LA's time as a Spanish colonial settlement onward, to force us to grapple with the wisdom of our current arrangements. "The hope is to promote civic engagement through engagement with this history and with the underutilized lands along the river," he said, gazing intently at the small wheel that stood between us and him.

It is unlikely that anyone has ever characterized the Metabolic Studio approach to the LA River as "cookie cutter." The scope and complexity of this project—perhaps best indicated by the sixty-eight permits from twenty-two public agencies that the group had to obtain before its 2019 project groundbreaking—signals the capacious ambitions behind it. This will be infrastructure not only intended to exploit the LA River's flows for public consumptive use within parks but also meant to educate the consuming public on the water management practices that marked the city's early years. Yet the complexities and particularities of the project are held together by a view of the river's flows as a resource to be exploited for public benefit *as water*—a perspective with a rich history in the context of environmental thinking and management of the U.S. west.

To early twentieth-century conservationists such as the U.S. president Theodore Roosevelt and Forest Service Chief Gifford Pinchot, stormwater was a substance to be carefully measured and rationally exploited, following the principles of the "gospel of efficiency" (Hays 1959). In their view, stormwater's tendency to "waste to the sea" was the underlying problem. Efficient management and exploitation of this natural resource would lead to the end of runoff "laying waste" in due course. Notably, water management struggles were integral to the process of establishing this as a broader approach to nonhuman nature (Hays 1959: 5):

> These views gradually became crystallized into an over-all approach and by 1908 emerged as a concept of multiple-purpose river development. The movement to construct reservoirs to conserve spring flood waters for use later in the dry season gave rise both to the term "conservation" and to the concept of planned and efficient progress which lay at the heart of the conservation idea.

Avoiding resource wastage takes on a clear moral dimension in these formulations. As in British colonial contexts, the American conservationists drew on Lockean notions of wild, undeveloped nature as morally hazardous "waste" in desperate need of improvement and containment (Ferry and Limbert 2008, Gidwani and Reddy 2011). They championed comprehensive, multipurpose river basin development, intended to maximize moral and economic returns to the nation and the market.

Like the "hazard" approach to stormwater discussed above, this view of water resources proceeds from the core notion that it is possible to control nonhuman nature in an instrumental way. In fact, one can easily argue that the "resource" approach to riverine management presumes a greater degree of control over landscapes and flows. Rather than merely cordoning off angry waters from private property and preventing harm, this view of riverine resources assumes that this can be done while adding value to the economy. William J. McGee, a high-level bureaucrat in Theodore Roosevelt's administration and a water development zealot, offers a particularly clear example of this thinking in a 1909 paper titled "Water as a Resource." Near the essay's end, he estimates that an annual national waterways investment of $50 million would eventually net an annual return of $1 billion, in the form of transportation savings, flood prevention, cheaper power, and improved agricultural production (McGee 1909:533). Notably, many of the tools and techniques proposed by McGee and his colleagues to "conserve" floodwater were similar to those favored in single-purpose flood control systems (e.g., dams, reservoirs, spillways, drains). In general, it was assumed that all of these large-scale, centralized water management infrastructures would be funded, owned, and operated by the state, though disagreements persisted as to the differentiation in roles between federal and local governments. This technocratic, expert-dominated approach has been accurately characterized as a high modernist state project of rationalization and legibility, intended to simplify the complexities of ecosystems for the purposes of efficient exploitation and capital accumulation (Worster 1985; Scott 1998; Scott 2006; Piper 2006; Muehlmann 2013).

LA's current array of prospective water supply projects suggests that an updated version of this perspective still marks mainstream environmentalist practice. During my fieldwork, one June 2015 day offered a particularly clear illustration of how these priorities are lived among this community. In the morning, I joined Ellen (the LA River expert mentioned at the chapter's outset) and several dozen other NGO workers, environmental activists, and concerned citizens at a meeting of the city's Recycled Water Advisory Group. There, most of the environmentalists focused on a shared line of questioning: Why wasn't the city moving faster toward building an advanced wastewater treatment plant that would produce water supplies clean enough for incorporation into the city's drinking water supply? That evening, I encountered many of the same faces at the rollout of the city's first-ever Stormwater Capture Master Plan, a document outlining how the city might maximize its use of local stormwater as a water supply source, thus reducing its dependency on cost and carbon-intensive waters imported from distant landscapes. Most of the queries posed by my interlocutors during the question and answer period were encouraging, gently pushing the plan's framers to build on their good work and think bigger. As these examples suggest, both large-scale wastewater recycling and enhanced stormwater capture represent environmentalist-supported sources for new and expanded local water supplies for the city's taps. Both new supplies also currently serve as sources of the LA River's flows.[2] In effect, those projects entail a managerial approach that understands wastewater and stormwater as substances to be managed as resources, rather than merely as hazards.

The Metabolic Studio's legal claim to and proposed infrastructure for the water of the LA River represents a slightly different materialization of the perspective that foregrounds the value of the waterway's flows as potential water supply resources. Rather than drinking water, the treated river flows will be used to irrigate public land. However, as Bon and other Metabolic Studio advocates have pointed out, exploiting the river for this purpose reduces the need to use potable supplies to water the same landscapes, allowing those flows to serve other functions within the city. As such, while making a private claim to and building a water wheel for the river's water may seem quixotic on one level, on another level the approach aligns neatly with an understanding of a river that can best serve the city by providing it useful water at a minimal cost. For all of their countercultural stylings, the organization is engaged in a very familiar form of techno-managerial practice within the region.

A PLACE OF (AND FOR) NATURE

Rain and flood were far from my mind as I waded into a soft-bottomed section of the LA River in August of 2014. Given that no precipitation had fallen locally since April and that the water I stood in was about a foot deep, I felt reasonably confident that I would not encounter the hazardous version of the river that has long shaped the work of LA's water managers. With assistance from my guide, a twenty-something Latinx woman I'll call Irma, I situated myself in the seat of a bright yellow kayak and used my paddle to push off the river floor and toward the group of our fellow boaters paddling slowly downstream. The river that day was calm and smooth. Its water smelled vaguely of chemicals, which was unsurprising given its main source was the highly treated effluent from the Donald C. Tillman Wastewater Treatment Plant.

Irma, my fellow kayakers, and I were drifting through the water that day as part of a program known as Paddle the River, run by the nonprofit LA Conservation Corps. Seeking such a guided boating excursion, I had searched online, found several providers, and comparison-shopped until I identified the tour that seemed to offer the best combination of value for my research funds and overall experience. Conversations among our group revealed that several of us had gotten the idea to boat the river from coverage of such trips on local blogs and newspapers. Someone mentioned the enormous photo of LA mayor Eric Garcetti grinning his almost-Hollywood smile from a kayak in the stream that had greeted travelers in the city's main airport since early that year. As if to underline the point that paddling the channel was "in" that summer, our group included a reporter for a local news station and a cameraman, who recorded our journey to use in a future segment about the trend.

A major reason for this excitement around boating in the river was that, until quite recently, it had not been legal to take to the waters in this way. Since the laying of the river's concrete lining in the middle of the twentieth century, access to the channel was severely restricted, separated from the rest of the city with fences and menacing signs in most sections. The choice to separate the city's residents from their river was attributed to fears of the watercourse's sometimes-hazardous nature, a danger highlighted by occasional news coverage of swift-water rescues in the swollen channel during winter storms.

Far-sighted Angelenos have long seen the river and surrounding lands as a more inviting sort of space. In 1930, a plan by the Olmsted-Bartholomew design firm outlined a comprehensive vision for riverside greenway development, intended to both limit flood damage and improve access to parks within the city. While the plan received little traction when initially proposed, similar ideas about the river corridor's potential as sylvan recreational area have reemerged in recent decades. Poet Lewis MacAdams, the engineer-baiting activist referenced above, founded FoLAR in 1986 with a self-proclaimed goal of giving the river "a voice" in public decision-making. FoLAR accumulated allies within the city's environmentalist and anti-racist activist groups through the 1990s and advocated successfully for developing parks on several prime riverside parcels. A 2007 comprehensive "revitalization" plan for the river, developed by LA County, included substantial new planned greenspace along the channel, a testament to the organization's enduring influence. Yet for all of this attention to the potential of land near the river, few of these efforts centered the question of legalizing direct access to the channel itself.

A rogue 2008 kayaking journey played a key role in shifting restrictions on channel access. That summer, a handful of Angelenos paddled the length of the river with a film crew in tow. The group, which included an Army Corps of Engineers biologist named Heather Wylie, was seeking to provide incontrovertible evidence that the waterway was "navigable in fact," a crucial legal distinction under the CWA. The 2006 Supreme Court decision *Rapanos v. United States* had limited federal protections under the law to watercourses found to meet that standard. Shortly after this finding, the Army Corps quietly classified the LA River as a waterway that failed to meet such criteria. Wylie leaked the memo outlining this shift to the public, then joined forces with local environmentalists to provide evidence contradicting the Corps' characterization of the river.

Wylie has described her actions as motivated by a desire to sustain the LA River's status a CWA-classified stream, which extends protections to tributaries throughout its watershed (Wylie 2008). Many of her local environmentalist collaborators, however, brought years of work toward remaking the waterway to the trip, grounded in particular visions of what the river could and should be for the city. To be clear, they also believed that CWA protection would benefit the riparian environment. They also believed that this legal classification was one small element of a larger project.

Rock the Boat (2011), a documentary film depicting the 2008 kayaking expedition, foregrounds the placemaking aspects of the effort. In addition to footage of the boaters, the film features interviews with local environmentalist leaders explaining how and why they see the trip as significant. In one scene, for instance, writer and historian Jenny Price addresses the kayakers during a rest period, highlighting the social role of traversing the channel (*Rock the Boat* 2011:21:00): "I think what you guys are doing is absolutely fantastic because you have to reintroduce Los Angeles River to Los Angeles, and one of the major ways to do that, why I give tours, is to bring people down to the river and have them use it and have them see it's a river and have them treat it as a river."

Others, including NGO founders, river-focused bloggers, and river restoration experts, echoed this assessment, emphasizing both the benefits of the trip itself (increased visibility for the river) and the broader benefits of Angelenos spending more time in and around the channel (a greater sense of investment in the river's health, leading to more public pressure for better management). Notably, the film also presents a powerful non-Angeleno expressing such a vision of the river in very explicit terms. In footage from the 2010 ceremony announcing the river's new status, EPA Administrator Lisa Jackson offers the following remarks (*Rock the Boat* 2011:47:00):

> When we talk about the environment, we cannot talk just about wide open, beautiful spaces, we have to talk about a river with a concrete bottom that flows through one of our nation's largest cities. We want this to be a place where people can walk and bike and picnic and learn again the importance of finding the solitude and solace that comes with being in America's great outdoors.

Emphasizing notions of both this-river-as-nature and nature-as-healing, Jackson here suggests that a well-managed LA River could serve Angelenos as a key respite from the city's manmade sprawl. Indeed, her words echo those of nineteenth- and early twentieth-century preservationists such as John Muir, characterizing the restorative powers of human encounters with nonhuman nature (Worster 2008). Though one would be loath to overstate the similarities between Muir's beloved Sierra Nevada Mountains and today's LA River, the assumed role of exposure to "nature" in human well-being reads as notably enduring. Further, the notion that even human-altered nature in the heart of an urban center can provide these benefits to the public highlights the importance of approaching these places on the same analytical plane as more remoted lands protected under the same rationale.

On our 2014 paddle down the river, Irma didn't speak about the river in quite such elevated terms. But she did offer us an account of the river's history and spoke in some detail about its past and present flora and fauna. To be sure, the trip's emphasis was on making sure that all participants had some good, safe, recreational fun. However, the educational components of the excursion were programmatically designed to build our understanding and appreciation of the river's role within the urban landscape. After exiting our boats that day, Irma and the other Conservation Corps staffers gathered us together to pose for a group photo ("We'll make you internet famous!"), then encouraged us to visit the river again soon, either as part of another organized excursion or on our own. We should, they seemed to suggest, see the river as our playground—and feel some attendant ownership and concern for its well-being.

CHALLENGES AND CONCLUSIONS

So, is the LA River most commonly understood as a hazard to be controlled, a water resource to be rationally exploited, or space of nature to be enjoyed and cared for by the public? As the discussion above attests, the answer is yes. Even the comparison between the "resource" advocates making legal claims to the river's flow bleeds into the consideration of the kayak-happy environmentalists seeking to "reintroduce the Los Angeles River to Los Angeles," as Jenny Price put it in 2010. In the contemporary LA contexts, advocates of both river recreation and water extraction seek to increase the waterway's visibility among everyday Angelenos. Yet approaches to the river are worth teasing apart, as research suggests that managing for both of those goals at once may not be possible and that advocates may soon need to prioritize policy measures associated with one perspective over the other.

In particular, recent writings from the research group of UCLA's Stephanie Pincetl suggest a coming conflict. Using a combination of socio-technical system analysis and hydrological modeling, these researchers find that management policies designed to maximize stormwater capture will adversely affect stream flows within the LA basin's watersheds, suggesting the need to accept tradeoffs between riparian habitat preservation and local water supply maximization (Mika, Gallo, and Porse 2018; Pincetl et al. 2019; Porse and Pincetl 2018). While noting the need for further study to adequately characterize the effects of new water management techniques on the local flow regime, this body of research highlights the inherent conflict between projects of riverscape restoration, or even preservation, and water supply enhancement.

On one level, these conflicts will feel familiar to anyone aware of past conflicts over nonhuman nature in the U.S. West. Debates over dams in remote, beautiful areas also pit the perceived public good of increased water supply against that of recreational spaces (or, in other circumstances, terrain sacred to Native communities), particularly since the 1960s (Wehr 2004). As in this case, these conflicts are driven largely by the dual character of riparian waterscapes as both places to be experienced and vessels containing a vital resource.

But the LA version of this conflict differs from hinterland examples in several significant ways. Densely settled and highly urbanized, LA is also a notably park-poor city, particularly in low-income and nonwhite majority neighborhoods (Wolch, Wilson, and Fehrenbach 2005). As such, preserving or enhancing the river's status as a natural or recreational space takes on an environmental justice dimension not common in other cases. Further, efforts to "localize" the city's water supply, by relying more on water sources that currently feed the LA River, hold the possibility of helping remediate distant landscapes degraded by LA's long-term practices of water extraction (such as the Owens Valley), and reducing the carbon footprint associated with the city's water supply, thus contributing to climate change mitigation. These overlapping scales of environmental "goods" and "bads" are all raised regularly in local environmentalist conversations regarding the river, underlining the complexity inherent in articulating or working toward a vision for a "sustainable" or "just" waterscape. The multiple senses of place that mark efforts to manage this contested waterscape suggest the possibilities for conflict within this ostensibly unitary project.

NOTES

1. Unless otherwise indicated, all first-name identification within the text uses pseudonyms.

2. Notably, not all of LA's proposed wastewater recycling efforts would directly affect the river's flows. At present, only the Donald C. Tillman Water Reclamation Plant and the LA-Glendale Water Reclamation Plant, both located in northeastern LA, discharge significant volumes of treated effluent into the river. Work is underway to build a pipeline between Tillman and the city-owned stormwater spreading grounds, infrastructures that direct water into the San Fernando Valley Groundwater Basin for storage and future use by the city. Current plans suggest that much of the water flowing through this pipeline will be displaced from discharges currently feeding the LA River. In contrast, most effluent the city's oceanside Hyperion Water Reclamation Plant is deposited in the Santa Monica Bay, not in the LA River (which is located several miles away from that plant). As such, the city's plans to further treat and eventually reuse all of Hyperion's flows, announced in early 2019, are not directly relevant to questions of river management.

REFERENCES CITED

Berg, Neil, and Alex Hall. 2015. Increased Interannual Precipitation Extremes Over California Under Climate Change. *Journal of Climate* 28(16):6324–34.

Christensen, Jon. 2015. Devices of Wonder: Artist Lauren Bon Reimagines the LA Aqueduct. *VQR Online* 91(3). https://www.vqronline.org/profiles-articles/2015/07/devices-wonder (Accessed December 23, 2019).

Cousins, Joshua J. 2017. Of Floods and Droughts: The Uneven Politics of Stormwater in Los Angeles. *Political Geography* 60:34–46.

Ferry, Elizabeth, and Mandana Limbert. 2008. Introduction. In *Timely Assets: The Politics of Resources and Their Temporalities*, edited by Elizabeth Ferry and Mandana Limbert, pp. 3–24. Santa Fe, NM: School for Advanced Research Press.

Gidwani, Vinay, and Rajyashree Reddy. 2011. The Afterlives of "Waste:" Notes from India for a Minor History of Capitalist Surplus. *Antipode* 43(5):1625–58.

Gumprecht, Blake. 2001. *The Los Angeles River: Its Life, Death, and Possible Rebirth*. Baltimore, MD: Johns Hopkins University Press.

Hays, Samuel. 1959. *Conservation and the Gospel of Efficiency: The Progressive Conservation Movement, 1890-1920*. Pittsburgh, PA: University of Pittsburgh Press.

Karvoven, Andrew. 2011. *The Politics of Urban Runoff: Nature, Technology, and the Sustainable City*. Cambridge, MA: MIT Press.

McGee, William. 1909. Water as a Resource. *Annals of the American Academy of Political and Social Science* 33:521–34.

Mika, Katie, Elizabeth Gallo, and Erik Porse. 2018. *Sustainable Water Project: Los Angeles*. Los Angeles, CA: University of California-Los Angeles Institute of the Environment and Sustainability.

Muehlmann, Shaylih. 2013. *Where the River Ends: Contested Indigeneity in the Mexican Colorado Delta*. Durham, NC: Duke University Press.

Orsi, Jared. 2004. *Hazardous Metropolis: Flooding and Urban Ecology in Los Angeles*. Los Angeles, CA: University of California Press.

Pincetl, Stephanie, Erik Porse, Kathryn B. Mika, Elizaveta Litvak, Kimberly F. Manago, Terri S. Hogue, Diane E. Pataki, and Mark Gold. 2019. Adapting Urban Water Systems to Manage Scarcity in the 21st Century: The Case of Los Angeles. *Environmental Management* 63(3):293–308.

Piper, Karen. 2006. *Left in the Dust: How Race and Politics Created a Human Tragedy in LA*. New York: MacMillan.

Porse, Erik, and Stephanie Pincetl. 2018. Effects of Stormwater Capture and Use on Urban Streamflows. *Water Resources Management* 33(2):713–23.

Scott, James C. 1998. *Seeing Like a State: How Certain Schemes to Improve the Human Condition Have Failed*. New Haven, CT: Yale University Press.

———. 2006. High Modernist Social Engineering: The Case of the Tennessee Valley Authority. In *Experiencing the State*, edited by Rudolph, L. and Jacobsen, pp. 3–52. New Delhi: Oxford University Press.

Wolch, Jennifer, John P. Wilson, and Jed Fehrenbach. 2005. Urban Geography Parks and Park Funding in Los Angeles: An Equity-Mapping Analysis. *Urban Geography* 26(1):4–35.

Worster, Donald. 1985. *Rivers of Empire: Water, Aridity, and the Growth of the American West*. New York: Oxford University Press.

———. 2008. *A Passion for Nature: The Life of John Muir*. New York: Oxford University Press.

Wylie, Heather. 2008. Floating to Save the LA River. *Los Angeles Times*. https://www.latimes.com/opinion/la-oe-wylie30-2008oct30-story.html (Accessed December 23, 2019).

Chapter 5

Chile and New Mexico

Identity, Difference, and Place

David Knowlton

New Mexico claimed me when I was three years old. Just after we arrived at our new home, my father went to a nearby restaurant in the railroad and college town of Las Vegas and brought home enchiladas. The first bite made this boy newly out of the South jump from his seat and race to the sink. "Daddy, I'm burnin' on the inside and burnin' on the outside."

From this fiery beginning, I learned to love chile—the hot peppers, that characterize New Mexico as a place—and to eat them frequently, and thus New Mexico, even while living far away. With that I was owned and learned to perform, especially as the story entered the store of family tales and came to justify my interest and my family's interest in chile, spicy food, things indigenous and Spanish, and New Mexico. We became in short New Mexicanizers.[1]

THE ENCHANTMENT OF ACTIVE ENGAGEMENT

New Mexico, a place, is not simply there but is actively created for people in their engagement with it over and over. Some people, such as I once I took the bite, were socialized and enculturated into New Mexico as children while others took it on as adults. Indeed, there are tales of becoming New Mexican as if it were a kind of baptism. David L. Caffey (1999:xi) acknowledges this tradition and locates himself in it when he writes that he was "born" into New Mexico at the "advanced age of fifteen" while camping on the Philmont Scout Ranch. In any case, the process is active and can lead to different degrees of absorption, differences of content, and varied experiences, all in the name of a place that sounds static, New Mexico.

Nonetheless, a place is many things and each can be transformative. Initially, we may think of place as a landscape before we notice that this includes not only nature but also the inhabitants and many overlapping sets of ideas. It is reported that "D.H. Lawrence, though worldly wise when he arrived in New Mexico, felt himself changed forever by a land of immense beauty, spiritual resonance, and mystery. 'It had a splendid, silent terror,' he wrote, 'and a vast, far-and-wide magnificence which made it way beyond mere aesthetic appreciation'" (Caffey 1999: 8). New Mexico can be narrative—such as Lawrence produced—history, paintings, ceremonies, architecture, society (and culture), food, and so much more.

One finds all of these registers represented in travel brochures and magazines, such as *New Mexico Magazine*. They are also enclosed in the state's nickname, "The Land of Enchantment." This sobriquet was developed in 1935 to brand and market the state for tourism. Although the oldest site of European habitation in the United States, New Mexico coined this slogan a mere twenty-three years after it became a state in 1912, for the purposes of drawing people to visit it and to reduce its complexity into a single attractive phrase. That phrase was not a simple descriptor but an enunciation of active enchanting.

This official wording is tellingly different from other nicknames (The Cactus State, The Spanish State, The Land of Sunshine, The Land of the Delight Makers, The Land of Opportunity, and The Land of the Heart's Desire) in that it suggests making place as something official, an enchantment which is about more than mere land (New Mexico 2019). A place is not simply a site, an ideology, or a marketing venture; enchantment communicates that. This term, Land of Enchantment, removes the focus from a material place and instead grants it to experience and, even more, to something that transcends simple experience to make it grander, more magical, and beyond the ordinary, even though this enunciation stems from officialdom—the New Mexico government and the federal government (including defense and the military which are so important in the state). By coining the term enchantment, New Mexico grants all this a reality as something bigger than ordinary life.

For the state of New Mexico, this transcendence begins with the natural environment: the qualities of sky and the landscape: mountains, alpine forests, prairies, desert valleys, and a good portion of one of the longest river systems in the United States. It also comes from important archaeological sites, villages, adobe houses, mines, and Indian reservations, public lands, private lands, and federal military sites that are conceptually attached to landscape. The heightening also depends on the state's conjoining of different peoples—Anglos, Latinos, Pueblo Indians (Acoma, Cochiti, Isleta, Jemez, Laguna Nambe, Ohkay Owingey, Picuris, Pojoaque, Picuris, Sandia, San Felipe, San Ildefonso, Santa Ana, Santa Clara, Santo Domingo, Taos,

Tesuque, Zuni, Zia), Apache (Fort Sill, Jicarilla, Mescalero), and Diné (Navajo). Not infrequently the people, other than non-folkloric Anglos, are also attached to the landscape that reifies them and denies them agency. As a result, one cannot forget the long history of Spanish and then American occupation and settlement through which this landscape and its people have been created.

New Mexico's enchantment also stems from what many people visiting and living in this place think of as culture, for example, Indian dances and festivities, Hispanic pilgrimages, fiestas, fairs, and museum events, in addition to well-known colonies of visual artists and jewelers. New Mexico relies for transcendence on a demography that is different from most of the United States, being some 11 percent Native and around 47 percent Hispanic. Alone, Hispanics almost comprise a majority. Placed together with New Mexico's original people, however, a non-Anglo majority appears.

Although the state has a substantial Native American population, whose tongues are spoken, Latinos and the state's living Spanish culture and its history seem to be the main focus within the state. In this is tension and contemporary colonialism since English is the dominant language and, though a minority in New Mexico, Anglos hold key eyes, ears, and bodies. Spanish shows up in the doubling of the slogan as Land of Enchantment/*Tierra del Encanto*, one in English and one in Spanish with the dominant language coming first, though Anglos are a minority. It also shows up in the common idea and slogan that New Mexico is the "state different." A word order from Spanish, this emphasizes the adjective and by implication shows that the state's main difference from the majority of the United States is in the history of Spanish colonization and in the continued presence of Hispanics whose Spanish language (which increasingly many do not speak) is subsumed within English.

New Mexico, therefore, is contradictory in that the marketing of it as a place stresses its varied landscape and particular light, as well as its multicultural and pluri-ethnic reality, while the slogan subtly emphasizes the state's almost majority, its colonial history, and the language inherited from the earliest European colonizers rather than from its indigenous population. Nonetheless, the agency of the descendants of the Spanish Empire (indigenous peoples and Hispanics) is often ignored unless people anglicize and leave behind their full ethnicity even when they are often not fully welcomed in Anglo society.

Still, New Mexico is commonly seen as the state where Spanish is spoken, particularly its own dialects of it, even though there are many other languages used, including various varieties of Tewa and Tigua, as well as Keres, Zuni, Navajo, and Apache. But, Spanish is the language that is celebrated centrally for the state's identity despite a history of ambivalence about it.

While focusing on Spanish, the slogan emphasizes more than the mere existence of the other ethnic groups—as if a wall of static variety in a museum—it stresses experience of the diversity. It involves going to the pueblos to be present during dances, listening to the languages on the streets of Santa Fe by the Spanish governor's palace, hearing Navajo on the radio as you drive among oil wells across the plateau between Cuba and Bloomfield, finding Spanish around you in Alsups, and hearing New Mexico Englishes while speaking your own dialect as you walk around and photograph the Camel Rock just off Highway 84.

Saying it like this suggests the experience is passive: you are there, and it envelops you. But it is active on your part, just as it is on the part of the diverse peoples of the state. They speak it and you hear it. It involves your feelings and movements and those of speakers of the other tongues. You engage them. They may engage you. Sometimes you pay no attention and other times your attention is as focused and detailed as a New Mexico landscape painting. Enchantment is a combination of all of these. It is being taken over by the place in its far-more-than-site reality—even if that reality is just realizing that Edward Abbey was educated at the University of New Mexico—and it is taking on the transcendent place. It is the lasting moment when all of this becomes more present than whatever else you might bring from other places you know, when it stings you like it did me. It is when you connect it all with the state's name, New Mexico, as a thing that is specific and purposive and has so much content that you can peruse it as if it were a great newsstand, library, or even Google.

ENCHANTMENT, PRESENCE, AND ABSENCE

New Mexico's nickname is felicitous since enchantment has a theoretical and academic reality, as Bærenholdt (2016) observes. He finds a significant and meaningful separation between one's enchantment with the place that is based on experiences with it and the enchantment of a place itself, both of which depend on many presence-absences. In this sense, decades ago, New Mexico's Tourist Board hoped to declare the state a place that enchants, that is, is both enchanted and claims people at the same time people actively claim it (Wilson 1997). But declaration alone, even if recognizing the history of locals' engagement with their place and outsiders' experience of New Mexico (including their fantasies—such as appeared in newspaper accounts of the territory once it was taken from Mexico and in short stories and novels penned to make the place real and filled with palatable and strange landscape, people, and ways) is only a piece (Caffey 1999). Without the ongoing history of portrayals of it, bureaucracies, and events structured to create identity, as well as locals' and outsiders' experiences with New Mexico, enchantment of the place would not have taken place (Wilson 1997).

The slogan was built on the ways in which New Mexico was seen by itself and by other Americans as different, and one of the biggest aspects of this difference has been the way that Spanish is maintained as a mainstream language of daily use and public life. Another is the continued existence of Indigenous Peoples in their own societies with their own languages and ways. As a result, New Mexico is a colonialist place where the present seems to conjugate with the past to make pasts visible whether in Native Peoples who did not go away or Spanish American villagers who remind of times before the United States came since the presumption of the present tends to be Anglo, as we shall see.

There is more to the temporality. New Mexico was a centuries-long colony of Spain—and then for some decades a colony of Mexico—before it was taken by the United States Nevertheless, it still appears as a colony. It was well settled in pre-United States times and had a functioning European-style government even though many New Mexicans were Native (First Peoples, Original Inhabitants). The centuries under Spanish rule left these peoples with a complex and intermingled relationship which the United States disrupted by locating Indians and Spanish Americans differently vis-à-vis Anglo Americans and the United States. It also disrupted them by creating around them and among them an Anglo modernity.

Harvey Ferguson wrote in *Rio Grande,* "that here alone change has not obliterated all that went before, that the past is present in patterns of life and types of men, that the face of the earth is not much altered" (Caffey 1999:9). Colonialism has not gone away.

With this begin the presences/absences as New Mexico seems to break both its existence as a landscape and a simple temporal flow from past to present. New Mexico has amazing and varied landforms, massive and marvelous archaeological sites and ancient cities, such as Pueblo Bonito in Chaco Canyon, as well as living Puebloan and Apache societies. It is famous for native jewelry, native art, and native cultures that themselves change and grow yet as if the old colonialism continued, maintained now by American state government, it is the Spanish that becomes the public claim to enchantment, subsuming the rest, including the land, all the while the English encompasses it.

However, this argument can tend to dismiss the vitality of New Mexico's Native peoples. They each have a long history, their own language and customs, as well as politics. Enchantment relies on them, even while reifying them in the landscape and the past, at the same time it grants discursive priority to Spanish colonialism and contemporary Hispanic claims on the state under the force of Anglo dominance. First Nation New Mexicans push the boundaries of this state of enchantment, with its presences/absences, in order to make space for themselves.

ANGLOS AS THE TARGET SUBJECT OF ENCHANTMENT

Another presence/absence is the backgrounding of American occupation and the Anglo-American population scattered in an uneven distribution throughout the state despite their dominant status. Anglos only form the majority population in an enclave in New Mexico's far northwest as well as on the eastern plains and the western mining and recreation areas; they are a minority in the state as a whole. Yet the Anglo, especially the outsider, is the person to be transformed in the making of enchantment. The slogan and its performance presume that, in the tourist experience of the state, those enchanted will be Anglos of a tourist, upper middle class; everyone else simply has ethnicity, culture, history, a different class, and race. Anglos are assumed to be the normative viewers, who either come from elsewhere to live in New Mexico or travel to more than visit, to experience the state's transcendence.

While in other states, such as California, the racial character of the dominant people is commonly spoken—they are Whites—in New Mexico the linguistic character with its ethnic and political implications is the focus of expression. Instead of being mostly labeled as Whites, they are Anglos. Race is backgrounded such that sometimes Blacks, Asians, and others can be Anglos given their relationship to the dominant cultural and linguistic form in the state just as lower-class Anglos also take position due to their race and their cultural relationship to more dominant Anglos who set the ideal.

Enchantment, then, is focused on silent and invisible work on Anglos and is filled with appropriations, the making rigid and thingifying of other peoples in the state. For example, the famous southwest style of furniture, decoration, and clothing that fills Anglo fairs in New Mexico while keeping local artisans working is, to a large extent, the product of conscious design choices to create distinctiveness and narratives by architects and employees of the Museum of New Mexico (Wilson 1997; Sheppard 1988). While these latter are usually Anglos, the former, the artisans and craftsmen, are Hispanos and Indians. The presences/absences go long ways toward creating Anglo regimes of power, including contemporary colonialisms. But these do not happen only among Anglos. From the beginning of the U.S. occupation, local elites of diverse ethnicities have taken part in the creation of this hegemony all the while others challenge them.

New Mexico was taken in the nineteenth century United States-Mexican War. It had a large population for the time and, as a result, presented difficulties for U.S. colonial administrators and politicians who suddenly had to work with a numerous, non-English-speaking, and racially diverse population. In this, they relied on Spanish American elites as brokers and on intermarriage with them to build a territorial and later state government. In addition, the United States depended on the presence of its military forces and the recruitment of Hispanic and Indigenous New Mexicans as troupes. As a result, the enchantment is conflicted. Even when presented as harmonious, it carries evidence of many historical and ongoing struggles.

For example, the capital city of Santa Fe, the Holy Faith, has carried out an annual celebration of the successful return of Spaniards, the conquistadors or conquerors, to the city following the seventeenth-century Pueblo Revolt, which had driven the Spaniards back to Mexico. Though the fiesta has a past as a continuous event (in which the word fiesta is merely a generic noun requiring some specifier such as "the fiesta of Our Lady of the Holy Faith"), it was reinvented as Fiesta (a name of a specific event enacting a narrative past) as part of creating New Mexico as a tourist and local object of identity including and reinforcing Spanish dominance in New Mexico for both the enactors and the tourists. Fiesta has become controversial of late for its portrayal of the "conquest" of Pueblo Indians by the Spanish and for biasing in favor of the Spanish instead of Mexicans. While the controversy has gone on for various decades, in 2018 the city announced the cancelation of the Entrada, or Entrance part of the Fiesta, which covers the return of the Spanish to New Mexico and their domination of the Pueblos in 1692. No one was mollified, supporters were angry at the removal, and the opposition felt it was not enough. An article describing this mentions a telling point about the broader context (Toren 2018). "Santa Fe attracts many people looking to experience its vibrant culture and history. But now, the celebration of a controversial part of that history is gone." The article locates the controversy and reduction of the Fiesta in the tourist experience of living culture and history, which has now changed.

Instead of keeping the focus on internal New Mexican events and New Mexicans' experience of place, it locates those experiences in a relationship between the place, its history and cultures, and outsiders who travel to experience it. In this reading of the controversy, the tourist gaze—as predefined and in interaction with a history of thinking about the presentation of the state—becomes the critical piece for evaluation of local controversies. Enchantment is not seen as general but as directed toward visitors, especially Anglos—potential converts—and their predefined experience, something that also is expected to influence local discussions and experiences of culture and history. In this view, New Mexican, despite the long and complex history of New Mexico, is chained to the ideal of "tourist."

Worth mentioning in that complex history is the U.S. nuclear project in New Mexico. While the controversy over Fiesta and its Entrada took place, there were also "controversial (and highly problematic) recuperative representations of the nuclear presence and its effects in New Mexico during the Doctor Atomic Opera" about the development of nuclear weaponry and the first explosion of a nuclear device. Both the opera and the history it relayed took place in New Mexico and Los Alamos, the site of the nuclear project, continues as part of the U.S. military and defense industry within the state (Masco 2006).

Continuing with the theme of absence and presence let me make another observation. While New Mexican tourist discourse speaks to generic tourists, it also tends to elide the Mexican as a theme and emphasize a synthesized view of the Spanish. Despite the state's name, which references Mexico, the Spanish are singled out and their European-ness exalted. In this is a cultural politics of race and ethnicity that gives preference to Whiteness. Nevertheless, New Mexico shows continuity with the history and culture of Mestizo and Indigenous America. The names of events and customs, towns and places in New Mexico often refer to Mexico and Latin America. For example, the word "Entrada," naming the pageant lost from Fiesta, defines the return of Spaniards from El Paso del Norte—contemporary Ciudad Juarez, Mexico—to Santa Fe. At the same time, an entrada, in lower case, is a main moment of a fiesta in Latin America, a procession and presentation in which the celebrants enter the central space of a town, traditionally the plaza. Similarly, the word fiesta remits to a tradition of public celebrations that were and are important to social-political life since the baroque (Knowlton 2018). They are part of organizing a society and a public. They present theatrical events to create and consolidate local identity even with controversies and division.

This particular presence/absence transports us out of the common frame of Anglo-American society and the formation of its publics. It leads to Mexico and the rest of Latin America both in history and today.

Notably, Fiesta is not officially about the American conquest when New Mexico became a colony of the United States and became one of the last states admitted to the Union. It is about a conquest centuries earlier and, as a result, empowers those generic Spaniards and the people who claim them as ancestors, all within the context of a dominant Anglo gaze with its conventions treating these people as past, as conquered objects. As a consequence, this plays a key role in the construction of New Mexican publics and identity all the while keeping American hegemony invisible, unquestioned, and intact. The period of Mexican independence and the imperialist war the United States waged on Mexico along with its take-over of New Mexico remain as vivid unspoken and unseen background all the while the U.S. military has a strong presence in the state. The Anglo tourist as idea is the one seeing New Mexico and its history and makes it a place.

Santa Fe, Taos, Española, Old Town Albuquerque, and New Mexico are not seen by the *visitadores* of New Spain or contemporary Spain but by envoys of the broader Anglo state, idealized tourists of the United States and their allies, Germans, Italians, French, English, Japanese, and now Chinese. This is a social-political reality of difference and inequality inscribed solidly within the tourist gaze. It is not necessarily the real Anglo tourist, but the idealized version of one, a role instantiated in the Anglo bodies present, and in my young body eating chile that early autumn in Las Vegas many decades ago.

WHO ARE THE HISPANIC NEW MEXICANS?

There is more. In Santa Fe's Fiesta, as well as New Mexico more broadly, we find the question of who the people are who descend from the Spanish Empire and, unspoken, its daughter Mexico. Fiesta is a celebration, by implication, of their survival and continuity in the United States even if in a partial way that enables the hegemony of Spanish purity over other realities and identities of descendants (Horton 2001: 14).

Under Spanish and Mexican rule, society included indigenous communities, as well as people who were Indian servants and slaves in Spanish households (Burnett 2016; Ebright 2015). They joined a range of people from the south including Spaniards, Jews, Africans, and the people of mixed heritage who later became the subject people of Mexico, mestizos, the Cosmic Race as they were later called (Sue 2013). The people were not divided strictly by race or by ethnicity, but by social position vis-à-vis the elite, and by pan Latin American discourses of colonial caste.

This changed when the Americans came with their racial ideas and laws. They applied their own categories to the seemingly under-defined population of New Mexico, separating them into Indian, Spanish, and Black. However, at the time and in practice, these people were integrated hierarchically by political ties, family ties, and connections to important men; they were not so neatly divided into distinct populations. Nonetheless, Americans were concerned to separate out races, especially Africans since slavery guided much of broader mid-nineteenth-century U.S. politics (Gomez 2018). They were also concerned to separate out Indians, dividing at the same time the so-called "civilized" Pueblos from the nomadic tribes. The more general Mexican population, encompassing a range of colors and social positions, tended to be defined as White and as Spanish even if it was of mixed blood and showed a range of skin tones. Many people seized on this usage of Spanish-said-in-English to define themselves both against Mexico and against Native Peoples who now had a different relationship to the governing powers.

The European-ness of Spaniards became a claim to racial identity similar to that of the Americans who migrated in increasing numbers to this land where the long Rio Grande flows south. Thus, the integration of Indians and Spanish (in a broad sense) celebrated in the Fiestas refers by implication to a disintegration of existing social categories of kinds of people under American governance or occupation.

Another issue arises in the long history of peoples who descend from those included in the Spanish Empire. Horton (2001) names it clearly when she speaks to Fiesta as an issue of Latino public history. Many categories have been used to refer to the descendants of that Empire, even though the very terms depend on being embedded in the Anglo world, which largely remains unaddressed. Among those categories are Spanish, Mexican, Chicano, Manitos, Hispano, Hispanic, Latinos, and Latinx. Each refers to a different regime of definition and existence with a strong emphasis on descent from the Spanish Empire (Myers 2009). However, this broad unifying category, exemplified in the simple and simplified archetype of the Spaniard in Fiesta is collapsing as people are discovering other ethnicities, from Mexican and Chicano to Sephardic Jew and Genízaro—the descendent of enslaved Native Americans (Burnett 2016; Ferry and Nathan 2000; Hordes 2008). The common denominator has fragmented into parts and new politics; all the while the local political and tourist gaze speaks to a common Spanish past and remains under the Anglo.

To be New Mexican and/or a New Mexicanizer—that is, someone who is actively exploring the state and its cultures and identity, who is in the process of enchantment—is to find oneself caught in the ethnic and colonialist dilemmas of the state and not just to be overwhelmed by its beauty and its "exotic" history. Indeed, it is to be suspended in dimensions of time where the past is ostensibly visible (in the buildings, the land, and the people—Spanish [Latinos] and Native Peoples, although not ostensibly Anglos who are visualized as present and modern). Time is not an irrevocable flow but is a river with many stones that came from upstream and carried with them, one supposes, that earlier time.

THE ENCHANTMENT OF CONSUMING PLACE

As we have noted, enchantment is an active process of giving oneself up and being taken over by something that appears transcendent and is filled with presences/absences; it is *an enchanting*, a New Mexicanizing. In this, we return to my three-year-old self and chile. I ate the enchiladas, things covered in chile, and as a result was transformed, or so goes the story. One can think of place as something that you consume in the process of living in multitudinous ways and that, as a result, transforms.

For many, land may seem the sine qua non of place—here the Rio Grande Valley and the mountains around it with their attached mesas, plateaus, mountains, and plains. Yet land, alone, is not enough. It must come with people and with ideas and histories as well as conflicts and dreams, with presences and absences, in order to be a place. That is why I do not start with the land, but with the food.

After I had my first enchiladas, and second and third, I learned about Spanish land grants and the Llano Estacado with its stag horn cacti and its wagon ruts heading eastward to Missouri, the Santa Fe Trail. Later I learned about the Great March and the suffering at Bosque Redondo, south on that plain that connected it with the Bisti Badlands of the north and the red stone valley just outside New Mexico's current border. Later, I heard about Socorro and the Jornada del Muerto, the Journey of the Dead Man. It was even later I saw the reservoirs on the Rio Grande, Elephant Butte and Caballo, that make agriculture flourish south of Socorro. I went to the dances of Puye where Indians were separated from tourists (Anglos mostly). I went to Santa Fe and saw the governor's Palace and the Plaza with their daily market of Indian jewelry and I climbed on the rock camel on the way to the Holy Ghost Ranch.

It was in my town, Las Vegas, that I learned that Old Town was mostly Hispanic and New Town mostly Anglo or at least symbolically so. I really did not understand Old Town and New Town until much later when I learned such were common in Anglo colonial governance of New Mexico. (I also learned a version of this division in the towns of the Andes where I did fieldwork; they have moieties of newcomers and original inhabitants.) To me, when young, a town was just divided in half with a stream—the Gallinas River—in between. By the stream, I learned stories of La Llorona when older boys encouraged me to hear her cries in the breezes that trembled the leaves of the river-bottom trees. At night, the same older boys, while we were standing under protective streetlights, told stories of a blue, hammer-headed man that would eat children if he caught them away from the light. They also identified neighborhood witches.

These tales suddenly made sense when, as an adult, I read Rudolfo Anaya's (1972) biographic novel located downstream on the larger Pecos River. In Anaya's telling, these were Spanish American stories, they came with ethnicity and ownership while to me they were just stories I heard. They did not have ethnicity per se. My experiences, took on greater weight when they connected with the tales of a prominent literary work, both in terms of where its story was located—in the broader river basin where I had been a child—and in terms of stories I had been told that frightened me and amazed me. An understanding of the complexity of ethnicity and cultural property slowly developed for me through other experiences and readings over much more time.

Not just through texts, my experiences also took form through the encouragement and interests of my parents. They were Anglos from somewhere else with a strong identity, Utah, and also had learned Spanish. They were intellectuals and artists who also studied the history and culture of this new place at the same time they explored its diverse social world. In many ways, classical academic romantics, they became New Mexicanizers, making sure among many other things that there was always a subscription to New Mexico Magazine with current issues laying around the house even long after we had left the state. I took on their interests, not as external curiosities, but as innate and dense realities, lifeworlds in which I was formed.

Enchantment is an active process and part of every New Mexican and every enthusiast's biography. While it takes the many forms that life takes, it is characterized by the opening of experience and the encounter with representations in text, film, art, and story, a recursive process of mutual support and consolidation that occurs over and over until one is enchanted and re-enchanted. Then it continues as enchantment moves on to become a way of life, even in places far removed from New Mexico.

RED CHILE AND GREEN CHILE

Now, we return to chile and that first burning bite. It stands as a synecdoche, connected not only with place but with every instance of eating hot peppers and spicy food that stretches over the course of my life and in geography over the United States, Latin America, and Europe. The bite, in the double sense of the word, is laden with the meaning of me, an Anglo boy transplanted from the South to the plains of New Mexico and encountering a world of the ay, ay, ay, ays when men in Old Town stood one night in an adobe house, someone pulled out a guitar, and they sang *Cielito Lindo*. Though the song is one of the Spanish Revolution, for me it was one of Las Vegas, New Mexico, my family, and it expressed emotion as part of good life. The refrain, "*Ay, ay, ay, ay, canta y no llores*" (ay, ay, ay, ay, sing and don't cry), stood as motto for how one should respond when the chile, or life, is too *picoso*, too hot.

Enchantment came with an ethos, a stance of gender and on life. As they say, the best chile is the one that burns you going in and burns coming out but you do not complain. Instead, you smile and stand with the men to sing.

Chile not only symbolizes New Mexico and a norm of masculinity for me, but it also is a norm of good food and good life, since good food has chile in it as condiment or as main ingredient. Just like life, it has its sting and also tastes damn good.

Though I can generalize about chile, there is still something particular about this pepper. It is like the state: one of fifty in our country and one of many subnational regions around the world, the same as chile, found in many states and most countries yet also different in specific locations, as every New Mexican knows.

Regionally, cultivars of chile developed in the Rio Grande Valley with flavors and spice typical of New Mexico, and particularly good ones developed in the north around the pilgrimage site of Chimayo (Hendrickson 2017).

If the miraculous sanctuary with its possible Tewa Puebloan or Spanish American origins and its Christ of Esquipulas—originally from Guatemala (Sullivan-Gonzales 2016) and related to Black Christs along the length and breadth of South and Central America, as well as Mexico—its devotion to the Santo Niño of Atocha, and its cult of miraculous dirt is not enough, or if you are not Catholic or not interested in local Pueblo or Hispano Catholicism, then the wondrous chile of Chimayo, celebrated by chefs throughout the United States, will draw you (Suri 2018). It is worth stopping to have some enchiladas fully sauced in it and buy a bag of delicate flavored, though hot, chile to take home.

Like the Christs and the state, chile extends outward as one of many varieties of capsicum. It too originated far down in what is now Latin America but as an heirloom is specific to the area of Chimayo and other parts of New Mexico's north. A landrace plant, it is under threat from pollen let off by improved varieties of chile (such as Hatch) from southern New Mexico that are grown for marketability at the same time that small-scale farmers are aging and their children no longer desire to farm landraces in such limited economies. As a result, this chile is subject to nongovernmental organizations aiming to protect it, in this case, the Chimayo Chile Project (Native Hispanic Institute n.d.)., and governmental legislation as a particular, recognized, and protected variety (Campos 2009). Chimayo Chile is challenged by modernization and the successful development of commercial cultivation of chile, especially the preferred kinds of New Mexico, either green or red.

The New Mexican press takes pride in the state's being the largest grower of chile in the United States even though there are presences/absences in this (Hawkes 2013; Walker 2018). Of preference in commercial New Mexico and the U.S. canning industry is not the red, very spicy, more mature chile of my first experience or of the Chimayo cultivar. Rather it is a much milder, long, green fleshy pepper, which has been bred for reduced piquancy and profitable cultivation.

The unripe chile, the green, chopped, and diced, is emblematic in all kinds of foods in New Mexico, including omelettes and green-chile hamburgers among many others. The long fresh peppers, peeled, stuffed with cheese, and fried in a beaten egg mixture, the chile relleno, is also an icon of the state although it is primarily from the middle and lower Rio Grande Valley rather than from the north such as Las Vegas or the Española valley near Santa Fe where indigenous chiles are thinner fleshed and smaller, nor is it from Chimayo. The large thick fleshed chiles for rellenos and for canning were developed in southern New Mexico at New Mexico State University in Las Cruces, now known for its Chile Pepper Institute, the leading capsicum pepper research institution in the world and an important contributor to the idea of New Mexico (New Mexico State University 2016).

The variety known as Hatch, after the chile growing town in the same county as Las Cruces, which calls itself the "Chile Capital of the World" in a kind of Midwestern civic hype, is a named and registered variety that has been commercially successful and is able to attract a relatively high price as quality chile (Streep 2012). Hatch and its less expensive mates, Big Jim and Joe E. Parker, among many others both named and numbered, came from the Chile Institute and form part of efforts to protect New Mexico chile from national and foreign competition similar to efforts elsewhere to define terroir and Designation of Origin (Coombe 2006; Paxson 2010; Smith 2018; Tracy 2013). Indeed, New Mexico chiles were earlier taken to California where they were developed and became the green grocer's named variety, Anaheim chile after the city of tourist enchantment containing Disneyland. More recently, another competitor was developed in the United States, the Pueblo chile in the region of the same name in Colorado, which is part of the traditional northern reaches of New Mexico chile cultivation. However, the greatest competition is coming from abroad: from Mexico, Peru, and, mostly, China (Knowlton 2014). New Mexico's industry and its government have been fighting to protect its now registered crop.

New Mexico has named chile a "symbol" of the state as the state vegetable, introducing along the way the difference between my first consumption of chile years ago when the spicy ingredient was simply associated indexically to my young self as a food in New Mexico unlike anything I had known before, or between my later learning of names and folklore, as well as literatures about chile, and the now official symbol related as such to the earlier state slogan "Land of Enchantment" (New Mexico Secretary of State, 2019). Chile entered me as an index, and only recently has become an official mark of New Mexico mediated by government, even though the very notion of New Mexico and enchantment originated with the government as did much of the boosterism that went into making the state a culture that enchants.

Consequently, we can speak of culture (with a little c) that exists in an indexical relationship with people in place, and Culture (with a big C) that is officially described, catalogued, and defined as typical of place by government, industry, and NGOs in conjunction with tourism in inscribed and carefully, legally delimited trademarks and brands.

Besides a symbol of the state, chile is tied deeply to the state's land. Nowadays, in the capital city, Santa Fe, as well as in much of the state, chile arrives from the south to be roasted and consumed, filling the air with scent and the streets with color, making it an experience of fall.

Chile is also an index of the so-called "New Mexico cuisine" more generally, as registered in a spate of cookbooks over the course of the twentieth century (e.g., Cameron 2017 and Cline 2015). Fabiola Cabeza de Baca Gilbert may have been the first to publish a cookbook of New Mexico cuisine. Called simply *Historic Cookery*, it appeared as circular 161 from the Agricultural Extension service of the New Mexico College of Agriculture and Mechanical Arts in the thirties. It is still printed, now as Historic Cookery: Authentic New Mexican Food, by Gibbs Smith, most recently 2019, with a copyright owned by La Galería de los Artesanos. The tradition of cooking stems from the red chiles that are ripe, dried, and generally ground and only more recently has it taken on green chile.

While the commercial, industrial varieties are also ripened and dried, the classic New Mexican cuisine comes from the landraces that are particular to a scattering of villages and valleys both in the north and in the south, in both cases along the reaches of the Rio Grande. New Mexico cuisine aggregates them into a whole, while they are separated by different types, flavors, and traditions of use. They tie deeply, as a result, into the diverse geography of the state at the same time, like the state, they come together in a categorical entity connected through government and commercial fiat to the state as a political and legal entity and not just a set of places.

Like the state and its enchanted, enchanting culture, chile also divides on ethnicity and history. Though many contemporary efforts locate chile and New Mexican cooking in the hands and fields of Pueblo farmers (Anaya 2014), others write that chile came northward with the Spanish (Peeples 2013). Unlike in Fiesta, where this division challenges a popular event, in issues of chile it is subtly and hegemonically settled, no matter what historians and archaeologists might say.

There are two spellings in American English for the pungent capsicum peppers, "chili" and "chile." The former is preferred in the United States and imitates the Nahuatl (Aztec) pronunciation of the pepper, *chilli*. The other spelling, the one with the "e," is dominant in Mexican Spanish where it engages the Caribbean *ají* and is also the dominant usage in New Mexico and hence the one used in this essay as well as the one that stems from my experience eating and then learning about the pepper (Merriam Webster 2019; Quinn 2014). It is Spanish in the New Mexican fashion, which is also Mexican even if many locals historically prefer to elide Mexico in favor of Spain.

TAKING CHILE HOME

When people from New Mexico prepare to return, they tend to talk to their friends, also from the state, to see if they want any chile brought back to them. There are New Mexicans living elsewhere who schedule a trip to the state every fall to get the best of the new crop of chile and to bring back bags of fresh, roasted, green chiles. Tourists also take little bags, jars, and strings of chile ristras home to remember and reinforce their enchantment. The state and its enchantment circulate as plastic, Ziploc bags of ground chile powder—green or red—and of roasted and peeled green chiles. This is a kind of life-blood, direct and piquant, which is edible. Other people make New Mexico delicacies, such as enchiladas, carne adovada, or even cookies called bizcochos to share in events and remind people of the state and even missionize the enchantment.

While this bears a certain similarity to the subscription to New Mexico Magazine that many people who have lived in the state continue, it is also different because it is about food. Eating moves the state and its enchantment inside you and makes it part of you, rather than leaving it as looking at the photos and articles in a glossy magazine.

In any case, chile represents the state, its people, history, land, and culture in all of their fraught social tensions and harmonies. Chile also demonstrates enchantment. Only the dirt from Chimayo, rubbed on the body or ingested with water in order to heal what ails you is a more direct connection of land, enchantment, and people.

NOTE

1. After "Judaizers" (Silverblatt, 2004).

REFERENCES CITED

Anaya, Rudolfo. 1972. *Bless Me Última*. Berkeley, CA: Tonatiuh International Inc.

Anaya, Rudolfo, et al. 2014. *How Chile Came to New Mexico*. Albuquerque, NM: Rio Grande Books.

Bærenholdt, Jørgen Ole. 2016. Experiencing the Enchantment of Place and Mobility. *Journal of Consumer Culture* 16(2):393–41.

Burnett, John. 2016. Descendants of Native American Slaves in New Mexico Emerge from Obscurity. *National Public Radio*. https://www.npr.org/2016/12/29/505271148/descendants-of-native-american-slaves-in-new-mexico-emerge-from-obscurity (Accessed December 14, 2019).

Caffey, David L. 1999. *Land of Enchantment, Land of Conflict: New Mexico in English Language Fiction*. College Station, TX: Texas A&M University Press.

Cameron, Sheila MacNiven. 1978. *The Best from New Mexico Kitchens*. Albuquerque, NM: University of New Mexico Press.

Campos, Marie Pilar. 2009. *Chimayo Chile: A Living History of Faith, Culture, and Art*. Chimayo, NM: Native Hispanic Institute.

Cline, Lynn. 2015. *The Maverick Cookbook: Iconic Recipes and Tales from New Mexico*. Santa Fe, NM: Leaf Storm Press.

Coombe, Rosemary J. 1996. Embodied Trademarks: Mimesis and Alterity on American Commercial Frontiers. *Cultural Anthropology* 11(2):202–24.

Ebright, Malcolm. 2015. *Advocates for the Oppressed: Hispanos, Indians, Genízaros and Their Land in New Mexico*. Albuquerque, NM: University of New Mexico Press.

Ferry, Barbara and Debbie Nathan. 2000. Mistaken Identity? The Case of New Mexico's "Hidden Jews." *The Atlantic* December.

Gilbert, Fabiola Cabeza de Baca. 2019. *Historic Cookery: Authentic New Mexican Food*. Layton, UT: Gibbs Smith.

Gómez, Laura E. 2018. *Manifest Destinies: The Making of the Mexican American Race*. New York: New York University Press.

Hatch Chile Store. 2019. New Mexico Chile History. https://www.hatch-green-chile.com/pages/new-mexico-chile-history (Accessed December 13, 2019).

Hawkes, Logan. 2013. More New Mexico Chile Acres, But Industry Faces Major Hurdles. *Western Farmer-Stockman*. https://www.farmprogress.com/vegetables/more-new-mexico-chile-acres-industry-faces-major-hurdles (Accessed January 13, 2019).

Hendrickson, Brett. 2017. *The Healing Power of the Santuario de Chimayó: America's Miraculous Church*. New York: New York University Press.

Hordes, Stanley. 2008. *To the End of the Earth: A History of Crypto Jews of New Mexico*. New York: Columbia University Press.

Horton, Sarah. 2001. Where is the "Mexican" in "New Mexican"? Enacting History, Enacting Dominance in the Santa Fe Fiesta. *Public Historian* 23(4):44.

Knowlton, David. 2014. Chiles Are Now Grown in Peru and Exported to Mexico. *Cuzco Eats*. http://cuzcoeats.com/chiles-are-now-grown-in-peru-and-exported-to-mexico/ (Accessed June 10, 2019).

———. 2018. Fiestas: Analytical Lacunae, Religious and Social Impact. Paper presented at the Society for the Scientific Study of Religion, Las Vegas, NV.

Masco, Joseph. 2006. *The Nuclear Borderlands: The Manhattan Project in Post-Cold War New Mexico*. Princeton, NJ: Princeton University Press.

Merriam Webster. 2019. Where in the World to Use 'Chili,' 'Chilli,' and 'Chile'. https://www.merriam-webster.com/words-at-play/usage-chili-chilli-chile (Accessed January 13, 2019).

Myers, Todd Mitchell. 2009. A 'Fantasy Heritage'?: A Review of the Changing Literature on Hispano Identity in New Mexico. *Journal of the Southwest* 51(3):403–21.

Native Hispanic Institute. n.d. Chimayo Chile Project. http://home.mindspring.com/~sfinhc/id2.html (Accessed January 12, 2019).

New Mexico. 2019. The State Nicknames. http://www.netstate.com/states/intro/nm_intro.htm (Accessed January 18, 2019).

New Mexico Secretary of State. 2019. State Symbols. http://www.sos.state.nm.us/Kids_Corner/State_Symbols.aspx (Accessed January 13, 2019).

New Mexico State University. 2019. Chile Pepper Institute: Devoted to Education and Research Related to Chile Peppers. https://cpi.nmsu.edu (Accessed December 13, 2019).

Peeples, Matt. 2013. Red or Green? Preservation Archeology Blog. *Archeology Southwest*. https://www.archaeologysouthwest.org/2013/09/03/red-or-green/ (Accessed January 13, 2019).

Quinn, Barbara. 2014. The Difference Between Chili and Chile. *Chicago Tribune*. https://www.chicagotribune.com/dining/recipes/sns-mct-bc-ntr-health-onnutrition-20141010-story.html (Accessed January 13, 2019).

Sheppard, Carl D. 1988. *Creator of the Santa Fe Style: Isaac Halton Rapp, Architect*. Albuquerque, NM: University of New Mexico Press.

Silverblatt, Irene. 2004. *Modern Inquisitions: Peru and the Colonial Origins of the Civilized World*. Durham, NC: Duke University Press.

Smith, Julia. 2018. Coffee Landscapes: Specialty Coffee, Terroir, and Traceability in Costa Rica. *Culture, Agriculture, Food, and Environment* 40(1):36–44.

Streep, Abe. 2012. The Chile Capital of the World. *New York Times*. https://www.nytimes.com/2012/10/14/magazine/the-chile-capital-of-the-world.html (Accessed January 13, 2019).

Sue, Christina A. 2013. *Land of the Cosmic Race: Race Mixture, Racism, and Blackness in Mexico*. Oxford, UK: Oxford University Press.

Sullivan-Gonzales, Douglass. 2016. *The Black Christ of Esquipulas: Religion and Identity in Guatemala*. Lincoln, NE: University of Nebraska Press.

Suri, Charu. 2018. Why This New Mexico Chile Has an International Cult Following. *Food and Wine*. https://www.foodandwine.com/travel/sante-fe-chimayo-chile-counterfeit (Accessed December 13, 2019).

Toren, Ariella. 2018. Santa Fe Removes Controversial Entrada Pageant from Annual Fiesta. *KRQE*. https://www.krqe.com/news/new-mexico/santa-fe-removes-controversial-entrada-pageant-from-annual-fiesta/1324192645 (Accessed December 13, 2018).

Tracy, Megan. 2013. Pasteurizing China's Grasslands and Sealing in Terroir. *American Anthropologist* 115(3):437–51.

Walker, Stephanie J. 2018. Red Chile and Paprika Production in New Mexico. College of Agricultural, Consumer, and Environmental Sciences, New Mexico State University, Guide H-257. https://aces.nmsu.edu/pubs/_h/H257.pdf (Accessed December 13, 2019).

Wilson, Chris. 1997. *The Myth of Santa Fe: Creating a Modern Regional Tradition*. Albuquerque, NM: University of New Mexico Press.

Part III

PRACTICES AND CONTEXTS OF COLLABORATION AND CONFLICT

Chapter 6

A Reckoning of the Nuclear West

Jonathan P. Thompson

Under a blanket of smoke from wildfires burning all over the West, the sun reduced to a blurry orange blob, I drove west from Idaho Falls, sailing past rolling plains of wheat, where huge thrashers looking more than two lanes wide kicked up big clouds of dust that vanished into the smoky haze. Raptors perched on nearly every fencepost or power pole I saw, scanning the lava flows and sage plains for lunch. And then the signal that I was amid the vast landscape coopted by the Idaho National Laboratories: bright yellow signs warning humans—and grazing cattle—to stay on this side of an invisible line.

It was August 2018, and I was out there in search of the future of nuclear power, which is increasingly being seen as a necessary component in the fight to stem a global warming catastrophe, by looking at its past, specifically Experimental Breeder Reactor I (EBR-I), where for the first time a nuclear fission chain reaction was used to generate and transmit electricity in 1951. But I was also on a tour through a small piece of what I'll call the Nuclear West, a myriad of landscapes scattered across the Western United States where the nuclear weapons and energy industries gouged into the earth in search of uranium ore, dumped the toxic and radioactive waste out in the open, obliterated huge swaths of desert, and desecrated land and water and sickened the population. Such is the plight of extractive communities everywhere, but the nuclear industry arguably has the most lasting and indelible impact, one that lingers long after every visible trace of the activities has been wiped away. The nuclear legacy becomes an integral part of the Place, with a capital "p," a truth that reaches from the uranium mining areas on the Navajo Nation to the dried-out husk of a community known as Jeffrey City, Wyoming, to the Nevada Test Site, to the milling town in southwestern Colorado where I grew up beneath a towering pile of toxic tailings that sat on the river's edge.

EBR-I is also one of those places. It appears today much as it did in 1963 when the team of workers clocked out for the last time and headed down to the bar at "Atomic City" before making the commute back to their homes in Idaho Falls or Pocatello. It's got an industrial retro-futuristic feel, with its control panels and knobs and valves and other apparatus that possess the characteristic sleek chunkiness of mid-century high-tech design. A temperature gauge for the "rod farm" goes up to 500 degrees centigrade, and if you look closely you'll see a red button labeled "SCRAM" that, if pushed, would have plunged the control rods into the reactor, thereby "poisoning" the reaction and shutting down the reactor. Outside sit two huge experimental jet-engine reactors, symbols of the promise nuclear energy once held.

Those were heady times. By whacking a uranium atom with a neutron and splitting it the technicians on that cold December day launched a chain reaction identical to the one that led to the explosions that annihilated Hiroshima and Nagasaki several years earlier. Mass is destroyed, energy created. Only this time the energy was harnessed not to blow up cities, but to create steam that turned a turbine that generated electricity that illuminated a string of lightbulbs and then powered the entire facility. During the reaction, loose neutrons are "captured" by uranium-238 atoms, turning them into plutonium-239, which is readily fissionable, meaning it can be used as fuel for future reactions and, potentially, warheads. The whole endeavor might look like a terrible trespass or a miracle that defies the laws of physics and creates an endless supply of energy. Scale that up and, for pennies per megawatt-hour, it could power our increasingly electrified society, all without burning any coal or oil or damming any rivers. Two years after EBR-I lit up, Dwight D. Eisenhower delivered his 1953 "Atoms for Peace" speech. Nuclear energy would help redeem the world from the terrible scourge of atomic weapons, the president said; it would be used to "serve the needs rather than the fears of the world—to make the deserts flourish, to warm the cold, to feed the hungry, to alleviate the misery of the world."

The pennies per megawatt-hour dream was never realized, and fears of meltdowns and the challenge of disposing of the waste sullied nuclear power's shine. Now, however, nuclear energy's golden days may be making a comeback. Climate hawks, scientists, energy wonks, eco-modernists, and a handful of politicians are pushing hard to bring nuclear back from the brink, touting the low-carbon-emitting electricity source as the best way to save the world and alleviate the misery to be brought by the impending climate catastrophe. When the entire fuel life cycle is taken into account, nuclear is among the most climate-friendly, emitting 100 times less carbon per megawatt-hour than coal and 50 times less than natural gas—even less than photovoltaics. Fission spews none of the nasty air pollutants emitted by burning coal, and only a fraction of the solid waste. And it would take hundreds of square miles of solar panels or wind turbines to generate the same amount of power as a nuclear plant the likes of Palo Verde outside of Phoenix, Arizona, which churns out a steady stream of juice that runs millions of lightbulbs and gadgets and air conditioners across Arizona, California, and New Mexico, all while generating a fraction of the solid waste—and none of the emissions—of fossil fuels.

A tour of the Nuclear West, however, reveals that this gleaming vision is incomplete. It conveniently ignores the fact that uranium must be mined, milled, converted, enriched, and go through a "fabrication" process. Each step produces waste. Each step potentially releases harmful substances into the environment and into peoples' bodies. Each step must take place somewhere, altering that place, for short-term betterment, perhaps, but often for the worse over the long term. Perhaps we, as a society, have little choice but to turn to nuclear power for future salvation. First, however, we must reckon with its past.

The Nuclear West dates back to 1898, long before anyone had thought of nuclear power or nuclear bombs, when Marie Curie discovered radium in unrefined pitchblende. Radium is a radioactive "daughter" of uranium that was once seen as a sort of miracle substance. Paint it on watch numbers or even clothing, and they'd glow in the dark. It purportedly could cure cancer *and* impotence and give those who used it an "all-around healthy glow," as one advertisement put it. During the early 1900s, it was added to medicines, cosmetics, and sometimes even food. The Denver-based Radioactive Chemical Company added radium to fertilizers. The Nutex Company made radium condoms. Makers of the "Radiendocrinator" instructed men (and only men) to wear "the adapter like any 'athletic strap.' This puts the instrument under the scrotum as it should be. Wear at night. Radiate as directed."

Shortly after Curie's discovery, a Colorado miner sent her a sample of uranium ore from western Colorado. Curie found that it, too, contained radium, and named the ore carnotite. That set off a mining boom in the area around Naturita, Colorado, in western San Miguel County. Hundreds of uranium mines and several extraction plants were built on the high desert mesas and valleys seeking carnotite ore from which was derived high-dollar radium ($100,000 or more per gram), along with vanadium, which is used to harden steel products.

The boom busted in the early 1920s when huge mines opened up in the Belgian Congo that were able to supply the globe's radium-hunger far more affordably. Not long after, radium's glow dimmed when the women who painted it onto watches began dying, and the inventor of the Radiendocrinator was stricken with bladder cancer. We now know that radium is highly radioactive and a "bone-seeker," meaning that when it is ingested it makes its way to the skeleton, where it decays into other radioactive daughter elements, including radon, and bombards the surrounding tissue with radiation. According to the Toxic Substances and Diseases Registry, exposure leads to "anemia, cataracts, fractured teeth, cancer (especially bone cancer), and death."

When the Manhattan Project was launched to build the first atomic bomb, the carnotite-mining infrastructure was brought back to life, and the mines began kicking out ore once again. The old extraction plants also were revived, as was the old metal ore smelter on the banks of the Animas River in Durango, Colorado, which would one day become my hometown. The Durango smelter had enabled the growth and success of the hardrock mining industry in the San Juan Mountains, but shut down in 1930, another victim of the Great Depression. In 1942, shortly after the United States joined World War II, the government came to the rescue. The Reconstruction Finance Corporation (RFC), a federal agency created to stimulate the economy following the Depression, purchased the shuttered smelter. The RFC then leased the site to the U.S. Vanadium Corporation (USVC), which converted the facility into a mill, purportedly to extract vanadium—which is used in steel alloys—from uranium ore. The real target was the uranium. Throughout the war, USVC secretly processed it for use in the Manhattan Project and the atomic bombs that would be dropped on Hiroshima and Nagasaki.

After the war ended, the mill—having served its purpose—shut down, along with many of the other facilities across the region. But when the Cold War and the arms race beckoned, the newly formed Atomic Energy Commission set out to manufacture a new uranium boom to provide the fuel for a massive nuclear arms arsenal and, perhaps, nuclear reactors that would power cities, submarines, and even airplanes. The federal government offered prospectors a cornucopia of subsidies, including bonuses of up to $35,000 for initial uranium ore production, and grubstake loans to finance mining operations. Most significantly, the government agreed to be the exclusive purchaser of ore and yellowcake, and guaranteed a price to be paid for it, thus eliminating financial risk from what otherwise would have been a high-risk, high-return proposition.

A frenzied boom erupted on the Colorado Plateau, transforming once-sleepy little towns like Moab, Utah, virtually overnight into bustling, chaotic mining camps. The mid-century equivalent of the Gold Rush infused popular culture. A 1949 cover story in *Popular Mechanics* instructed readers on building their own Geiger counters, in 1953 a *New Yorker* article cheekily chronicled the writer's trip to Moab to get into the uranium business. A board game called "Uranium Rush," included a "Geiger counter" that "lights and buzzes your way to fun and fortune." Prospectors from across the demographic spectrum descended on the sparsely populated region with their Geiger counters and combed canyons and mesas, looking for the next bonanza. To facilitate the craze, federal land agencies and counties webbed with roads some of the most remote land remaining in the lower forty-eight. Ranchers were pushed off ancestral grazing lands, and quiet little towns erupted into boisterous ones almost overnight. The Atomic Energy Commission leased the Durango mill out to Vanadium Corporation of America, and in 1949 it was once again resurrected, this time milling uranium ore and producing yellowcake, piling up the waste just across the river from the growing town.

In 1955, a thirty-three-year-old doctor named George Moore arrived in Durango, then a town of 7,500 people, to oversee the San Juan Basin Health Department, which served four counties of southwestern Colorado. Moore, who served in the military and later worked in Kathmandu, Nepal, for the U.S. Public Health Service, might have expected a staid office job in a healthy community; instead, he found a leaderless organization in disarray, in a region full of health hazards and illness. Rico, a small mining town to the northwest, had a tuberculosis outbreak. Mesa Verde National Park, an hour away, lacked sanitary drinking water. The Southern Ute Indian Reservation had high rates of obesity, alcoholism, pneumonia, tuberculosis, and infant mortality—along with an epidemic of sexually transmitted diseases brought by the recent wave of oil and gas workers.

To top it off, the massive uranium mill and mountain of radioactive tailings loomed along the shores of the Animas River. Moore didn't like the looks of the operation, so he sent staffers to check it out. They "brought back dead fish heavy with uranium ore," he later wrote. The mill, he learned, had been giving tailings to area highway departments and construction companies, to use as road base, on streets and sidewalks, and even in homes in Durango's burgeoning, postwar suburbs. He notified his former colleagues at the U.S. Public Health Service, but it took three years before the agency finally sent a team of researchers to assess the situation. What they found was unnerving.

Each day, the mill churned through about 500 tons of ore per day. The chunks of pale yellow rock were pulverized into a sandy powder, and then processed with a chemical soup. One ton of ore yielded around six pounds of uranium, the remainder ending up as waste. The Durango mill kicked out some 997,000 pounds of tailings per day, containing leftover uranium, a host of naturally occurring toxic metals, and leaching chemicals, including sulfuric acid, salt and soda ash, tributyl phosphate and kerosene.

Nick Niedler (a pseudonym) was in the seventh grade in Farmington, New Mexico, in 1958. His family had moved to the region not long before, and his father was a big fan of the mountains, so nearly every weekend they all drove up the Animas River and past the uranium mill. "The (mill) had several large ponds next to the river that were usually full and a deep green"; Nick, a tall man with a friendly demeanor, who worked for years as a scientist with the New Mexico Health Department, told me. "Many times when we drove by the ponds, the dirt walls and dikes retaining the acid process wastewater would be breached. The ponds would be empty, and on the river shore you could see where the contents went into the river."

What the young Niedler did not see was a separate liquid waste stream that flowed directly into the river at about 340 gallons per minute, depositing at least 15 tons per day of spent ore solids, leftover acid leaching chemicals, and an iron-aluminum sludge.

At the time, the Animas and San Juan rivers were the primary drinking water sources for at least 30,000 people downstream. Farmers irrigated thousands of acres of crops with the water, and their cows, sheep, and goats drank it. Of all the nasty ingredients, radium-226—with a half-life of 1,600 years—was of most concern to the researchers.

The government scientists sampled river water, milk from cows that drank the water, and crops that were irrigated with river water for seventy-five miles downstream from the mill. They found that the Animas River was polluted with chemical and radioactive materials. Water, mud, and algae samples taken two miles below the mill were 100–500 times more radioactive than the control samples taken above the mill. Another twenty miles downstream, farmers were drinking and irrigating with water that was twelve to twenty-five times as radioactive as the Animas above the mill, double the Public Health Service's "maximum permissible concentration."

Water that Niedler drank from the taps in his Farmington home had ten times the radioactivity of Durango's tap water. Cabbage, sweet corn, apples, and other crops from downstream farms tested similarly high in radioactivity. Downstreamers who drank from the river and ate local food were taking in at least 250 percent of the maximum permissible concentration of radiation. This was added to the strontium-90, another bone-seeker, that wafted in high concentrations over most of the Interior West as a result of the extensive nuclear bomb testing at the Nevada Test Site during the same period.

The river also had high levels of other toxic metals, both from upstream metal-mining tailings and the uranium mill, and was virtually devoid of "bottom fauna," such as aquatic bugs and algae, and fish, for nearly thirty miles downstream from the mill. "The river was a pea-green color during low flow near the state line," Jim Smith (a pseudonym) who was in the elementary school in Aztec when the study occurred, told me. "The river was mostly dead, except for a few suckers."

Clearly, the Vanadium Corporation was violating the laws and regulations. But since the same laws were virtually toothless, there was little the feds could do except ask them to stop. Shortly after the results were revealed to the general public, Vanadium officials vowed to build a treatment facility to reduce the poisoning of the Animas River, prompting the government to report that the "situation was brought under control before the population of the area had ingested sufficient amounts of this radioactive material to cause detectable health damage."

The declaration, while calming, is dubious. By that time, downstreamers had been drinking tainted water for at least a decade, if not more, and no one had done a systematic investigation of the effects on human health. In 1959, Public Health Service officials launched a study to much fanfare, asking Farmington and Aztec school kids to skip the Tooth Fairy and turn their baby teeth over to them. In return, the children would receive a lapel pin that read: "I gave a tooth for research!"

And yet, there's no record of the study ever being completed, nor was any other epidemiological study ever done on the downstream residents, who for nearly two decades had consumed radioactive and otherwise poisonous food. Fearing more public outcry and grappling with a drop in uranium prices, Vanadium shuttered the Durango mill in 1963, and moved its operations to Shiprock, New Mexico. There, Vanadium took over the Kerr-McGee uranium mill, constructed in 1954 on the banks of the San Juan River, on the Navajo Nation. It's hard to see the move as anything but a blatant act of environmental injustice—a continuation of late-nineteenth-century policies when Native Americans were forcibly relocated to make way for greedy extractive industries. Nearly everyone for hundreds of miles downstream from the Kerr-McGee mill was Diné. There was no George Moore to sound the alarm, nor government scientists at hand to get to the bottom of pollution problems. In 1960, when Kerr-McGee was operating the mill, one of the evaporation ponds broke, sending at least 250,000 gallons of highly acidic raffinate, containing high levels of radium and thorium, into the river. None of the relevant officials was notified, and people continued to drink the water, put it on their crops, and give it to their sheep and cattle. It wasn't until five days later, after hundreds of dead fish had washed up on the river's shores for sixty miles downstream, that the public was alerted to the disaster.

Durango's mill was far from the only such facility in the region—similar ones were scattered everywhere, from Mexican Hat, Utah, to Tuba City, Arizona, to Rifle and Grand Junction, Colorado—nor was it the biggest or the worst polluter, by far. Every company running every mill followed more or less the same procedures, dumping radioactive waste into rivers, piling toxic tailings up near populated areas, showing no concern for workers or people living nearby. For every mill there were dozens of mines—some 750 were active across the Colorado Plateau in the mid-1950s—many of which were on the Navajo Nation and employed mostly Navajo miners. Most of the mines were fairly small, underground operations. While mine operators may have adhered to the terribly lax standards of the day concerning worker safety, none took into account, or tried to mitigate the health effects of working underground for hours on end in air saturated with dust from radioactive ore.

Decades before the U.S. boom got going, researchers had firmly established that European uranium miners (before Curie, uranium was used to make dye) got lung cancer at much higher rates than the general populace—a phenomenon that had been observed as early as the 1400s. In 1942, W.C. Hueper, a German scientist who had immigrated to the United States, published *Occupational Tumors and Allied Diseases*, in which he theorized a link between radon—another radioactive "daughter" of uranium found in at dangerously high levels in mines and mills—and the lung cancer in the European miners. A decade later, even as the uranium boom was in full swing, the U.S. scientists confirmed the theory by uncovering the mechanism by which radon caused lung cancer, and throughout the 1950s a variety of studies showed that uranium mining and milling were hazardous to workers' health, because miners and millers were inhaling both radon gas and radioactive nuclei that had attached themselves to dust particles. The same studies found that simply ventilating the mines would potentially reduce risk. Yet the miners were never informed of the perils of their occupation, nor were meaningful protective measures taken. In fact, the federal Atomic Energy Commission actively withheld or downplayed this information in a cover-up that ultimately benefited the corporations and sacrificed the lives and health of thousands of people in order to keep the nuclear weapons machine running at full throttle.

The government stopped buying ore in the 1960s, and yellowcake in the 1970s, but continued to prop up the nuclear industry as a whole with a slew of subsidies. Many of the smaller uranium mines and mills shut down, or were purchased by larger corporations, and consolidated into big operations, yet almost none of them attempted to fix the broken land.

When Vanadium Corp. left Durango in 1963, it left a festering mess behind. Two huge piles of tailings lay piled up at the mill site, perilously close to the Animas River. No lining was installed below the piles to prevent leaching into the groundwater, and no cap put on the piles to prevent tailings from running off into the water. Wind picked up the fine dust and blew it over the river onto town. The closest neighborhood to the pile was low-income and predominantly Hispanic. Kids played in the tailings, reveling in the sandy beach-like texture; one local told *High Country News* in 1980 that it was "the biggest, best sandpile in the world." For a long time, folks would go over to the mill and fill a truck with the tailings, to break up the clay-like soil in gardens, or use in the foundations of homes, or under the concrete sidewalk. In September 1970, a huge rainstorm dumped onto the San Juans and sent torrents running down the Animas River, swelling it to double the volume of the peak spring runoff. The rushing waters didn't quite reach the bottom of the uranium tailings piles, but the event reminded residents of the potential for such a catastrophic event.

I was born in a Durango hospital just days after the floodwaters subsided, and while I was still an infant, my family moved from a little trailer on my grandparents' farm into a house in town, a couple of blocks from the river and about one mile north (upstream) of the old uranium mill and its tailings piles.

The river, which twisted through Durango like a scoliotic spine, was our playground. We spent hours on the Animas, wading, swimming, fishing, and chasing minnows. We'd dislodge old cottonwoods that had drifted downriver, drag them into the current, and grip them with our skinny legs, riding maybe twenty yards before the log bucked us into the icy waters. My brother, a trout-whisperer of sorts, reeled in a half-dozen fish a day, feeding the family all summer long. When we got older, we'd head to the river on warm summer nights, strip down and leap from the footbridge into the deep, dark cold.

We mostly had the river to ourselves. But always, in the background, the tailings piles loomed. We traversed the rocky banks of the river just below, where rattlesnakes posed a more immediate danger than radon or thorium. Occasionally, on nights after a snowy winter storm, people would sneak up the piles and ski down their steep slopes, illuminated under the orange glow of streetlights. When I was eight years old, fifteen years after the Durango mill stopped operating, a scientist examined river bottom sediment downstream from the old mill site. One sample registered 800 picocuries-per-gram (pCi/g) of radium-226, which is 160 times the Environmental Protection Agency's limit for drinking water, and at least as radioactive as a typical uranium mill's wastewater.

In the late 1970s, when I was still a boy, a local doctor named Scott McCaffrey noticed what seemed to be an unusually high number of lung cancer cases in town. When state health department researchers took a closer look, they determined that McCaffrey's statistics were off, but they did notice anomalies on the south side of town, where folks were being dosed with elevated levels of radon-222, which can cause lung cancer. They cautioned against alarm, claiming the sample size was too small to be conclusive. A more systematic epidemiological study was never performed.

A handful of mills and mines across the Colorado Plateau were still operating at the time, but their days were numbered. In March 1979, one of the reactors at Three Mile Island Nuclear Generating Station in Pennsylvania experienced a partial meltdown, thanks in part to a stuck valve. While a devastating catastrophe was narrowly averted, the accident was enough to spark fear in a populace among which an antinuclear weapon movement was already growing. A few months later an even more damaging accident occurred on the Navajo Nation, when a uranium mill tailings dam owned by the United Nuclear Corporation was breached near Church Rock, New Mexico, sending 1,100 tons of tailings and 94 million gallons of radioactive liquid into the Puerco River, affecting livestock and contaminating drinking water wells of countless people downstream. *The China Syndrome* hit theaters that same year, and a rousing, star-studded "No Nukes" concert rocked Madison Square Garden, with Jackson Browne, Carly Simon, John Hall, and Bonnie Raitt imploring the world to "take all your atomic poison power away."

Even as public perception of nuclear power took a turn for the worse, and the U.S. utilities stopped building new reactors, uranium mining and milling operations were ramping up in other countries, leading to a global glut and a uranium price crash. With cheaper yellowcake flooding in from overseas, the domestic industry withered shutting down and leaving behind dozens of mills and thousands of abandoned mines, including more than 500 on the Navajo Nation. At nearly every one of them, the millions of tons of tailings containing radioactive daughters of uranium such as thorium and radium, along with heavy metals such as copper, arsenic, molybdenum, and vanadium, remained.

In late August 2018, a few weeks after my aforementioned trip to Idaho Falls and EBR-I, I went to another corner of the Nuclear West. Monticello, Utah, sits at the foot of the Abajo Mountains with an expansive view of a good slice of uranium country. Monticello had its own uranium mill, which operated from 1942 to 1960, and it sits just a couple dozen miles from the White Mesa Mill, the last operating uranium mill in the United States. The Monticello Mill, like the one at Durango, produced millions of pounds of tailings, contaminated the soil and groundwater with a litany of toxic and radioactive materials, and left an indelible stain on the land and on the collective health of the local residents. For years after the mill shut down, local kids played in the raffinate ponds or on the tailings piles. As in Durango, suspicions eventually arose that high incidences of cancer and other health problems were related to the mill. But as in Durango, these suspicions were pushed aside and downplayed and eventually forgotten.

I was in Monticello to visit with Shirley Franks (a pseudonym), a tenacious activist who is determined to keep the world from repeating the nuclear-related mistakes of the past. We chatted on a cafe patio under cloudless skies. The wind had blown the smoke away, and the air was clearer than it had been for much of the summer, but the short-lived monsoon had vanished, leaving behind blistering heat at the end of one of the driest years for the Four Corners Country on record. Franks is the founder and sole employee of Uranium Watch, and has been a thorn in the side of Utah's uranium industry for nearly forty years.

In 1987, Franks and her husband and kids moved from San Luis Obispo—just a couple miles inland from the then-new Diablo Canyon Nuclear Power Plant—to Moab, Utah. There, the Atlas uranium mill, located on the edge of town along the banks of the Colorado River, was about to shut down for good, thanks to the crash of the domestic uranium market. The owners and the federal government had to figure out what to do with the sixteen million tons of radioactive tailings that sat onsite and that was leaching into the water supply of millions downstream. Fields jumped into the fray, watchdogging the process for the Sierra Club and Friends of Glen Canyon before starting her own one-woman show, Uranium Watch, in 2006.

The Atlas pile was just one shard of the toxic legacy left behind by the U.S. uranium industry. Discussions around nuclear waste usually focus on what's known within the industry as spent fuel, the radioactive leftovers of the electricity generation process. Pro-nuclear energy advocates often emphasize the relatively small volume of spent fuel compared to the solid waste produced by coal. They tend to forget about the far larger stream that comes from the earlier phases of the fuel cycle, such as mining and, especially, milling. The International Agency on Atomic Energy estimated that the U.S. uranium mills had produced 190 million metric tons of uranium tailings for energy production, alone.

Franks is trying to re-inject this inconvenient truth back into the conversation. With a shy smile, big blue-gray eyes, and straight silver hair, she is tireless in her activism, most of which is funded by her. She puts countless miles on her decades-old Toyota station wagon driving to hearings and conferences and site visits. She has learned the art of activism on the fly, brought herself up to speed on the myriad technical issues of her focus issue. And she's an expert at badgering agencies with Freedom of Information Act requests to get them to cough up pertinent documents such as letters concerning a 26,000-ton pile of uranium tailings that was inundated by Lake Powell in the 1960s. Federal officials had determined that it would be better to flood a defunct mill near the mouth of White Canyon with water than to bother cleaning it up, first. Now the tailings are still there, mixed in with a several-meter layer of silt.

Over the years, Franks has continued to monitor the Atlas Mill cleanup—which won't be completed until approximately 2030—and fought hard to stop a proposed nuclear plant in Green River, Utah. She's kept an eye on the White Mesa uranium mill outside of Blanding, Utah, as well as the Daneros uranium mine that lies just outside the boundaries of the Obama-drawn boundaries of Bears Ears National Monument. Both the mill and mine are owned by Energy Fuels.

When we met, she wasn't expecting any sort of flurry of uranium mining, even if new nuke plants get built. That's because globalism has reduced mining and milling in the United States to a mere shadow of its Cold War self. In 2017, the U.S. uranium producers kicked out a record low of just 1,150 tons of uranium concentrate, or about 5 percent of the fuel consumed by domestic nuclear plants (compare that to the 600 million tons of coal burned in the U.S. plants last year). The other 95 percent is imported, mainly from Canada, Australia, Russia, and Kazakhstan. These countries can supply uranium for far cheaper, in part thanks to government subsidies like those that propped up the U.S. uranium industry from the 1950s to the 1980s. Plus, because of uranium's high energy density, it is relatively cheap to ship overseas.

But a new round of government meddling and support could bring the industry back to life. In recent years, the few remaining U.S. uranium producers, led by Ur-Energy and Energy Fuels, have lobbied the Trump administration to step in and do something, specifically to limit the amount of reactor fuel the U.S. utilities could buy from overseas. The administration balked, in part because that would effectively increase fuel prices for already struggling U.S. nuclear plants. Instead, it proposed infusing the industry with cash by purchasing large quantities of uranium for a national reserve. If that ultimately gets the go-ahead, it could immediately and substantially up demand—and prices—for domestic uranium, potentially raising production to levels that haven't been seen in decades. It could breathe new life into Energy Fuels' Canyon Mine, which is near the Grand Canyon, along with its Daneros Mine and White Mesa Mill. Ur-Energy, meanwhile, would see more demand for its products from the spill-prone Lost Creek in-situ facility in Wyoming near Jeffrey City, a community that bet everything on the uranium boom in the 1970s, only to see it all crash a few years later, leaving the town a husk.

Energy Fuels is looking for a lifeline from overseas, too. Currently, it is hoping to import nuclear waste from Estonia, which it would then reprocess in its White Mesa Mill.

If any of that happens expect Franks to be there, pushing back, hard.

In 1986, the Department of Energy came to Durango and spent $500 million in taxpayer dollars to clean up the mill mess—a mess it had originally financed with taxpayer dollars. I was in high school, and I vividly remember going out onto the roof of the school to watch the demolition of the original smelter, its tall brick chimney crumbling into a cloud of dust. Over the next five years, the detritus from mill and smelter were scraped away and removed. Especially egregious hot spots around town, where tailings had been used for construction, were also cleaned up. The site of the once-sprawling industrial complex is now a dog park, and was once slated to become the city's official homeless camp. The place where the radioactive water once poured into the river is the biggest rapid in town and a favorite of rafters and kayakers alike.

Mills all over that part of the West were cleaned up at around the same time, from Uravan to Grand Junction to Monticello. Today, you can find the former mill sites by studying satellite maps on Google Earth, and looking for the telltale tombs—big, gray, featureless monoliths in which the tailings reside—out among the sage or the sandstone or the blood-red earth. No matter how many millions of tons of tailings are removed, and how many millions are spent to "reclaim" the land, the toxic legacy endures, somewhere, somehow. Studies in Shiprock have found elevated levels of birth defects, kidney disease, cancers, and other persistent health problems. Radioactive, heavy-metal-laden water continues to seep into Many Devils Wash, adjacent to the site of the Shiprock mill, and then into the San Juan River, flummoxing scientists. Groundwater beneath the Durango dog park still swims with high levels of uranium, lead, and other contaminants, and the town itself is still riddled with hotspots that weren't cleaned up before. We can only guess at what lurks in the silt of the Animas riverbed.

For the most part, the people of Durango managed to forget that part of their town's history, as remembering might disturb the logic behind dropping a million dollars or more on a house. Mass amnesia serves as a form of economic development and a gentrifying force.

There are those, however, who will never forget. The surviving mill workers whose friends died painful deaths won't forget. Those who lived downwind or downstream from the mill—anyone whose grandmother, father, aunt, or friend died of cancer or kidney failure—will always wonder if it was the tailings, the Nevada nuclear tests, not enough sunscreen, or just terrible luck that killed their loved ones. The science and the statistics won't be much help. Sure, living next to an old uranium mill or gas well may elevate your cancer risk, but it's by an infinitesimally small amount, they say. While the federal government finally recognized that working in a uranium mine or mill, or being downwind from a nuclear bomb test, could lead to cancer, and started compensating the sick, it has yet to conclude the same for those living downwind or downstream from a mine or mill. Studies of the folks living in uranium country at Grants, New Mexico, and Uravan, Colorado, have failed to turn up unusually high cancer rates among the folks who lived near the mills but didn't work in the mines. And when a cluster is found, as was the case in Moab not long ago, the researchers and health officials attribute it to elevated smoking rates or natural background radiation.

Maybe the scientists are right. Maybe there is no direct, causative link between the mines and the mills and the cancer. It cannot be denied, however, that the *place*—the interaction between the people and the land and water—did change somehow as a result of all of that industrial violence. And when that happens, the people who draw physical and spiritual sustenance from the water or the land or the sky are altered as well. Once a mountain is mined, it is diminished, a place out of balance, transfigured. When dynamite and draglines chomp apart traditional grazing lands, they take away more than just grass, rocks, and shrubs; they shatter a delicate balance that existed between humans and the land for thousands of years. When a cluster of oil wells and holding tanks explodes, rending the night, the place is tainted. This diminishment, or unbalancing, produces a trauma that wends its way into our psyches and into our cells, maybe even our genes.

I thought about this as I drove back to Idaho Falls from EBR-I during that smoky summer. I saw a shimmer through the haze, something that resembled the polished dome on a mosque, or a structure on a colony on Mars from a Ray Bradbury story. It was the containment building for—and a sort of monument to—a second experimental breeder reactor, EBR-II, which was shut down and razed in the 1990s, following the Chernobyl disaster, when public opinion of nuclear power was at a low point.

I found it odd that they would leave that part behind, because not so far away from there was another landmark of the Nuclear West known as Stationary Low Power Reactor Number One (SL-I). Only there was nothing apparent to remember it by, no monument, not even a simple sign. In 1961, one of the three workers there, perhaps intentionally, had pulled the control rod too far out of the reactor, causing the chain reaction to go haywire. The reactor facility exploded, the water pressure so strong it impaled a man onto the ceiling of the containment structure. The other two died, as well, making it the first fatal nuclear reactor accident ever. Rumor has it the men are buried in lead caskets.

REFERENCES CITED

Arnold, Carrie. 2014. Once upon a mine: the legacy of uranium on the Navajo Nation. *Environmental Health Perspectives* 122(2):A44–A49.

Brugge, Doug, and Rob Goble. 2002. The History of Uranium mining and the Navajo people. *American Journal of Public Health* 92(9):1410–19.

Hart, Stephen S., and Eric Twitty. n.d. Colorado's 'Lost' Radium Boom: Early 20th Century Mining and Processing Landscapes on the Colorado Plateau and in Denver. http://montrosecounty.granicus.com/MetaViewer.php?view_id=2&clip_id=141&meta_id=10184 (Accessed June 29, 2020).

Holaday, Duncan. 1967. Radiation Exposure of Uranium Miners. Joint Commission on Atomic Energy Subcommittee on Research, Development, and Radiation. Idaho National Laboratories

National Research Council. 1999. *Health Effects of Exposure to Radon: BEIR VI*. Washington, DC: The National Academies Press.

Thompson, Jonathan P. 2018a. *River of Lost Souls: The Science, Politics, and Greed Behind the Gold King Mine Disaster*. Salt Lake City, UT: Torrey House Press.

———. 2018b. Is Nuclear Energy the Key to Saving the Planet? *High Country News*. https://www.hcn.org/issues/50.21/nuclear-energy-a-new-generation-of-environmentalists-is-learning-to-stop-worrying-and-love-nuclear-power (Accessed June 29, 2020).

———. 2018c. Nuclear Energy is Clean—If You Ignore All the Waste. *High Country News*. https://www.hcn.org/issues/52.1/nuclear-energy-nuclear-power-is-emissions-free-but-at-what-cost-waste (Accessed June 29, 2020).

———. 2019. Will the Trump administration boost uranium? *High Country News*. https://www.hcn.org/issues/51.9/mining-will-the-trump-administration-boost-uranium (Accessed June 29, 2020).

United States Department of Energy. https://www.energy.gov (Accessed September 28, 2020).

United States Environmental Protection Agency. https://www.epa.gov (Accessed September 28, 2020).

Chapter 7

Public Lands Security

The Dispute over Federal versus Local Law Enforcement

Jacqueline J. Russell

The questions at the root of the United States' western public lands paradigm are echoed in the public lands' security debate. This is the discussion as to whether law enforcement should be the sole purview of local authorities or enforced at the federal level with the presumed cooperation of local law enforcement, as it is currently. Shadowing this issue are attempts to diminish federal law enforcement's authority, which could deliver a critical blow to federal control. The possibility of losing federal law enforcement's presence on western lands brings into question the degree of effectiveness and zeal that local law enforcement would demonstrate to protect western public lands properly in the face of conflict of interest with constituents. Local law enforcement currently serves a central role in ensuring public safety on federal lands and is a necessary ally in the success of the mission of the Bureau of Land Management (BLM) and the United States Forest Service (USFS). The federal government contends that the role of a federal conservation authority on public lands is necessary to provide comprehensive land management and to assure adherence to environmental legislation. This debate intensifies each time the government attempts to prosecute violators of federal laws or steps up enforcement of conservation protections. Because the federal system's failure to educate the public and to make clear the full extent of the long-term consequences of short-term actions, opponents to federal control of public lands gain a vocal, enthusiastic following in this debate.

To put the vastness of these public lands into perspective, consider that almost half of the western United States has been set aside by the federal government in trust for the American people. These parcels were either given to the United States by the states upon entering statehood or were acquired later through purchase or trade. The bulk of this land is managed by the BLM and USFS. Other agencies such as the National Park Service (NPS), Fish and Wildlife Service, Bureau of Indian Affairs, and the military are also responsible for certain aspects of land management in the west. The majority of BLM lands were originally considered unwanted and/or unusable state lands. Much of the USFS lands were designated during the conservation movement that began in the late 1800s and was championed by President Theodore Roosevelt. The BLM and USFS agencies have served as the government's martinet in the decades-old war of the interests: east versus west, state power versus federal power, and local rights versus the authority of the distant federal politicians.

As of 2008, there were seventy-three federal agencies employing over 120,000 full-time federal law enforcement agents (Reaves 2012). Each of these 120,000 law enforcement officers is authorized to make arrests and carry firearms. These numbers are even more significant when considering that this number does not include officers of the military, Central Intelligence Agency agents, or Transportation Security Administration Air Marshals. In striking contrast, the BLM employs only about 255 law enforcement officers to oversee 245 million acres; about one officer per million acres (Reaves 2012). Additionally, many positions in very rural locations go years without being staffed and millions of acres go without patrol by federal or local law enforcement for extended periods. The USFS manages 191 million acres and has about 644 full-time law enforcement personnel; about one officer for every 300,000 acres (Reaves 2012). The saturation is slightly greater in the NPS: as of 2008, they had about 1,400 officers to cover 84 million acres or one officer for every 60,000 acres (Reaves 2012). Roughly, 58 percent of USFS-managed lands are in the western region of the United States, and almost all of the BLM lands are in the west.

THE HISTORY OF LOCAL-FEDERAL STRUGGLE

The seeds of the power struggle over the western wilderness and resources took root in Washington D.C. as a conservation movement. Theodore Roosevelt, identifying wanton waste and abuse of American resources including hunting and logging, was the defining force behind the American conservation efforts. The Forest Reserve of 1891 was, in part, spurred by the abuses of the Timber Culture Act of 1873 and the overgrazing of areas across the west (Steen 1992:210). Grasslands, ranges, and lush riparian areas along waterways were ravaged by the overgrazing of sheep and cattle. Large expanses of forest were leveled for industry or grazing lands. At the time, limited local outcry over the devastation of western land areas prompted the conservation legislation. Only when the Organic Act of 1897 was passed did all Westerners really start to take notice. This act established the purpose of forest reserves and authorized the Secretary of the Interior to make rules that would ensure timber supply, preserve water flow, and conserve wild areas. In addition, the Organic Act established the Forest Service structure, which included the hiring of the first rangers. Many in the west did not have a clear understanding of the implications of this legislation and, at that time, there was little or no enforcement at the local level. When the U.S. Department of Agriculture took over, national forest management fees were instituted, more rangers were hired, and new rules were published and enforced. With the new visibility of the Forest Service, Westerners felt the impact of the new policies both at home and in their pocketbook (Steen 1992:211).

Acts of protest from western states began immediately in response to the designation of forest reserves and the associated restrictions. The first case law was established when the Supreme Court heard the case of Pierre Grimaund, a sheep farmer, who in 1907 began illegally grazing his sheep on the Sierra Forest Reserve (Miller 2012:86). After several years and multiple conflicting lower court rulings, the Supreme Court determined that the Congress could, in fact, delegate authority to the Department of Interior (DOI) and other governmental agencies. Several subsequent cases have reaffirmed the ability of the federal government to own and manage lands and the constitutionality of federal law enforcement presence on these lands.[1]

Protests against the Organic Act centered on many of the same grievances heard today. Protestors argued that the laws governing public lands put western states on an unequal footing from eastern states. They believed land restrictions limit access to the raw materials that were available to Easterners who had already exhausted them in the process of making their fortunes. In addition, they argued that administrators far removed from the local issues and environment had too much authority and control over land adjacent to communities that needed the resources of the lands for the prosperity of their families, communities, and for their livelihoods. They believed that conservationist legislation locked up taxable land and prevented rural areas from growing through lack of revenue (Miller 2012:86).

These views have persisted for centuries. Beginning in the late 1800s, Westerners have argued that decreasing grazing allotments and restricting logging, mining, or any other industrial activity was, and still is, effectively extinguishing a way of life in the west. Then and now, many Westerners feel that these laws were written by Easterners and protected by federal rangers directed by Eastern elites, neither of which have concern for the effect on those who had built a life in these areas. A recent example is the 2016 lawsuit by Utah's Kane and Garfield counties against the BLM and DOI. The lawsuit claims that if the federal government continues to deny new coal leases on public lands, it will "economically devastate rural Utah communities, eliminating hundreds of jobs and closing crucial mine sites" (Tanner 2016).

Since the establishment of western public lands, disregard for federal land laws such as that of the sheep farmer Grimaund has been common. The people of the west continue to fight against perceived oppression in their home counties. They continue to cut timber without the required permits, graze livestock, mine, and live as they have historically. This cavalier attitude toward the public land laws has been perpetuated throughout the last century. When forest rangers first began to enforce land laws, they were met with contempt and in the early 1990s began to carry firearms for personal safety (Steen 2012:188). Today, there are numerous incidences of caviar poached from Columbia River sturgeons, Native American artifacts and dinosaur bones destroyed or sold from public lands, rattlesnakes taken from Arizona lands to sell as pets, big horned sheep killed for their horns, and many other natural resources crimes that are common on Forest Service and BLM managed lands (Goldfarb 2017). Much like the highly publicized revolt of Cliven Bundy of Clark County, Nevada, Grimaund grazed his sheep in protest of the restricted access to lands that had been previously open with unhindered grazing. As with Bundy, he was also part of a widespread pattern of abuse of the lands and blatant disregard of federal law.

Even after passing the 1897 Sundry Civil Bill with Pettigrew Amendments which assured open prospecting and timber and livestock access, the government never really allowed such access, creating a pattern of uncertain enforcement. The required permits were almost impossible to obtain, the process took months, and the authorities were required to compile an excessive amount of information (e.g., whether the trees had reached maturity, how the cutting of trees would benefit the forest, etc.). After all this was completed; permits might still be denied (Miller 2012). Locals who tried to follow the rules were thwarted. The public lands' governmental agencies of the day created the perception that they could not be trusted, and this core belief held by the local population has been passed on to subsequent generations.

Almost a century later, during a time of record high levels of permitted grazing on BLM managed lands, Congress passed the 1976 Federal Land Policy Management Act (FLPMA). Before the enactment of FLPMA, the BLM's planning process consisted of multifaceted competitive planning models that required a management framework plan (MFP). It was believed by some that the MFP primarily benefited ranching interests. The grazing and mining areas of the BLM profited by a more substantial budget and, therefore, exerted more influence in the planning process. As a result, it was difficult to reach a resolution when there were resource conflicts. This period of BLM grazing mismanagement caused an imbalance in the ecosystem and damage to the ranges and riparian areas (Nolen 1996:771).

After the National Environmental Policy Act (NEPA) of 1970 and FLPMA in 1976, planning changes shifted the approach to the management of public lands and required land management agencies to consider environmental impacts in all the decision-making. It also ushered in the use of Environmental Impact Statements and Environmental Assessments, which required proposals to include the impacts of any actions to the environment and to include any unavoidable adverse effects, alternatives to proposals, short-term productivity versus long-term environmental consequences, and all irreversible commitments to resources (Andrews 1976). Because not all decisions were required to be made based on the environmental implications, but only with consideration of them, it provides a less-biased decision-making process than pre-FLPMA (Nolen 1996:771). Additionally, the Archeological Resources Protection Act was passed primarily because of "the need to provide more effective law enforcement to protect public archeological sites" (NPS n.d). The new weight given to environmental and archaeological considerations requires experts to observe and evaluate environmental impact and trained law enforcement to ensure adherence to the conservation laws and regulations (State of Utah 2014). However, in compromise with the passing of FLPMA, the western industry ensured that law enforcement was kept to a minimum, a deficiency that the BLM and USFS still suffers from today (Cowart and Fairfax 1988:393).

THE ADVENT OF BLM LAW ENFORCEMENT

Congress acknowledged that law enforcement capacity was an important step in legitimizing the BLM and its mission. FLPMA, which authorized the hiring of law enforcement officers for the BLM, was heavily opposed by land users and western politicians alike. When it was ultimately passed, it authorized "Federal personnel or appropriate officials to carry out his law enforcement responsibilities with respect to the public lands and their resources" (State of Utah 2014). In 2002, because of the second landowner revolt known as the Sagebrush Rebellion, the DOI published *Disquieting State of Disorder: An Assessment of the Department of Interior Law Enforcement.* The report determined that the DOI law enforcement agencies needed a stronger and clearer chain of command. BLM law enforcement was a structural challenge from the start because of insufficient funding and no clear leadership echelons. This was a crucial flaw that had been identified repeatedly by those working with the BLM in the west, leading to charges that BLM officers had no culpability for their behavior, used intimidation tactics, and lacked integrity. As a result of the report, a Director of Law Enforcement position was established and appointed. However, even after reinforcing chain of command

and accountability procedures, complaints from county commissioners and sheriffs remain frequent. They argue that BLM officers continue to have little accountability (Burr 2014).

In the past, the BLM spent thirty years as a land management agency that relied solely on local law enforcement. The process was summarized by Charles S. Watson Jr.:

> If a Bureau field man spots a hundred minibikes wrecking the side of a mountain or catches someone walking off with a rock adorned with petroglyphs, his only recourse is to hop in his truck, drive to the nearest sheriff's office or police station, wait for the deputy to finish with the wreck on the interstate, and bring him back to the scene of the crime—by which time, of course, the dust of the minibikes would have settled and the rock be either gone or tossed to the ground. (Watson quoted in Harvey 1979)

This scenario illustrates how difficult it was to address conservation-related violations when the only available resource was local law enforcement. Furthermore, local law enforcement has not been reliable in enforcing any law that may adversely affect the local economy (Smyth 1979:462).

A serious failing of USFS and BLM is the inconsistent presence and enforcement of federal laws and regulations. For several decades, public offenses on public lands had little or no repercussions, and only the most egregious were prosecuted. In July 1980, several county commissioners and other officials gathered with 300 other protestors as local officials facilitated the bulldozing of a road into a prospective Wilderness Study Area (WSA) in Utah. They claimed that the federal government had become a "cancerous" growth and that FLPMA was a disaster to the country. One of the county commissioners, said, "We will take control of our destiny in Southeastern Utah and not delegate it to bureaucracy" (Cawley 1993:6). The government's response to the commissioners was a certified letter telling them that they needed to repair as much of the damage done as possible (Cawley 1993:6).

A more recent example of these inconsistencies in enforcement are the actions that led to the Bundy Standoff in 2014. For decades, Cliven Bundy grazed his cattle on public lands and refused to pay the accumulation of almost a million dollars in grazing fees. In 2014, after years of planning, the federal government finally decided to remove the cattle from the Nevada public lands. The federal contractors and BLM and NPS law enforcement were met with gun laden protestors and after a dangerous escalation of force during the Standoff, the government backed down. It took two years and the 2016 occupation of the Malheur National Wildlife Refuge before any charges were filed. Any new attempts by BLM and USFS to enforce federal laws and regulations further reinforce the claims by state representatives that these officers are "Rambo," "jack-booted thugs," and militarized (Free Range Report 2017).

THE CATCH-22 OF BLM LAW ENFORCEMENT

Just as all peace officers have to undergo training within their state, all federal land management law enforcement officers are required to attend the Federal Land Enforcement Training Center's (FLETC) seventy-nine-day Land Management Police Training (LMPT). After graduation, officers undergo an additional twelve weeks of closely supervised training with a field training officer. This police training is specifically for officers responsible for protecting natural resources and public lands but also provides basic policing skills. LMPT instruction uses an interdisciplinary approach to meet the unique requirements of land management law enforcement officers. Additionally, the program changes based on needs that are "identified through systematic program monitoring in the form of validation studies and continuous research, which includes feedback from Partner Organizations (POs)" (FLETC n.d.). The personnel who deploy to the nation's immense public lands are well-trained, especially given their niche specialization in conservation law enforcement.

The use of primarily administrative actions and the inconsistency with policy enforcement, however, makes the USFS and BLM appear to be a paper tiger. There is often a lack of support of federal law enforcement from agency administrators due to the risk of local backlash. Federal agencies will send out certified letters or other official correspondence for the most significant violations and offenders rarely respond. One example is a criminal trespass case in Utah. An individual dug canals for water, created roads, and built a shelter on public lands.[2] The BLM delivered certified letters to this individual for over ten years, yet administrators still refused to take any other action. Cases that are handled by administrative action are, by far, the most common and are frequently ignored. When offenders do face major consequences for acts that have been ignored in the past or have been supported by local government, it causes anger toward the federal government and toward those that they believe do not have the authority to address them. Inconsistent action emboldens anti-government Westerners to continue illegal protests or activities, and when law enforcement finally pursues legal options, it threatens their sense of entitlement.

While state and local police perform 90 percent of law enforcement on public lands, they seldom provide regular policing and rarely actively patrol these areas. Additionally, they very rarely investigate conservation crimes. This follows the historic pattern (Perry n.d.). Federal agencies investigate or prosecute only a small portion of crimes, and while most western public lands are proprietorial jurisdiction, state and local police are still a predominant presence on public lands near population centers (Perry n.d.). Proprietorial jurisdiction are areas that the federal government has the authority to conduct policing activities pursuant with the Property Clause and the enabling acts (Shephard 1984). In areas of proprietorial jurisdiction, local law enforcement remains in charge of general policing, and federal officers enforce federal laws and regulations that are applicable to the designated areas (McLane n.d.a). In addition, the Assimilative Crimes Act allows federal law enforcement to use an appropriate state law in federal court when there are situations where there is no applicable federal statute (McLane n.d.b). This allows local, state, and federal officers to effectively prosecute crimes that occur on or against public lands. In general, land management agencies prefer to remain proprietorial because they lack the organizational infrastructure to effectively provide general law enforcement (McLane n.d.b).

CLASHING LOCAL AND FEDERAL AUTHORITY

The ability for federal officers to enforce state law to prosecute crimes has not gone without protest. In 2013, a federal judge blocked a Utah attempt to pass HB 155, a bill that would have prevented federal officers from using Utah state law to prosecute crimes. The judge ruled that this bill violated the Supremacy Clause of the U.S. Constitution and could result in criminal penalties for performing legitimate law enforcement duties on public lands. As is common, particularly in Utah and Nevada, rural sheriffs were at the forefront of the push for change. They believed that passing that bill would prevent law enforcement abuses that use state law to prosecute crimes by federal officers (Maffly 2013). In 2014, Nevada pursued similar legislation spurred on by the Bundy Ranch Standoff and the shooting death of a twenty-year-old Nevada man by a BLM officer after the man reached for a state highway patrolman's rifle (Botkin 2014).

The rise of local revolts and Wise-Use Movements created traction for the County Supremacy Movement in the political arena. In 1995, an Idahoan congressional representative tried to pass the Civil Rights Act. This would have required federal law enforcement to get permission from the county sheriff prior to enforcing laws in that county (Blumenthal 1995). That same year, an Idahoan congressional representative and senator openly disputed the rights of federal law enforcement officers to carry firearms (McLane 2011:509). In 1996, an Alaskan congressional representative attempted to eliminate all law enforcement funding from the BLM. The most recent resurgence of attempted legislation to undermine BLM and USFS law enforcement in Utah is the introduction of HR 622, Local Enforcement for Local Lands Act, in 2017. Two bills, HR 622 and HR 621, were proposed by a Utah congressional representative (Blevins 2017). Both of these measures were an effort to decrease or undermine federal presence and authority in the west. HR 621 or "Disposal of Excess Federal Lands Act of 2017," which would have allowed the sale of 3.368 million acres across much of the west, was withdrawn after significant pressure from hunting and outdoor groups.[3] The designated parcels were those identified in 1997 as "suitable for disposal or exchange for the purpose of conducting restoration activities in the Everglades region of Florida." However, the term "suitable for disposal" is misleading because, as stated in a 1997 letter from the Assistant Secretary of the Department of the Interior, the sale of those "disposal" lands would have to resolve the "high disposal costs, threats to critical natural or cultural resources and habitat, mineral claims and leases, and hazardous conditions" (Cohen 1997).

Unlike the minimal support for HR 621, HR 622 the "Local Enforcement for Local Lands Act," was cosponsored by six other representatives from western states.[4] Representatives from Utah, California, Nevada, and Arizona all sponsored the bill. HR 622 cuts funding for the Department of the Interior or law enforcement officers working for the USFS and the BLM (5 percent for the BLM and 7 percent for the USFS, respectively). Written into the bill as explanation is the clause, "Federal agencies do not enjoy the same level of trust and respect as local law enforcement that are deeply rooted in local communities." In addition, the representative from Utah argued that removing police power would allow the USFS and BLM to focus on managing public lands and would improve transparency and accountability. HR 622 would also provide block funding to county sheriffs for local patrols based on the amount of public lands in that area. For those in favor of local control of public lands, this is an attractive solution to perceived federal overreach. It brings funding to counties and allows for local authorities to decide how and when to enforce federal laws. Many rural areas would welcome the opportunity to deal with only their locally elected sheriff and not the bureaucracy of the BLM and USFS. However, these types of funding agreements are already routine in some rural counties through paid partnerships and Memorandums of Understanding, which the BLM contracts for patrols and dispatch services with local law enforcement. Illustrating the problems with these arrangements in 2014, eight of the twelve Utah BLM/County contracts were not renewed. In some cases, this was a result of counties not filing the required reports or performing the required services; in others, it was because the contract needed to be reassessed or was no longer required (Scott 2016). HR 622 would require county sheriffs to file annual reports on public land patrols to the federal government, which has already proven to be problematic.

THE FAILURE OF LOCAL-FEDERAL PARTNERSHIPS AND COLLABORATION

Law enforcement partnerships are a critical component to successful multiple-use land management. However, each partner must be willing to commit to the coordination, interdependence, and trust of each agency in order for the state, local, and federal offices to be effective partners (Mohr and Spekman 1994). There is a significant history of discord and mistrust between the federal agencies, especially the USFS and BLM versus county sheriffs. The trouble arises from both sides. For instance, the BLM had spent years working with the county sheriff prior to the Bundy Ranch Standoff. The first attempt to round up Bundy's illegally grazing cattle was in 2012, but after collaborative planning with the sheriff's office fell through at the last minute, it was cancelled. Again, in 2014, the BLM spent months of joint planning just for the sheriff to withdraw his aide at the beginning of the operation. The county sheriff and his deputies watched the situation escalate from the sidelines and did nothing, thus endangering federal personnel (Taylor, Heikkinen, and Yachnin 2014).

Similar to a 1980 incident in Moab, in 1996, elected officials from three Southwestern Utah counties led an effort to bulldoze through land that was being considered for WSA (Warren 1996). Two of the counties were accused of creating more than fifteen miles of roads in several different WSAs. In 2003, a county sheriff in Utah assisted the county commissioner in taking down BLM signs that restricted wheeled vehicle access. Two years later, they erected new signs announcing that those roads were open. In 2014, a county sheriff in Utah was an integral part of the Recapture Canyon protest ride where multiple ATVs were ridden on restricted lands. The county commissioner that participated in that ride was later convicted on federal charges of conspiring to operate off-road vehicles on public lands closed to motorized vehicles, and of operating vehicles on those lands. The county sheriff was also an integral part of the protest but was not charged (Thompson 2015). There are numerous other examples of incidents in which sheriffs either condoned, participated in, or simply looked the other way when crimes against the USFS, BLM, or public lands were openly committed (Chaloupka 1996; Coppelman 1997).

ANTI-FEDERAL MOVEMENTS

The threats from militias, anti-government protestors, proponents of the County Supremacy Movement, and anti-environmental Wise-Use Movements continue to result in disregard for federal law and threaten the safety of federal employees in the west. Additionally, there is heightened hostility toward federal authority in states and counties that have the largest percentage of federally owned lands. For instance, Nevada, which is 85 percent public lands, is home to numerous incidences of illegal protest events.[5] Many of the western anti-government extremist groups (i.e., Oath Keepers, Three Percent, Constitutionalist Sheriffs, Border militias, etc.) continuously show up at occasions such as the Bundy Ranch Standoff, the Malheur National Refuse Takeover, the Recapture Canyon protest, the 1994 takeover of the Garfield County courthouse, Ruby Ridge, and other events of significance involving the public lands of the west. Emboldened by many of these events, radicalized individuals continue to threaten the federal employees whom others seek to disarm. Each of these events directly affects public land law enforcement, civilians, and other employees (Wiles 2015).

The anti-government group that has had the greatest influence on anti-federal law enforcement legislation are the Constitutionalist Sheriffs. Constitutionalist Sheriffs created and continue to facilitate the Sheriff Supremacy Movement which contends that the constitution holds the sheriff as the highest law authority in a county, superior to federal officers, and seeks to increase county authority and decrease federal power (Coppelman 1997:32). This movement is one of the largest threats to federal law enforcement authority. In the last fifty years, western county sheriffs have been at the root of every legislative proposal and illegal attempt to disarm federal law enforcement. They also stand to gain the most if federal law enforcement were to leave or be rendered impotent. To rural Westerners, county sheriffs are elected officials beholden to the citizens of that county, and federal law enforcement are outsiders with no perceived local accountability. County sheriffs are accountable to their constituents, local special interest groups, and county commissioners. They are often concerned with reelection, and their decisions can be, and often are, swayed by economic and political considerations. In rural western counties, many county commissioners and sheriffs are ranchers with a clear conflict of interest. Local politics do not always align with federal mandates, and the economic interests of the county are not always the priority of the federal government.

Abuse of power, conflict of interest, and/or corruption are, however, just as possible among federal officers as they are among state and local law enforcement. In many cases, one BLM ranger may be the only federal law enforcement officer with which an entire county would work. A strained relationship can create an atmosphere of anger and distrust. For example, one overzealous BLM ranger in the early 2010s created significant discord with the sheriff of county in southern Utah. The BLM ranger's behavior gave credence to the sheriff's arguments of BLM's disregard for local authority. The sheriff testified in front of the House of Representatives' Public Lands Subcommittee regarding the complete lack of respect for local ranchers and citizens from the ranger assigned to his county. This disregard extended to visitors to the Grand Staircase-Escalante National Monument, local law enforcement, and the sheriff, himself.[6] His testimony also provided a litany of other frustrations and abuses his county experienced while working with BLM.

The county sheriff testified that when he addressed his concerns to the BLM ranger's supervisor, he was received with condescension and disrespect.[7] His time in office had been fraught with constant conflict with the BLM field office, the state BLM law enforcement supervisor, and the BLM ranger working in his county. While that sheriff may have reason to resent the idea of working with BLM federal law enforcement, he had also perpetuated some of this animosity himself. In 2014, he had openly threatened to arrest any federal law enforcement officer who would try to close off trails or any public areas (Siegler 2016). That same year, he proclaimed through written ordinance that federal law enforcement authority was not recognized in his county. In fact, he had arrested one BLM non-law enforcement employee under dubious circumstances and, in 2014, attempted the arrest of a law enforcement ranger for a similarly spurious reason (Wiles 2016). He has been adamant about the lack of coordination, communication, and respect from the BLM district office; and he openly condemns the presence of any BLM law enforcement. As a BLM spokeswoman stated in 2014, after the BLM ended its contracts with five Utah county sheriff's offices, "But when you are trying to negotiate an agreement, and you're trying to find common ground, when one side continues to poke you in the eye with a stick, it is frustrating and it makes it very hard to continue to have productive talks" (Scott 2016).

The rift between federal and state, resources of the west and east, and the rights of one faction over the rights of the other has also divided local law enforcement against federal law enforcement. In some cases, an impasse occurred where neither acknowledged the authority of the other. In 2014, five Utah county sheriffs declared that they would not acknowledge the authority of federal law enforcement officers in their counties. The most recent justification was that federal authority is a threat to "the health, safety, and welfare" of their citizens (Taylor, Heikkinen, and Yachnin 2015). Each of the five counties passed similar resolutions that banned federal law enforcement within the border of those counties. Clearly, these resolutions have no legal standing, but they can and do have real-world consequences.

This is history repeating itself because as early as 1996 in Owyhee County, Idaho, a veteran county sheriff, declared BLM law enforcement was no longer allowed to carry firearms in the line of duty in Owyhee County (Chalpoupka 1996:163). In 1993, Nye County, Nevada, which is roughly 93 percent federal public lands, was the first to issue a County Supremacy ordinance against the federal government (Coppelman 1997:31). The ordinance declared that the county had authority over the federal government concerning all environmental planning and grazing permits and threatened to shoot any federal employees that objected (Chaloupka 1996). This type of ordinance was dubbed the Nye County Ordinance. In 1996, courts found in the federal government's favor.[8] Another type of ordinance is the Catron County style. Catron County, New Mexico was the first county to issue an ordinance against BLM and USFS law enforcement. This type is deemed a customs and culture ordinance and is more common than the Nye style. Customs and culture ordinances require that the county sheriff give permission for federal law enforcement to take any actions on public lands (Coppelman 1997:31). As of 1996, there were fifty-six counties that have tried to enact similar ordinances (Chaloupka 1996:164). These ordinances have not found favor from the courts but have sent a clear message to the residents of the counties as to the weight given to adherence to federal laws.

DISCUSSION AND CONCLUSION

Were the persistent attempts to disarm federal land management officers successful, they would set a precedence for all other federal law enforcement agencies. Further opportunities would open up to question the authority and relevance of all law enforcement employed by the government's seventy-three agencies. The USFS and BLM's ability to protect federal property as they are dictated to do by Congress would be hindered and their personal safety, when faced with armed violators, would be endangered. Each argument for only local law enforcement authority on public lands assumes that the local law enforcement is able and willing to enforce federal laws such as the Endangered Species Act, archaeological protections, and FLPMA. These are laws and regulations that local sheriffs have openly disdained or defied. However, the USFS and BLM are required by Congress to enforce them.

Additionally, many western county sheriffs have sent a clear message to their constituents that illegal protests against the federal government are acceptable and, in some cases, encouraged. Several counties that received funding from the federal government for law enforcement activities were nevertheless uncooperative. If left to their own devices, they would be unlikely to take up investigations of timber poaching with the same vigor as a USFS law enforcement officer or destruction of petroglyphs as the BLM would. Local law enforcement would need extensive and expensive conservation law enforcement training to fill the roles of federal officers, which in sparsely manned jurisdictions would be a burdensome requirement and would take officers away from their routine duties.

In many cases, it simply does not make sense for local law enforcement to patrol public lands that are nowhere near population centers. Before BLM federal law enforcement, a remote call could take hours for sheriff's deputies to respond, taking them away from the priorities in their assigned cities and towns. Should funds be redirected to counties through bundled grants, public lands would once again be placed under the care and charge of the state from which they were previously controlled before the BLM established law enforcement, with unenforced laws (Skillen 2009:104). Even with local assistance, looters at archaeological or Native American sites are almost never caught, and when they are, they are rarely prosecuted. Federal officers are also better able to work cases that cross county and state lines, providing continuity that local offices are not able to offer.

Federal law enforcement has been put in the untenable position of having to choose between thorough enforcement of the law or the weakest manner in order to avoid conflict with the very people who should be their partners. The perception that the federal government is "protecting" those living in western states from themselves induces deep resentment and feelings of paternalism (Miller 2012:87). Additionally, the groundwork was set for a region with a history of mistrust of the government and no understanding of how compliance would benefit them. Federal law enforcement, the most visible and seemingly threatening extension of this paternalism, are the enforcers of these repugnant restrictions. Federal conservation law enforcement officers are considered the face of an oppressive and callous federal bureaucracy.

Even so, there are many western counties that have a collaborative working relationship with their federal partners. These counties take an active role in seeking compromise and working together. In these places, local law enforcement, sheriffs, BLM, and USFS are allies, working toward a common goal of protecting people and natural resources and upholding their sworn duties. For example, in 2015, a BLM ranger in southern Utah caught images of several students from Texas stealing dinosaur fossils from BLM and state-trust lands. The state of Utah and the BLM worked together to build a case against the students and bring charges (Maffly 2016). These counties can serve as both a blueprint and an inspiration for cooperative law enforcement.

Western public lands have been the center of heated debate for well over a century. Those who call these states home are generally a patriotic and independent group. Many residents have deep roots in a cowboy culture, a heritage that is revered across the world. The open and abundant lands are the resources from which generations of families have carved their lives. Some seek to serve Western interests through local control of public lands and, to that end, eliminate conservation law enforcement. Squeezed between local protests and endless environmental lawsuits, federal law enforcement must uphold the policies, regulations, and laws that they have sworn to uphold.

They must also provide public education and serve as the public face for agencies.

The ultimate questions are who will provide law enforcement on public lands and how and who gets to decide the answers. To restate the issue, the questions may be phrased, who gets to control what laws are enforced on public lands, what form the enforcement will take, and who has the authority to perform the enforcement. Decades of case law says that Congress has that authority, but this does not diminish the rural west's conflicting ideals and fundamental beliefs. Differing interpretations of the U.S. Constitution and animosity toward the perceived inequity of the federal government's interference and attempts to exert control at the local level are the foundation of the public lands law enforcement dispute. It is contingent upon all stakeholders to reach a reasonable conclusion of this dispute to protect the individuals affected and the interests of the public both now and for future generations.

NOTES

1. *Kleppe v. New Mexico*, 426 U.S. 529, 49 L. Ed. 2d 34, 96 S. Ct. 2285 (1976), power over public lands is entrusted to Congress without limitations. *Camfield v. United States*, 167 U.S. 518, 17 S. Ct. 864, 42 L. Ed. 260 (1897), the government has police powers over its property similar to those of the states.
2. Law enforcement personnel. Personal communication. May 15, 2017.
3. Chaffetz, Jason. H.R.621–115th Congress (2017–2018): Disposal of Excess Federal Lands Act of 2017. https://www.congress.gov/bill/115th-congress/house-bill/621
4. Chaffetz H.R.622.
5. 1995, The USFS office in Carson City, NV and Reno, NV BLM office were bombed. 2014 Bundy Ranch Standoff. See McLane 2011.
6. "Testimony of Sheriff James D. Perkins." Garfield County, Utah before the U.S. House of Representatives Committee on National Resources, July 24, 2014. http://docs.house.gov/meetings/II/II10/20140724/102552/HMTG-113-II10-Wstate-PerkinsJ-20140724.pdf
7. As of 2017, this BLM supervisor is under investigation for abuse of power.
8. US v. Nye County, Nev., 920 F. Supp. 1108 (D. Nev. 1996).

REFERENCES CITED

Andrews, Richard N. L. 1976. *Environmental Policy and Administrative Change: Implementation of the National Environmental Policy Act*. Lanham, MD: Lexington Books.

Blevins, Jason. 2017. Utah Congressman Pulls Federal Land Transfer Bill, But Fight to Keep Federal Lands Public Continues. *The Denver Post*. http://www.denverpost.com/2017/02/02/federal-land-transfer-bill-withdrawn/ (Accessed March 01, 2017).

Blumenthal, Sidney. 1995. Her Own Private Idaho. *The New Yorker*. http://www.newyorker.com/magazine/1995/07/10/her-own-private-idaho (Accessed March 1, 2017).

Botkin, Ben. 2014. Hansen Seeks to Limit BLM, Forest Service Police Powers. *Las Vegas Review-Journal*. http://www.reviewjournal.com/news/nevada/hansen-seeks-limit-blm-forest-service-police-powers (Accessed March 27, 2017).

Burr, Thomas. 2014. 'Gestapo' BLM Officers Decried in House Hearing. *The Salt Lake Tribune*. http://archive.sltrib.com/story.php?ref=%2Fsltrib%2Fpolitics%2F58221221-90%2Fblm-county-federal-law.html.csp (Accessed March 27, 2017).

Cawley, R. McGreggor. 1993. *Federal Land, Western Anger: The Sagebrush Rebellion and Environmental Politics*. Lawrence, KS: University Press of Kansas.

Chaloupka, William. 1996. The County Supremacy and Militia Movements: Federalism as an Issue on the Radical Right. *Publius* 26(3):161–75.

Cohen, Bonnie R. 1997. Land Disposal Report. https://chaffetz.house.gov/sites/chaffetz.house.gov/files/land%20disposal%20report.pdf (Accessed July 4, 2019).

Coppelman, Peter D. 1997. The Federal Government's Response to the County Supremacy Movement. *Natural Resources and Environment* 12(1):30–33, 79–80.

Cowart, Richard H., and Sally K. Fairfax. 1988. Public Lands Federalism: Judicial Theory and Administrative Reality. *Ecology Law Quarterly* 15(3): 375–476.

Federal Law Enforcement Training Centers (FLETC). n.d. Land Management Police Training. https://www.fletc.gov/training-program/land-management-police-training (Accessed February 1, 2017).

Free Range Report. 2017. Utah Congressman Introduces Bill to Strip Police Powers from BLM, Forest Service. http://freerangereport.com/index.php/2017/01/26/utah-congressman-introduces-bill-to-strip-police-powers-from-blm-forest-service/ (Accessed March 1, 2017).

Goldfarb, Bob. 2017. Busting the Tree Ring. *High Country News*. http://www.hcn.org/issues/49.5/busting-the-tree-ring (Accessed March 20, 2017).

Harvey, D. Michael. 1979. Support Your Local Sheriff: Federalism and Law Enforcement under the Federal Land Policy and Management Act. *Arizona Law Review* 21(2):461.

Maffly, Brian. 2013. Judge Blocks Utah Law Limiting Federal Authority on Public Lands. *The Salt Lake Tribune*. http://archive.sltrib.com/story.php?ref=%2Fsltrib%2Fpolitics%2F56517102-90%2Fagencies-enforcement-federal-judge.html.csp (Accessed March 1, 2017).

———. 2016. Texas Students Charged in Utah Dinosaur Fossil Theft. *The Salt Lake Tribune*. http://www.sltrib.com/news/3805427-155/texas-students-charged-in-utah-dinosaur (Accessed March 1, 2017).

McLane, Dennis. n.d.a Land Management Law Enforcement. http://www.landmanagementle.com/le/Fed_Jurisdiction.cfm (Accessed March 15, 2017).

———. n.d.b Federal Jurisdiction. http://www.landmanagementle.com/le/Fed_Jurisdiction.cfm (Accessed July 4, 2019).

———. 2011. *Seldom Was Heard an Encouraging Word: A History of Bureau of Land Management Law Enforcement*. Guthrie, OK: Shoppe Foreman Publishing.

Miller, Char. 2012. *Public Lands, Public Debates: A Century of Controversy*. Corvallis, OR: Oregon State University Press.

Mohr, Jakki, and Robert Spekman. 1994. Characteristics of Partnership Success: Partnership Attributes, Communication Behavior, and Conflict Resolution Techniques. *Strategic Management Journal* 15(2):135–52.

National Park Service (NPS). n.d. NPS Archeology Program: The Archaeological Resources Protection Act of 1979 (ARPA). https://www.nps.gov/archeology/tools/Laws/ARPA.htm (Accessed March 26, 2017).

Nolen, Kelly. 1996. Residents at Risk: Wildlife and the Bureau of Land Management's Planning Process. *Environmental Law* 26:771–840.

Perry, Steve. n.d. Territorial Jurisdiction on Federal Property. *Federal Law Enforcement Training Centers*. https://www.fletc.gov/audio/territorial-jurisdiction-federal-property-mp3 (Accessed July 4, 2019).

Reaves, Brian A. 2012. *Federal Law Enforcement Officers, 2008. Report no. NCJ 238250*. Washington, DC: Office of Justice Programs, Bureau of Justice Statistics, U.S. Department of Justice.

Scott, Dylan. 2016. The New BLM Throwdown: Utah County Sheriffs Cry 'Retribution.' *Talking Points Memo*. http://talkingpointsmemo.com/muckraker/blm-utah-county-sheriffs- (Accessed March 1, 2017).

Shephard, Blake. 1984. The Scope of Congress' Constitutional Power Under the Property Clause: Regulating Non-federal Power to Further the Purposes of National Parks and Wilderness Areas. *Environmental Affairs Law Review* 11: 479–85.

Siegler, Kirk. 2016. Utah Sheriffs Threaten To Arrest Rangers If They Try To Close Public Lands. *National Public Radio*. http://www.npr.org/2016/05/31/480100279/utah-sheriff-threatens-to-arrest-rangers-if-they-try-to-close-public-lands (Accessed March 1, 2017).

Smyth, Paul B. 1979. Federal Law Enforcement on Public Lands: Reality or Mirage? *Arizona Law Review* 21(2):462.

State of Utah. 2014. Federal Statutes and Regulations Governing Federal Lands. le.utah.gov/interim/2014/pdf/00004976.pdf (Accessed March 01, 2017).

Steen, Harold K. 1992. *The Origins of the National Forests*. Durham, NC: Forest History Society.

Tanner, Courtney. 2016. Kane and Garfield Counties Sue BLM and Interior, Say Coal Lease Moratorium Threatens Rural Utah. *The Salt Lake Tribune*. http://www.sltrib.com/home/4655949-155/kane-garfield-counties-sue-federal-government (Accessed February 15, 2017).

Taylor, Phil, Niina Heikkinen, and Jennifer Yachnin. 2014. Public Lands: Sheriffs are Key to BLM Mission, but Local Politics Intrude. http://www.eenews.net/greenwire/stories/1060003061 (Accessed March 27, 2017).

Thompson, Jonathan. 2015. Recapture Canyon Protesters Found Guilty in Utah. *High Country News*. http://www.hcn.org/articles/recapture-canyon-protesters-found-guilty (Accessed February 2, 2017).

Warren, Larry. 1996. Utah Counties Bulldoze the BLM, Park Service. *High Country News*. http://www.hcn.org/issues/92/2868 (Accessed March 1, 2017).

Wiles, Tay. 2015. New Data Released on Violent Threats to Federal Employees. *High Country News*. http://www.hcn.org/articles/new-threats-harassment-of-federal-land-agency-employees-cliven-bundy (Accessed March 1, 2017).

———. 2016. In Southern Utah, a Ranger is Jailed Under Questionable Circumstances. *High Country News*. http://www.hcn.org/articles/blm-ranger-jailed-escalante-ellison-utah-sheriff (Accessed March 1, 2017).

Chapter 8

Restoring Wild Bison in the Heart of Cattle Country

Yellowstone's Political Firestorm

Scott Turner

When entering Yellowstone National Park from the north in Gardiner, Montana, visitors pass through the triumphal Roosevelt Arch. The rusticated masonry and scale of the structure convey a significant sense of leaving one place and entering another. Some will pause to read the inscription that spans the top of the imposing stone monument: "For the benefit and enjoyment of the people." The intellectually curious may access the fading Wi-Fi signal to discover that the words derive from the 1872 Organic Act that established Yellowstone as the first national park. Like all successful propaganda, the phrase commands easy ascent by appealing to shared political mythology, while avoiding the sausage-making details of political reality.

By crossing onto public land, the epigram suggests, we are partaking in the very promise of America—read "benefit" as general welfare, "enjoyment" as the pursuit of happiness, and "the people" as democracy itself. But to employ a somewhat anachronistic metaphor, that simplistic representation is only the first transparency on the projector. As we overlay additional slides in our presentation, we find that Yellowstone National Park and the region that lies just north of it in Montana make up a complicated tapestry of political jurisdictions. That tapestry is further complicated by competing claims regarding the purpose of the park and how it should be managed. This chapter profiles the contested use of this public space by several primary stakeholders in regard to the management of Yellowstone's bison.

Contemporary scholarship requires a sober reconsideration of Wallace Stegner's gushing ode to national parks, popularized by the Ken Burns documentary series: "The best idea we ever had. Absolutely American, absolutely democratic, they reflect us at our best rather than our worst." As Mark Spence

(1999) compellingly argues in *Dispossessing the Wilderness*, the establishment of the first national parks cannot be entirely separated from the contemporaneous policy of forcible relocation of Native American populations to reservations. Both policies were manifestations of westward expansion or American imperialism. Once the park was established, Yellowstone was no longer accessible to indigenous people for traditional uses such as hunting. The park's spectacular features, such as geysers and hot springs, were protected primarily for eastern tourists.

Nevertheless, Yellowstone soon played a central role in the preservation of a keystone species: the American bison. Once numbering in the millions, bison had been steadily reduced by intensified hunting, a process that reached a fevered pitch in the 1870s in response to the market demand for hides, including from Europe's burgeoning leather industry (Robbins 1999; Taylor 2007). By the beginning of the twentieth century, fewer than one thousand bison remained, with twenty-three of those protected by the U.S. Army in Yellowstone National Park (Glick 2012; Keitner 2013).[1]

Despite its pivotal role in saving the species, for decades the park managed its surviving herd in a semi-domesticated fashion. On the one hand, bison were culled and castrated to limit the population to only a few hundred head, while on the other they were corralled and hay-fed at the park's Buffalo Ranch to help them survive the region's harsh winters (Sellers 1997). The prevailing conservation theory of the time centered on carrying capacity, an estimate of how many animals could be sustained by the rangeland and cultivated hay fields inside the park.

Such heavy-handed management was contemporaneous with the park's predator eradication practice, whereby personnel intentionally killed off presumably dangerous animals like wolves. This was consistent with the original concept of national parks as popular "pleasuring-grounds," where tourists could safely take in the natural wonders and be entertained by wildlife. As late as the 1950s, visitors routinely fed bears from their automobiles and were even invited to sit in bleachers to observe bears congregating at garbage dump sites to eat discarded food. Parks were managed more as natural amusement parks than wilderness preserves.

But managing national parks for public amusement had troubling consequences. Predator eradication contributed to an explosion of the elk population, to which park rangers responded by shooting more than 4,000 of the animals in the winter of 1961–1962. The slaughter triggered a public outcry, which prompted the Secretary of the Interior Department, Stewart Udall, to establish the Advisory Board on Wildlife Management, chaired by A. Starker Leopold, to review park policies. The resulting Leopold Report would mark a sea change in management philosophy. National parks, the report argued, should "represent a vignette of primitive America," and the "the biotic associations within each park [should] be maintained, or where necessary recreated" (Pyne 2017).[2]

The resulting changes at Yellowstone National Park could not have been more dramatic. No more feeding bears or eradicating predators, no more dousing of naturally occurring forest fires, and no more corralling, hay-feeding, or culling elk and bison.[3] Park management had met modern ecology. The new approach was essentially to let nature take its course, and even to restore as much as possible of the park's historic ecosystem that had been disrupted by past management practices, as demonstrated by the reintroduction of wolves to the park in the 1990s, for example (Keitner 2013). The park ceased treating bison as semi-domesticated livestock and allowed them to roam free, as they had in the early nineteenth century when a massive herd had halted the Lewis and Clark expedition for an hour at the mouth of the Yellowstone River (Taylor 2007).

The National Park Service enacted a moratorium on the culling of bison in 1969. As a result, the population grew rapidly, from 397 head in 1967 to over 2,500 by 1988. While a cause for celebration among wildlife advocates, this dramatic recovery of Yellowstone's wild bison herd would soon stir a tempest in the teapot of public lands management in the Greater Yellowstone Area. The larger population led to many animals exiting the park in winter to seek forage in lower elevations, and that in turn brought them—and the National Park Service—into conflict with cattle ranchers and their political allies in Montana, where wild bison posed a potential threat to private property and, more controversially, to the health of cattle herds due to the potential spread of the infectious disease brucellosis (Keitner 2013; Adams and Dood 2011). While hunting inside of Yellowstone National Park has been prohibited since 1894, in the 1980s Montana responded to bison migrations by authorizing public hunting and lethal removal by state agents of bison that crossed out of the park and into the state, resulting in 489 bison killed in 1989 alone (The Oregonian 2013). This situation prompted the National Park Service to negotiate with the state of Montana on a common management plan, leading to a resumption of periodic culling operations in the 1990s (Loomis 2013). By that time, environmental and animal rights activism was becoming increasingly intense and well organized, setting the stage for a seemingly intractable controversy. It involved a coalition of ranchers, the Montana Department of Livestock, and locally elected politicians on the one hand; environmental and animal rights groups, Native Americans, and ecologists on the other; with Yellowstone National Park administrators, seeking to balance ecological values with political pressures, caught in the middle (McBeth et al. 2010).

THE INTERAGENCY BISON MANAGEMENT PLAN

In 1995, Montana sued Yellowstone National Park for failing to curtail the flow of bison into the state. Court-ordered mediation produced the Interagency Bison Management Plan (IBMP) in 2000. Under the plan, eight governing entities representing a range of often competing interests jointly manage Yellowstone bison:

- Montana Fish, Wildlife & Parks
- Montana Department of Livestock
- National Park Service
- U.S. Forest Service
- U.S. Department of Agriculture's Animal and Plant Health Inspection Service (APHIS)
- Confederated Salish and Kootenai Tribes
- Nez Perce Tribe
- InterTribal Buffalo Council (ITBC).

The objectives of the IBMP include the following:

- Maintain a wild, free-ranging bison population
- Manage bison that leave Yellowstone National Park and enter the state of Montana
- Reduce the risk of brucellosis transmission from bison to cattle
- Maintain Montana's brucellosis-free status for domestic livestock (Winter Operations 2019).

The Native American groups joined the IBMP because of treaty hunting rights on certain federal lands near the park, as well as their interest in restoring bison on reservations. Under the IBMP, the park commits to managing the bison population at around 3,000 head. In return, a limited number of bison are permitted to migrate out of the park in winter to designated areas in Montana (IBMP 2019).

The plan was revised in 2011 to permit bison in the Gardiner Basin, just north of the park, between November 1 and May 1 each year (NPS n.d.a). The spatial and temporal restrictions are intended to minimize the opportunity for bison to come into contact with cattle, which are brought in late spring to graze on nearby land leased from the federal government. In 2015, Montana Governor Bullock approved further habitat expansion, allowing bison year-round on 250,000 acres west of the park.

However, the cooperative management plan and habitat expansions have not mollified all stakeholders. Many ranchers are dissatisfied that the park has not stuck to the 3,000 head limit designated in the IBMP (Adams and Dood 2011).[4] The habitat expansion into Gardiner Basin was immediately challenged in court by local cattle interests, though the lawsuit was ultimately unsuccessful (Ecologist 2014). Nor has the plan satisfied animal rights activists, since the park continues to participate in regular culling, sometimes slaughtering more 1,000 animals per year. To accomplish this, bison that have crossed into Montana are lured or "hazed" to the Stephens Creek Capture Facility near the park's northern boundary. There, the animals are tested for brucellosis. Calves and yearlings that test seronegative are vaccinated and released into the park. All animals that test seropositive for brucellosis are shipped to slaughterhouses. The meat, which is safe when cooked, is donated to charities and Indian tribes (IBMP 2012, 2019).

THE BUFFALO FIELD CAMPAIGN

In the winter of 1996–1997, the Montana Department of Livestock shot an estimated 1,100 bison that had exited the park, which was the largest number killed since the unrestrained hunting that brought the species to the brink of extinction in the nineteenth century. In response, environmental activist Mike Mease and Lakota elder Rosalie Little Thunder co-founded the Buffalo Field Campaign (BFC) to protest and document what the group's members see as the mistreatment of the sacred animal. The organization's stated mission is:

> To stop the harassment and slaughter of Yellowstone's wild buffalo herds; protect the natural habitat of wild, free-roaming buffalo and other native wildlife; and work with all people—especially Indigenous Nations—to honor and protect the sacredness of the wild buffalo. (BFC n.d.)

Members conduct "regular patrols" and "remain prepared to initiate nonviolent action as necessary to defend these magnificent animals" (BFC n.d.). Video documentation of harassment of bison is published on the organization's website, YouTube, and other media outlets, and the website posts a running tally of bison killed. On one video, volunteer Andrea Abrams describes witnessing four separate hazing operations, which she describes as "barbaric" and "cruel." She decries the attempt by Montana officials to "rid an entire state's landscape of its native species," and observes that "a lot of the locals moved here to be around the wildlife" and "welcome and appreciate bison." They have "Bison Save Zone signs in their windows." She describes law enforcement officers hazing bison on private property, against the wishes of the owners (BFCMEDIAa 2010). Her story is consistent with another video that features landowner Ed Ryberg confronting a Montana Department of Livestock agent who is attempting to haze bison from his property. Only when an unnamed woman informs the agent that she has called 911 does he leave (BFCMEDIAb 2014).

In 1999, BFC co-founder Rosalie Little Thunder led forty Lakota on a 507-mile march from South Dakota to Roosevelt Arch at the northern entrance to Yellowstone National Park to perform a Native American ceremony in protest of bison slaughter (Zantec 2007). In March 2014, twenty-year-old Comfrey Jacobs, in a brazen act of civil disobedience, handcuffed himself to a fifty-five-gallon barrel full of concrete to block the access road to the Stephens Creek Capture Facility. He succeeded in stalling the transport of bison to slaughter for more than two hours. His stated demand included Yellowstone National Park withdrawing from the IBMP because of its "ineffectiveness in maintaining a wild, free-roaming bison population." Mr. Jacobs was arrested, fined, and banned from the park for three years (BFC 2014a, b, c). His action exemplified the passion and conviction that BFC activists bring to the cause. The following statement was published on the organization's website:

> BFC shares Mr. Jacobs' goals for wild, migratory buffalo populations that are respected and valued as native wildlife and free to roam and flourish beyond Yellowstone's borders, in Montana, and beyond. (BFC 2014a)

In early 2018, there were two separate incidents of sabotage at the Stephens Creek Facility that resulted in the release of several dozen bison (Kudelska 2018). Activists are determined to bring a media spotlight to what they view as Yellowstone National Park's complicity in the mistreatment of a majestic animal that should be permitted to roam as freely as it once did in the region.

CATTLE COUNTRY

The Leopold Report's vision of restoring a "vignette of primitive America" in the parks is a fiction not only because the primitive America settled by people of European and African descent had already been considerably impacted by centuries of human habitation but also because parks, even ones as vast as Yellowstone, are defined by political rather than ecological geographies. Biologist William Newmark demonstrated that most national parks in the west have lost species to extinction because, laudable as their conservation mission may be, they provide insufficient habitat to sustain viable populations (Keitner 2013). When Yellowstone's administrators temporarily permitted the park's bison to reproduce naturally following the Leopold Report, the population almost immediately expanded beyond the park's arbitrary political boundaries.

BFC has a point. If the park is serious about restoring bison, the animals need wide-open range like other wildlife species. But Montana's ranchers have a point too. If the bison population is not curtailed, it will rapidly spread and impose significant costs on the cattle economy that is not only the ranchers' source of livelihood but the essence of their lifestyle. Just as the activists with Buffalo Filed Campaign are passionately committed to wildlife protection and restoration, so too are many ranchers passionate believers in their way of life. To them, the western ranching life represents independence and freedom, and the regulatory reach of the federal government, which the park embodies, is an affront to those values. When ranchers hear calls for expanded habitat for a free-roaming bison population, they may be reminded of the notorious proposal by two Rutgers University professors in the 1980s for a Buffalo Commons to replace cattle country with a vast new national park across ten prairie states (Popper and Popper 1987).

American settlement of the west in the nineteenth century meant the replacement of open range for millions of bison with a cattle economy that now covers over 95 percent of Great Plains grasslands (Gates et al. 2010). Montana has 2.5 million cattle, about 2.5 times its number of people, and 500 times the number of bison in Yellowstone National Park. About 64 percent of land in Montana is used for farming and ranching, and livestock accounts for over a billion dollars of the state's annual receipts (MFBF n.d.).

If one talks to ranchers whose cattle graze near Yellowstone, the first topic of concern is brucellosis, which may cause spontaneous abortions in cows. More than half of Yellowstone's bison test positive for the disease. However, male bison do not transmit brucellosis, and only about 15 percent of seropositive females are infectious. While there are no confirmed cases of brucellosis transmission from bison to cattle in the wild, the transmission was demonstrated under laboratory conditions by researchers at Texas A&M in 1990 (APHIS n.d.; NPS n.d.a). Elk is the most likely source of cattle infections, which in the past resulted in the U.S. Department of Agriculture's APHIS downgrading Montana, Wyoming, and Idaho from brucellosis "class-free status" (Gates et al. 2010). Loss of class-free status can have devastating economic consequences for the cattle business. In the past, federal regulations required that if a single cow tested positive for brucellosis, the entire herd had to be slaughtered, and nearby herds had to be tested (MFBF n.d.).[5] Mandatory testing in 2008 was estimated to cost ranchers from $6 to $12 million (Wray 2008). Loss of class-free status can also stigmatize the state's beef and hurt out-of-state sales (MFBF n.d.).

From her home in Paradise Valley, north of Gardiner, Druska Kinkie explained the challenges and rewards of ranch life in learned detail. Her living room's big storm window framed beautiful snow-topped mountains in the distance. She and her husband owned about 300 head of cattle on a ranch situated inside of the 6,000 square mile Designated Surveillance Area established by the Montana Department of Livestock in 2010, where it considers the risk of brucellosis infection from elk and Yellowstone bison to be the greatest. For Druska, the issue of bison migration is simple economics. She had joined with other area ranchers in an unsuccessful legal effort to stop the expansion of bison habitat into nearby Gardiner Basin. She complained not only about the expense of testing her cattle, but also observed that such testing causes weight loss. While she acknowledged the sincerity of her environmentalist adversaries—groups such as Earthjustice and Buffalo Field Campaign—she contrasted their commitment to an "abstract cause" to her own more practical concern with "livelihood." Yet the pathos in her voice revealed more than attention to a balance sheet. "What right does the park have to send their bison onto my private property" (Kinkie 2014)? With that rhetorical question, Druska expressed the heart of a conflict between private landowners and public—mostly federal—land managers that has flared up repeatedly across western states for decades. Her sentiment is echoed in an article found on the Montana Farm Bureau Federation's website:

> Many of the ranches near Yellowstone National Park are nearly as old, or older, than the establishment of Yellowstone National Park itself. Is it appropriate for federal and state agencies to determine that bison supersede the heritage of those ranches and the rural lifestyle that they have given to generations of people? (MFBF n.d.)

As Andrew McKean (2013) observes, what may appear to outsiders as a somewhat mundane controversy over wildlife management has taken on near-mythical proportions for area stakeholders:

> To traditional ranchers, a bison isn't just a wild cow. It's code for the systematic dismantling of the ranching culture. But bison are equally emblematic to wildlife advocates, who view the animals as the single species capable of restoring wildness to one of the largest ecosystems on the continent, the short-grass prairie that stretches from central Canada to Oklahoma.

From Druska's home, I traveled to another ranch belonging to Bruce Malcolm, an elderly state legislator who lived twenty-three miles north of Yellowstone National Park. We sat on bales of hay in his barn, accepted his offer of lemonade, and began with small talk about his legislative work. By Montana standards, he was considered a moderate Republican, known for working across the aisle on controversial issues such as wolf management. He complained of the intractability of his fellow Republican "Tea Partiers" and spoke fondly of one of his Democratic friends, who he identified as a vegetarian—no doubt an iconoclastic lifestyle in Montana—and remarked with some embarrassment that "she's married to another gal." We diplomatically changed the subject to bison.

When asked his opinion of the park's management practice, he sneered and answered, "There is none." That was a call back to the suspension of culling following the Leopold Report in the 1960s. He explained that the soil and vegetation in Lamar Valley, inside the park, are depleted from over-grazing, and predicted the area will be a desert within a few decades. This was not mere political flame throwing, but a reference to the sober ecological principle of carrying capacity. Yet political resentment was not far behind. He referred to the park as a "dictatorship," and a "terrible neighbor." Like other ranchers, he resented the park's refusal to strictly manage the bison population. He recounted that federal officials required his daughter to slaughter 600 of her cattle following a brucellosis outbreak (Brown 2008; Malcolm 2014).

Yet another rancher, Pat Povah, complains not only of the cost of brucellosis testing but also of repairing fences and trampled rangeland. After all, bison are the largest North American land mammal. Mature males range from 10 to 12 feet long, up to 6.5 feet high, and may weigh up to 2,500 pounds. They can run at a sustained speed of 40 mph, and jump six-foot-high fences. For ranchers, protecting their property means constructing eight-foot-high rail fences that, according to Povah, would interfere with the movement of other wildlife (Taylor 2007; Loomis 2013).

But again, rancher resentment is as much philosophical as practical. As David Samuels (2011) writes, to many ranchers bison represent "the desire of conservationists to destroy their way of life in the pursuit of a whimsical dream of returning to an imagined Eden." Consequently, a variety of anti-bison bills have been introduced in the Montana state legislature, such as one that would permit county commissioners to block restoration of wild bison in their counties, even on tribal and federal lands. The bills were backed by Republican senator John Brenden, who has referred to bison as a "creeping cancer" and, even more colorfully, as "wooly tanks." In contrast to the conservationist vision of restoring wild herds to the plains, Brenden says, "We don't talk about bringing back the dinosaurs, but that's exactly what big herds of free-roaming buffalo are. . . . Their time has passed" (McKean 2013; Voggesser 2013).

A number of Senator Brenden's anti-bison bills were vetoed by the state's Democratic governor, Steve Bullock, who likewise approved the substantial expansion of bison habitat on state land west of Yellowstone in 2015. This is emblematic of the complicated patchwork of political agendas and jurisdictions within the state, which includes counties and conservation districts that are generally responsive to local cattle interests. Even within state government, rival management philosophies compete for influence in different agencies. In the late 1990s, the state legislature shifted primary responsibility for managing migratory bison from the Department of Fish, Wildlife and Parks to the Department of Livestock, reflecting the position that bison should not be viewed as free-ranging wildlife (Zantec 2007). The patchwork also includes various federal jurisdictions, including lands managed by the U.S. Forest Service within the U.S. Department of Agriculture, and others managed by the Bureau of Land Management within the Department of the Interior, both of which lease grazing land to ranchers but are also potential sites for expanding bison habitat. As noted earlier, cattle ranchers are likewise subject to federal regulations under APHIS within the USDA, whose monitoring of brucellosis and certification of class-free status can have a profound impact on their industry's profitability. Then there is Yellowstone National Park, under the NPS within the Department of the Interior, which pursues a conservation strategy within the strictures of competing political pressures. Finally, Montana is home to seven separate Indian Reservations and eleven recognized tribes.[6] It is to the latter, Native American groups and their cultural relationship with the bison, that we now turn.

RESTORING THE BUFFALO NATION

For many Native Americans, bison are not only an important food source but also a linchpin of cultural identity. As early as the nineteenth century, Native American leaders saw a parallel between the near eradication of bison and the genocide of their people.[7] In the words of the famed Lakota leader Sitting Bull: "A cold wind blew across the prairie when the last buffalo fell—a death wind for my people." Similarly, the Mountain Crow Chief Plenty Coups observed: "When the buffalo went away we became a changed people. Idleness that was never with us in buffalo days has stolen much from both our minds and bodies" (Zantec 2007).

However, in recent decades, many tribal groups have committed to renewing their relationship with bison by seeding herds on reservation lands. To that end, in 1992, several tribal groups came together to form the InterTribal Bison Cooperative, now called the ITBC. Its mission is "reestablishing buffalo herds on Indian lands in a manner that promotes cultural enhancement, spiritual revitalization, ecological restoration, and economic development." Today, the ITBC includes sixty-three tribes in nineteen states, with a collective herd of approximately 20,000 bison, and it is estimated that reservation lands could potentially sustain up to 120,000 bison. The organization seeks the transfer of surplus bison from national parks to tribal lands (ITBC n.d.; Zantec 2007). While management practices vary among tribes, some manage the bison as "conservation herds." This is part of the essential role that tribes play in national conservation efforts, and they have received millions of federal dollars to assist with conservation programs (Schweber 2014). The ITBC advocates that tribes maintain herds in free-range conditions, while practicing sustainable harvesting (Zantec 2007). In this way, they provide a source of lean protein for the tribes, while being managed as wildlife rather than livestock.

As a member of the IBMP, the ITBC advocates expanded habitat throughout the Greater Yellowstone Area (Ecologist 2014). This approach has brought the ITBC into conflict with some Native ranchers, who like other ranchers worry about brucellosis, and who see bison harvesting as unwelcome competition to the cattle industry (Zantec 2007). But to others, restoring the historic connection of Native peoples to the bison has a potent spiritual appeal. The Lakota spiritual chief Avrol Looking Horse explains: "When we first came upon the earth, we were the 'Buffalo People.' . . . We must do what we can to protect the buffalo. Whatever happens to them, happens to us" (Brown 2008). In 2014, several U.S. tribes and Canadian First Nations gathered on the Blackfeet Territory in Montana to sign the Buffalo Treaty, a commitment to cooperate in restoring bison to tribal lands in the interest of both conservation and cultural renewal (Andersen 2018).

The eagerness of many tribes to receive bison on reservations may appear at first blush to be an obvious solution to Yellowstone's management dilemma. Rather than consigning hundreds of animals to slaughter, why not simply capture and transfer them to welcoming reservations? Again, the problem lies with ranchers' anxiety over the spread of brucellosis. Montana law prohibits transporting wild bison within the state when they have been exposed to brucellosis (NPS n.d.b). However, in 2005, the Montana Department of Fish, Wildlife & Parks department, and the USDA's APHIS launched a study whereby bison calves that tested negative for brucellosis were held in quarantine for observation. By 2010, the program was judged a success and the first group of some eighty certified brucellosis-free bison were approved for transfer to Ted Turner's Green Ranch in Montana. Subsequently, sixty-one additional brucellosis-free bison were transferred to Montana's Fort Peck Reservation, home to Assiniboine and Sioux tribes, with plans to move a contingent of those animals to Fort Belknap Reservation (Glick 2012; Robbins 2014; NPS n.d.a). However, in 2012, a state court issued an injunction on further transfers in response to a lawsuit filed by a group called Citizens for Balanced Use. The injunction was appealed by Defenders of Wildlife and the National Wildlife Federation, represented by Earthjustice. The following year, the Montana Supreme Court approved the transfer of bison to Fort Belknap Reservation, home to Assiniboine and Gros Ventre tribes, and a federal Environmental Assessment subsequently greenlighted additional transfers (Voggesser 2013; Andersen 2018). Consequently, the quarantine program provides a mechanism for seeding Yellowstone's genetically pure wild bison on reservations and potentially other sites. However, given the extensive time requirement and limited capacity of the quarantine program, it does not solve Yellowstone's management dilemma. The transfer of a few dozen disease-free animals each year is hardly a drop in the bucket compared to the several hundred bison that the park is routinely compelled to send to slaughter.

DEFUSING THE LANDMINE

While the competing passions and interests among activists, environmentalists, ranchers, Native Americans, various government agencies at both the federal and the state levels, not to mention the few million tourists who visit Yellowstone each year, may give the appearance of intractable political gridlock, it is important to recall that for two decades a range of stakeholders have in fact cooperated in negotiating and overseeing a management plan for Yellowstone bison. Nevertheless, the sincere expressions of dissatisfaction among various stakeholders highlight the need for further revision of the plan. On the conservation side, Glen Hackett of the Gallatin Wildlife Association articulates the problem with Yellowstone National Park's ongoing culling program:

> The act of corralling and sending animals to slaughter within Yellowstone is completely contrary to the basic idea of a national park—particularly as buffalo are the iconic logo of the U.S Park Service. (NRDC 2008)

This sentiment reflects an ecological ethic, grounded in the Leopold Report, that the park's bison should be managed as a wildlife species, not corralled and slaughtered like livestock. However, groups such as the Gallatin Wildlife Association and National Wildlife Federation are not opposed to fair chase hunting as a means of controlling the population that exits the park. The problem is that hunting alone is unlikely to mollify the concerns of all ranchers, and killing a large number of animals near the border of the park is not likely to sit well with bison activists, tourists, or the public at large. Consequently, the National Wildlife Federation has also tried to address rancher concerns head-on. Its Wildlife Conflict Resolution Program raises funds to pay ranchers for retiring their grazing allotments on federal lands. This strategy has retired around 600,000 acres around Yellowstone and helped to secure the habitat expansions described previously. Likewise, the National Resources Defense Council has a fund to help ranchers pay for improved fencing to secure their livestock and other property against free-roaming bison (Adams and Dood 2011; Skoglund 2014). Despite progress on the conservation front, however, the ongoing presence of ranches north of the park will mean continued controversy over the park's interest in maintaining a free-ranging bison population. Likewise, the park's culling policy will continue to distress environmentalists. Nevertheless, the quarantine program described previously is poised to help build new herds elsewhere.

While the seeding of new herds is encouraging, however, ecologists worry that many of them are too small to sustain healthy genetic diversity (Skoglund 2012). Consequently, groups such as the World Wildlife Fund aim at securing several Yellowstone-size herds. Fort Peck, which for now is the primary destination for certified brucellosis-free bison from Yellowstone, may be well on its way with several hundred animals. Another exciting prospect is the privately owned American Prairie Reserve (APR) in northeast Montana, which had grown its wild herd to around 860 as of 2017, with the goal of reaching 10,000 within the next decade (Adams and Dood 2011; APR 2016-17)!

CONCLUSION

As a private conservation project, APR provides an ironic parallel to the deep-seated ideology of private property and independence held by the ranchers who have been the foil to Yellowstone's truncated effort to manage bison in accord with natural processes. If the APR reaches its goal of 10,000 bison, it will be because it has bought enough land and bought out enough ranchers to make the vision of its financiers a reality. It will have re-wilded a large swathe of the west not through a federal land grab but through private land purchases and will not be subject to the political strictures that national parks such as Yellowstone must contend with.[8]

Yellowstone National Park, on the other hand, is subject to the full array of political pressures and public demands that, for good or bad, are the hallmark of pluralist democracy. While the public comments of park administrators suggest their ongoing affinity with the management philosophy espoused by the Leopold Report, the fact that the park is an ecological island in a stormy political sea compels administrators to facilitate and publicly justify the unsavory practice of capturing and slaughtering a portion of the park's wild bison population, often by the hundreds. Otherwise, they risk losing the limited tolerance for bison outside the park to which Montana has grudgingly acquiesced. Nevertheless, given the growing interest among Native American communities in restoring bison on tribal lands, Yellowstone's quarantine program for certifying brucellosis-free animals for transfer, and bold undertakings such as the APR, the prospects for wild bison appear promising. The tapestry of federal, state, and tribal jurisdictions, combined with ambitious private initiatives, may yet facilitate the recovery of America's national mammal more effectively than Yellowstone National Park can do in isolation.[9]

NOTES

1. There are around half a million bison in North America today. However, the vast majority of these have been interbred with cattle and are raised as livestock. Yellowstone bison make up one of the few extant genetically pure wild herds.

2. Assumptions about the natural conditions that prevailed in "primitive America" were somewhat arbitrary, as in fact humans had been impacting the area around Yellowstone for centuries. Essentially, the Leopold Report pointed to the prevailing ecological conditions at the time of first European contact in the mid-nineteenth century as the baseline for primitivism.

3. The Yellowstone National Park website lists 1952 as the last year of "supplemental feeding" of bison.

4. The park's estimated bison population in August 2018 was 4,527 (NPS n.d.a).

5. In 2010, federal regulations were revised to replace the slaughter requirement with quarantine and testing.

6. The Little Shell Tribe of Chippewa Indians is a state-recognized tribe but does not have a reservation.

7. While the term genocide was not crafted until the twentieth century, it is applicable to the experience of numerous indigenous peoples of the Americas in previous centuries.

8. This is not to say that the American Prairie Reserve is free of controversy, as local resentment has prompted efforts by the Montana legislature to restrict its use of federal grazing allotments for conservation purposes.

9. This official designation of bison as the national mammal was awarded by Congress in 2016.

REFERENCES CITED

Adams, S. M., and A. R. Dood 2011 Background Information on Issues of Concern for Montana: Plains Bison Ecology, Management, and Conservation. *Montana Fish, Wildlife, and Parks*. http://fwp.mt.gov/fishAndWildlife/management/bison/plainsEcology.html (Accessed June 5, 2019).

American Prairie Reserve (APR). 2016–17. Bison Report. https://www.americanprairie.org/sites/default/files/APR-Bison-Report_2014.pdf (Accessed June 6, 2019).

Andersen, Chamois.2018. Treaty Signed for the Return of the Buffalo. *Medium*. https://medium.com/wild-without-end/treaty-signed-for-the-return-of-the-buffalo-97af243bc584 (Accessed June 4, 2019).

Animal and Plant Health Inspection Service (APHIS). n.d. Brucellosis and Yellowstone Bison. https://www.aphis.usda.gov/animal_health/animal_dis_spec/cattle/downloads/cattle-bison.pdf (Accessed September 25, 2014).

Bison Field Campaign (BFC). 2014a. Man Blocks Road to Yellowstone Bison Trap. https://www.buffalofieldcampaign.org/man-blocks-road-to-yellowstone-bison-trap (Accessed October 14, 2014).

———. 2014b. Bison Activist Charged and Released. https://www.buffalofieldcampaign.org/bison-activist-charged-and-released (Accessed October 14, 2014).

———. 2014c. Bison Activist Convicted of Blocking Yellowstone's Wild Bison Trap. https://www.buffalofieldcampaign.org/bison-activist-convicted-of-blocking-yellowstone-s-wild-bison-trap (Accessed October14, 2014).

———. n.d. Mission.https://www.buffalofieldcampaign.org/mission-vision-values (Accessed June 5, 2019).

Brown, Matthew. 2008. American Indians Honor Spirit of Bison. *Helena Independent Record*. https://helenair.com/news/state-and-regional/american-indians-honor-spirit-of-bison/article_633db064-8931-5dee-b40a-e86f9d0bbfe1.html (Accessed September 24, 2014).

Buffalo Field Campaign Media. 2008a. (BFCMEDIA). A Buffalo Field Campaign Volunteer's Experience. *YouTube*. On-line video clip, May 23, 2010. https://www.youtube.com/watch?v=6PKfVTZi4Jk (Accessed June 25, 2019).

Buffalo Field Campaign Media. 2008b. (BFCMEDIA) 2014 DOL Trespass. *YouTube*, On-line video clip. June 25, 2014: https://www.youtube.com/watch?v=_i1qcpyXaQI (Accessed June 25, 2019).

Ecologist. 2014. Yellowstone Bison Have 'Right to Roam.' http://www.theecologist.org/News/news_round_up/2320798/yellowstone_bison_have_right_to_roam.html (Accessed August 19, 2014).

Gates, C. Cormack, Curtis H. Freese, Peter J. P. Gogan, and Mandy Kotzman, eds. 2010. *American Bison: Status Survey and Conservation Guidelines 2010*. Gland, Switzerland: International Union for Conservation of Nature. http://www.nationalmammal.org/pdf/IUCN-American-Bison-Status-Survey-and-Conservation-Guidelines-2010.pdf (Accessed September 18, 2014).

Glick, Daniel. 2012. Bison Homecoming: A Long Effort by American Indians and Conservationists Brings Genetically Pure Bison to the Fort Peck Reservation in Montana. *National Wildlife Federation*. https://www.nwf.org/Magazines/National-Wildlife/2012/OctNov/Conservation/Bison-Homecoming (Accessed June 5, 2019).

Interagency Bison Management Plan (IBMP). 2012. Joint Bison Management Plan Operating Procedures. http://ibmp.info/Library/20121127/OperationsPlanIBMP_Oct2012_PJW2.pdf (Accessed June 5, 2019).

———. 2019. Winter Operations Plan. http://www.ibmp.info/Library/OpsPlans/2019_IBMP_Winter_Operations_Plan_FINAL.pdf (Accessed June 6, 2019).

InterTribal Buffalo Council (ITBC). n.d. InterTribal Buffalo Council Website. https://itbcbuffalonation.org/ (Accessed June 6, 2019).

Keitner, Robert B. 2013. *To Conserve Unimpaired: The Evolution of the National Park Idea*. Washington, DC: Island Press.

Kinkie, Druska. 2014. American Democracy Project, Civic Engagement in Action: The Stewardship of Public Lands Seminar on Politics and the Yellowstone Ecosystem, Paradise Valley, MT.

Kudelska, Kamila. 2018. Bison Intentionally Released at Stephens Creek Facility for Second Time this Year. *Wyoming Public Media*. https://www.wyomingpublic media.org/post/bison-intentionally-released-stephens-creek-facility-second-time-year#stream/0 (Accessed June 7, 2019).

Loomis, Molly. 2013. Bison & Boundaries: Can Yellowstone's Signature Mammal and the Region's Ranchers Just Get Along? *Sierra The National Magazine of the Sierra Club* November/December, pp. 28–31, 70.

Malcolm, Bruce. 2014. American Democracy Project, Civic Engagement in Action. Paper presented at the Stewardship of Public Lands Seminar on Politics and the Yellowstone Ecosystem, Paradise Valley, MT.

McBeth, Mark K., Elizabeth A. Shanahan, Paul L. Hathaway, Linda E. Tigert, and Lynette J. Sampson. 2010. Buffalo Tales: Interest Group Policy Stories in Greater Yellowstone. *Policy Sciences* 43(4):391–409.

McKean, Andrew. 2013. The New Bison War. *Outdoor Life*, September, pp. 44–48.

Montana Farm Bureau Federation (MFBF). n.d. History of Bison and Bison Management in Yellowstone National Park. http://mfbf.org/wp-content/uploads/2010/09/MFBF-Bison-Study_1007.pdf (Accessed October 7, 2014).

National Park Service (NPS). n.d.a. Yellowstone: Bison. *Yellowstone National Park*. www.nps.gov/yell/naturescience/bison.htm (Accessed September 26, 2017).

———. n.d.b. Yellowstone: Bison Management. *Yellowstone National Park*. https://www.nps.gov/yell/learn/management/bison-management.htm (Accessed June 5, 2019).

National Resources Defense Council (NDRC). 2008. NRDC Proposes a Way Out of Needless Buffalo Slaughter. https://www.nrdc.org/media/2008/080410 (Accessed September 14, 2014).

The Oregonian. 2013. Hunters Kill 250 Bison Migrating from Yellowstone in Largest Harvest Since 1989. *The Oegonian*. https://www.oregonlive.com/pacific-northwest-news/2019/06/deschutes-prosecutor-cited-for-neglect-after-police-discover-baby-asleep-in-vehicle.html (Accessed October 7, 2014).

Popper, Deborah Epstein, and Frank J. Popper. 1987. The Great Plains: From Dust to Dust. *Planning* 53(12):12–18.

Pyne, Stephen J. 2017. Vignettes of Primitive America: The Leopold Report and Fire Policy. *Forest History Today*. Spring:12–18.

Robbins, Jim. 1999. Historians Revisit Slaughter on the Plains. *New York Times*. https://www.nytimes.com/1999/11/16/science/historians-revisit-slaughter-on-the-plains.html (Accessed June 7, 2019).

———. 2013. On the Montana Range, Efforts to Restore Bison Meet Resistance. *New York Times*. https://www.nytimes.com/2013/04/02/us/efforts-to-restore-bison-on-the-montana-range-resisted.html (Accessed September 8, 2014).

Samuels, David. 2011. Where the Buffalo Roam. *Mother Jones*, March/April 2011:36–45.

Schweber, Nate. 2014. Moving Back Home Together. *New York Times*. https://www.nytimes.com/2014/08/26/science/rarest-native-animals-find-haven-on-tribal-lands.html?_r=2 (Accessed September 27, 2014).

Sellers, Richard West. 1997. *Preserving Nature in the National Parks: A History*. New Haven: Yale University Press.

Skoglund, Matt. 2012. Sharing the Range: A Place for Wild Bison on Today's Landscape. *National Resources Defense Council*. https://www.nrdc.org/resources/sharing-range-place-wild-bison-todays-landscape (Accessed September 19, 2014).

———. 2014. American Democracy Project, Civic Engagement in Action. Paper presented at the Stewardship of Public Lands Seminar on Politics and the Yellowstone Ecosystem, Gardiner, MT.

Spence, Mark D. 1999. *Dispossessing the Wilderness: Indian Removal and the Making of the National Parks*. New York: Oxford University Press.

Taylor, M. Scott. 2007. *Buffalo Hunt: International Trade and the Virtual Extinction of the North American Bison*. Cambridge: National Bureau of Economic Research, Working Paper 12969.

Voggesser, Garrit. 2013. Kill the Bad Bills, Not the Buffalo. *National Wildlife Federation*. https://blog.nwf.org/2013/04/kill-the-bad-bills-not-the-buffalo/ (Accessed September 11, 2014).

Wray, Tom. 2008. Montana Loses Brucellosis-free Status. *The National Provisioner*. https://www.provisioneronline.com/articles/90698-montana-loses-brucellosis-free-status-1 (Accessed June 6, 2019).

Zantec, Ken. 2007. *Buffalo Nation: American Indian Efforts to Restore the Bison*. Lincoln: University of Nebraska Press.

Chapter 9

Through a Forest Wilderness

Native American Environmental Management at Yosemite and Contested Conservation Values in America's National Parks

Rochelle Bloom and Douglas Deur

The creation of the United States' national parks is a widely celebrated achievement in the history of land conservation worldwide, often credited as America's "best idea." Early national parks served to protect some of the most dramatic landscapes, geology, and natural habitats in North America. Yet, there has been growing awareness of the way in which park creation served to displace Native American peoples, practices, and traditions from the American landscape. Consequently, the traditional ecological practices that had sustained Native peoples and ecosystems were also displaced, contributing to the decline of both Native cultures and the habitats on which they have traditionally depended.

For many Native American tribes whose traditional lands were incorporated into national parks, the experiences of the tribes traditionally associated with Yosemite National Park are both representative and instructive. Founded in 1864 and designated a national park in 1890, Yosemite National Park was one of the first national parks in the world. Significantly, however, before its founding as a wilderness park, Yosemite was home to many Native American tribes. The enduring connection between these tribes and Yosemite is reflected today by the concept of "traditional association," which is enshrined in the legal frameworks of modern federal land management. This status denotes "a longstanding relationship of historical or cultural significance between an Indian tribe and a park area predating the establishment of the park area" (United States Code of Federal Regulation 2016 [36 CFR 2.6]). Today, there are seven tribes traditionally associated with Yosemite: the Tuolumne Band of Me-Wuk Indians, the Bridgeport Indian Colony, the Bishop Paiute Tribe, the North Fork Rancheria of Mono Indians, the Picayune Rancheria of Chukchansi Indians, the Mono Lake Kutzadikaa, and the Southern Sierra Miwuk Nation (a.k.a. the American Indian Council of Mariposa County).

The establishment of the national parks was rooted in nineteenth-century conceptions of "wilderness." "Wilderness," as used by nineteenth-century environmentalists in the United States, was derived from the tenets of European Romanticism. The philosophy conveyed a nostalgic yearning for a nature that was "untouched" and "unspoiled" by human influence, hearkening back to the days before industrialization (Haila 1997:129). Significantly, these conceptions of supposed "wilderness" relied upon an assumption of human-nature duality and *terra nullius*, the perceived absence of actual or meaningful prior indigenous occupation of the land. Wilderness was defined in diametric opposition to "civilization," or any area inhabited or utilized by humans. It was viewed as a space in which humans had not historically had any lasting impact, and in which they were to be prevented from doing in order to protect it from their harmful influence. With the creation of national parks, "pristine" landscapes were set aside in order to protect them from the extractive uses suffered by industrialized areas.

This understanding of "wilderness" is demonstrative of the way in which early Euro-Americans misunderstood the processes that shaped the landscape that they so admired. The perception that Native peoples had a negligible impact on the landscape is reflected in the writings of John Muir. In *My First Summer in the Sierra*, Muir (1911:54–55) provides the following description of Native people in order to contrast their practices with the destructive impacts of non-Native settlers:

> Indians walk softly and hurt the landscape hardly more than the birds and squirrels, and their brush and bark huts last hardly longer than those of wood rats, while their more enduring monuments, excepting those wrought on the forests by the fires they made to improve their hunting grounds, vanish in a few centuries.

This perception ignored the extensive millennia-long contributions of Native peoples to shaping the Sierra-Nevada landscape and its biota. In many parts of the Americas, this colonial fiction was made manifest as Native people were displaced from their "wilderness" homes.

Park creation served to displace Native peoples from designated parklands and disrupted traditional lifeways that included widespread plant harvesting and associated activities—cultural, social, economic, dietary, and spiritual. Prior to their designation as parks, lands throughout the United States were traditionally modified through annual or semiannual burning. Many of the habitats today preserved and managed as "natural" landscapes within national parks are in fact the product of long-term cultural interventions. As a result of these misperceptions, park managers prohibited Native management traditions and restricted their ability to gather. The natural and cultural consequences of these restrictions have been far reaching; tribes have experienced an erosion of their sovereignty and lifeways while park-directed regulations have brought about the deterioration of culturally significant habitats (Pyne 2015; Boyd 1999).

Based on these factors, it is unsurprising that the view of wilderness propounded by nineteenth-century conservationists is diametrically opposed to the Native conception of what constitutes a healthy landscape. Anderson (2005:3–4) elucidates the Native perception of the so-called "wilderness" and how the removal of human influence is detrimental to both plants and animals:

> Interestingly, contemporary Indians often use the word *wilderness* as a negative label for land that has not been taken care of by humans for a long time, for example, where dense understory shrubbery or thickets of young trees block visibility and movement. A common sentiment among California Indian is that a hands-off approach to nature has promoted feral landscapes that are inhospitable to life. "The white man sure ruined this country," said James Rust, a Southern Sierra Miwok elder. "It's turned back to wilderness" (personal communication 1989). California Indians believe that when humans are gone from an area long enough, they lose the practical knowledge about correct interaction, and the plants and animals retreat spiritually from the earth or hide from humans. When intimate interaction ceases, the continuity of knowledge, passed down through generations, is broken, and the land becomes "wilderness."

Ironically, going by this understanding of the term, Yosemite is indeed returning to true wilderness—a place where Native people do not have an active hand in resource management. In 1929, Totuya, also known as Maria Lebrado Ydarte, a survivor of the Mariposa Battalion's incursion into Yosemite, visited Yosemite Valley for the first time since she and her family had been forced out in 1851. Upon looking at the meadows covered with trees and shrubs, she is reported to have shaken her head and remarked that it was "too dirty; too much bushy" (Taylor 1932:4–5). Without the continuation of traditional management, there has been a measurable decrease in biodiversity, deteriorating plant health, and obstruction of the scenic vistas valued by both environmentalists and recreationists. Dense, young conifer forests overrun traditionally managed meadows and oak groves, as the Western fiction of "wilderness" becomes manifest in the landscape (Catton 1997; Keller and Turek 1998; Loendorf and Nabokov 2004; Spence 1999; Kantor 2007; Stevens 2014).

Nevertheless, this concept of wilderness has persisted throughout the history of the U.S. national parks, codified in such legal instruments as the 1964 Wilderness Act (Deur and James 2020). To this day, this concept—fundamentally unexamined as to its ontological context and implications—actively shapes national parks policy. One major change, however, is the growing understanding and acceptance among resource managers that Native management techniques were necessary for producing the landscape and conditions necessary for the mosaic of species found within the valley to survive. Over the last few decades, Native peoples have exerted greater pressure on the government to allow gathering, and the park service has slowly begun to see the importance of implementing Native methods of management. As a result, gradual changes to regulations indicate that the paradigm is slowly beginning to shift.

The following pages recount the historical impacts of "wilderness" on park service regulations, and the resulting suppression of traditional management and gathering in Yosemite. The experience at Yosemite may serve as a cautionary tale, but also offers a potential path forward for resource managers attempting to restore park species to their historical vitality and abundance.

TRADITIONAL ECOLOGICAL MANAGEMENT IN YOSEMITE VALLEY AT THE TIME OF CONTACT

Yosemite Valley abounds with seeds, grasses, clovers, bulbs, corms, tubers, roots, fungi, berries, and other vegetation that have long provided Native peoples with sustenance, medicine, and materials (Anderson 1990; Bibby 1994; Clark 1904:78–87). Seeds and nuts provided the bulk of the Native diet and included acorns and buckeye nuts as well as the seeds of herbaceous plants and wild grasses such as clarkias, wild oats, red maids, and California buttercup (Anderson 1990; Barrett and Gifford 1933). Native harvesters gathered seeds using a seed-beater, and then winnowed, parched, and pulverized them in bedrock mortars (Barrett and Gifford 1933:151–155). Harvesters collected acorns when they fell from the oaks, beat the acorns off the trees with a long, slender pole, or removed them from branches pruned from trees before they were ripe enough to fall (Barrett and Gifford 1933:142; Clark 1894:15). Bulbs, corms, and tubers, often referred to as "Indian potatoes" or "wild potatoes," included brodiaeas and other lilies. Harvesters typically extracted these with a digging stick, and then cooked within an earth oven or roasted in coals (Anderson 1990:15; Barrett and Gifford 1933:155–158). In addition to food, plants were also a significant source of medicines, basketry materials, and other items. Barrett and Gifford (1933:165–176) identify at least sixty-seven plants used medicinally by tribes associated with Yosemite Valley. Additionally, native communities of Yosemite Valley have traditionally harvested various grasses, shoots, and fibers for the production of baskets, cordage, and other traditional crafts. Harvesters have widely perceived Yosemite Valley as a place of cultural importance and cosmological power, so that they often describe the valley's plants as being imbued with more power—medicinal, cosmological, nutritional, and otherwise—than the same species obtained from other locations. Additionally, gathering in ancestral lands provides a link to one's ancestors. These factors contribute to a distinct preference for plants gathered within the park (Deur 2007). Though traditional foods may no longer form the bulk of Native American diets, they retain a place of significance within their culture. The act of gathering itself, and particularly in the land used by one's ancestors, is considered by some cultural practitioners to be "one of the last traditional practices" (NPS 2016c:2).

The abundance of culturally preferred natural resources was not merely "natural" phenomenon but represented a cultural artifact of considerable antiquity. Traditional resource management was intensive, particularly on the valley floor. Contemporary tribal members and ethnohistorical literature have consistently reported a wide range of traditional management methods employed within Yosemite. Accounts demonstrate that these methods were responsible for keeping meadows free from underbrush and conifer encroachment, protecting large trees from being destroyed by fire, reintroducing nutrients into the soil, maximizing plant diversity, eliminating insects and pathogens from plants, prolonging the life of dry meadows, enhancing the production of basketry and cordage materials, and preserving open scenic vistas (Anderson 2002:45; Anderson 2005). Various historic accounts describe how Native peoples managed the floor of Yosemite Valley to maintain a "park-like" landscape with clear views of the surrounding meadows, granite walls, and waterfalls (Clark 1894:14–15; Clark 1927:14; Markham 1892:6–7; Martin 1996). Some methods were practiced historically, but have been discontinued in the valley as a consequence of the park's establishment. Other practices have endured, though typically at a reduced scale and outside the areas trafficked by park visitors. The wide range of management methods are presented here to suggest the extent of Native American engagement with the plant habitats of Yosemite and their significant role in shaping the landscape and its biota.

Anthropogenic burning is the most commonly cited form of traditional management for Yosemite Valley. It was frequently mentioned by early writers, such as Willis Baxley (1865:476), who observed:

> A fire glow in the distance, and then the wavy line of burning grass, gave notice that the Indians were in the Valley clearing the ground, the more readily

> to obtain their winter supply of acorns and wild sweet potato root. (huch-hau [*Brodiaea spp.*])

The literature holds many descriptions of its beneficial impacts on the landscape and associated species. Native peoples used fires to clear conifers and shrubs from the valley floor, maintaining an open landscape, and perpetuating and enhancing a mosaic of culturally significant wetland, meadow, shrub, and forest communities. Burning promoted the quality and abundance of subsistence staples, such as edible lily bulbs (especially *Brodiaea* spp.) and the acorns of California black oak (*Quercus kelloggii*), caused the release of nutrients from accumulated biomass, and triggered the germination of fire- and heat-stimulated seeds (Anderson and Lake 2013:68; Ernst 1949:40; Kuhn and Johnson 2008:4; Reynolds 1959:159–160; Stewart 2002:294). Burning brush also increased the availability of surface water and increased the flow of springs by reducing water appropriation by less culturally preferred species (Anderson and Rosenthal 2015:22; Wickstrom 1987:8).

In addition to promoting the growth and health of preferred species, anthropogenic burning is important for protecting them from threats. Regular and systematic burning decreases the risk of destructive wildfires by eliminating underbrush, dead leaves, pine needles, and other debris (Kuhn and Johnson 2008:4; Stoy 1890:26). Research also demonstrates that it assists in controlling pests and pathogens, and limits the spread of root fungus, partly by keeping trees scattered and isolating the disease (Anderson and Rosenthal 2015:22; Champion 1986; Kuhn and Johnson 2008:4; West 1986:2).

In addition to burning, several interviewed tribal members have also reported "smoking" certain species in order to increase their output and deter the insects that infest certain preferred plants (Anderson and Rosenthal 2015; Goode 2014:6). Pruning is another common management technique. Tribal members cut off the fruit- or flower-bearing parts of branches while they are harvesting plants such as elderberry and manzanita (Anderson 1988:132). Similarly, in his letter to the Board of Commissioners of the Yosemite Valley and Mariposa Big Trees Grove, Galen Clark (1894:15) attested to Yosemite Native peoples pruning black oaks as they harvested acorns and enumerated the benefits of the practice:

> In order to get the necessary supply early in the season, before ripe enough to fall, the ends of the branches of the Oak trees were pruned off to get the acorns, this keeping the branches well cut back and not subject to being broken down by the heavy snows in winter, and the trees badly disfigured as is the case since that practice has been stopped.

Pruning also serves to remove diseased limbs from trees and is reported to improve the health and output of plants (Anderson 2005; NPS 2014:2; Stevens 1998). Basketry plants, such as redbud (*Cercis occidentalis*) and willow (*Salix* spp.), were also pruned in order to produce the long, straight shoots necessary for weaving (Anderson 1988:133; Anderson 2005:319).

"Knocking" is another management technique that occurs in conjunction with traditional gathering. Gatherers would use long, flexible poles to knock acorns off of higher branches that could not be reached from the ground; this encouraged acorns to fall without damaging branches or bark (Anderson 2005:141; Long et al. 2016:44). While using this harvesting and management technique, gatherers simultaneously remove dead and diseased wood from the trees, reducing the likelihood of disease or catastrophic fire that might affect the living tree, and also stimulate new growth (Martin 1996). As one tribal member associated with Yosemite noted, when Native people hit the trees with sticks to harvest acorns, what they were really doing was pruning, but park service didn't understand that (NPS 206d:3). Knocking is also beneficial to the reciprocal relationship between the trees and tribal members; the practice is described as "a kind of massage for the tree, to give it energy and continue the relationship between the harvester and the tree" (Goode 2014:6).

Individuals and families also manually removed conifer seedlings, weeded, cleared underbrush, and raked leaf litter around the bases of trees. These actions made it easier to gather, prevented crowding out of preferred plants, reduced the competition among different plants for sunlight and water, and promoted light surface fires that reduced the likelihood of destructive fires (Anderson 1988; Bibby 1994; Martin 1996).

Tribal members practiced selective harvesting by only harvesting larger plants and leaving the smaller ones to continue growing. They also left parts of various tubers, bulbs, corms, rhizomes, and mushrooms within the soil so that the remaining parts could regenerate. Selective harvesting ensures that culturally significant plant communities are not overexploited and functions to promote genetic diversity (Anderson 2005; Anderson and Lake 2013).

Digging bulbs in meadows with the use of digging sticks loosened soil and resulted in both deliberate and inadvertent soil aeration. This stimulates the growth of bulbs, helps convey water to drier soil, and produces straighter stems appropriate for weaving (Anderson 2005; Reynolds 1959; Ortiz 1991; People of Yosemite n.d.; Stevens 1998).

In addition to mechanical management methods, tribal members stress the importance of less quantifiable actions and interactions. Tribal interviewees assert that the plant species of Yosemite were gifted to them by the Creator, along with the responsibility to care for them. These caretaking obligations are both mechanical and metaphysical in nature; ensuring the health of plant and animal communities necessitates a holistic combination of traditional management, gathering and use of the species, and demonstrating respect for them. Failure to perform these duties, as mandated by the Creator, threatens the well-being of both land and people (Deur 2007:59). As such, tribal members describe the reciprocal relationship between themselves and the plant species as a crucial component of their care (NPS 2014:1). Instead of just "cold management," the plants thrive when tribal members sing to them, talk to them, and dance for them (NPS 2016b:3). Harvesting and managing the plants in a culturally appropriate manner demonstrates a "respect" for them, which is reciprocated by the plants returning more abundantly in the future (Anderson and Lake 2013; Deur 2007). The importance of fulfilling caretaker responsibility entails that even if they are not gathering, they continue to check the crop to ensure its well-being (NPS 2016b:6).

Most significantly for the purposes of this chapter, tribal members stress the interconnectivity of gathering and caring for the plants. As is demonstrated by the descriptions and results of the management techniques above, gathering and management are two inseparable byproducts of the same actions. These management techniques are, in fact, implemented as part of the gathering process, and not within a vacuum for purely aesthetic, recreational, or even conservation purposes. These methods are implemented to create the conditions ideal for gathering, to improve the quality of the gathered species, or in the course of undertaking gathering. Historical references to management techniques explicitly describe them as employed for subsistence purposes. These conditions demonstrate that the management of the landscape is inseparable from gathering. As such, tribal consultants state that by implementing some of their management techniques without also restoring gathering traditions, they will not work (NPS 2016a, b). Fundamental to this concept of gathering as a form of management is the principle that "if you don't use it, it goes away" (NPS 2016b:5). Tribal members often express that "the plants want to be used" and that the plants flourish and return when people care for and respect them (Deur 2007:59). In this sense, the inability of tribal members to harvest species may have negative effects on plant communities that respond positively to human management for biological and/or spiritual reasons.

PARK CREATION, SURVEILLANCE, AND THE DISPLACEMENT OF TRADITIONAL ECOLOGICAL PRACTICES

The management of Yosemite Valley's anthropogenic landscape changed abruptly as Euro-Americans arrived and it eventually became a park. First under control of the State of California, and later under federal control, fire and other forms of mechanical management were actively suppressed. For a generation or two, traditional management persisted, usually clandestinely and on a much smaller scale than before. As the park quickly developed, tribal communities were relocated and their previously dispersed villages were consolidated. Over time, however, only tribal members who worked for the park as laborers or in interpretive roles were allowed to remain (Spence 1999; Turek and Keller 1997). With this displacement, the extent and intensity of traditional management practices declined. As park-imposed land-use regulations became stricter over the decades, most of the management and gathering activities described above were largely extirpated within the park boundaries. Implementation of these regulations, which codified nineteenth-century beliefs about a pristine untouched wilderness, had deleterious impacts on the health of plant species and valued scenic views within Yosemite.

Euro-American settlement began in Yosemite Valley in the 1850s. Though disruption of traditional Native practices began soon after the Mariposa Battalion entered the valley in 1851, plant gathering practices persisted into the 1850s and 1860s (Deur 2007:9–10). In 1864, President Lincoln signed the Yosemite Grant Act, which gave Yosemite Valley and the Mariposa Grove to the State of California to be set aside for preservation and public use. The Yosemite Park Commission was charged with upholding the management of the park. In this period, authorities sought to suppress fires and prohibit traditional anthropogenic burning. An 1866 letter from the secretary of the Yosemite Commission, W. Ashburner, to Galen Clark, the appointed Guardian of Yosemite, is illustrative of their management of park resources. Clark was instructed to inform the sub-Guardian that in order to protect the valley from "future depredations," he was to ensure

> that no trees are to be cut or injured, that no fires are to be made where by running in the dry grass or undergrowth they will destroy or injure the large trees; that the Indians are to be especially warned from breaking the boughs of oaks in search of acorns. (Ashburner 1866:8)

An article in the *Mariposa Gazette* in 1869 attests to the implementation of these instructions:

> It is the custom with the Indians to commence gathering [acorns] for food very early in the Fall by cutting off the branches of the trees before the acorns are ripe enough to fall. While on a recent trip to the Valley, Mr. Galen Clark, one of the Commissioners and Guardian of the Valley, had a talk with the Indians living there, requesting them not to cut off the branches of the trees, but wait until the acorns fell off and then gather them. They replied that he had never

> paid them for their acorn trees nor the Valley, neither had anyone else paid them. . . . The Guardian explained to them that it would be better for them not to injure the trees by cutting them even if they had never been paid. (*Mariposa Gazette* 1869:2)

By the 1880s, written accounts indicated that suspension of management activities had resulted in obscured vistas, overgrowth of underbrush, and rapid colonization of meadows and other plant habitats by young conifers (Briggs 1882:10–11; Gibbens and Heady 1964:11). In 1882, M. C. Briggs, Secretary of the Yosemite Commission, detailed the valley's rapid devolving landscape:

> In our brief report of 1880, we called attention to the rapidly increasing breadth of underbrush and second growth pines, and need not restate our convictions with respect to the importance of counterworking this spreading infestment. While the Indians held possession, the annual fires kept the whole floor of the valley free from underbrush, leaving only the majestic oaks and pines to adorn the most beautiful of parks. In this one respect protection has worked destruction. (Briggs 1882:10–11)

These observations were stressed yet again a decade later in the *Report of the Commissioners to Manage the Yosemite Valley and the Mariposa Big Tree Grove* (1891–1892):

> As this Commission has already demonstrated, the valley originally was a forest park, dotted with open meadows. Its Indian owners kept the floor clear of underbrush. It is known that besides the careful use of fire for this purpose they annually pulled up unnecessary shrubs and trees as soon as they sprouted. This protected the large trees from destruction by fire and left a free view of the walls, waterfalls, and beauties of the valley. Letting nature have her way in choking every vista with underbrush has obscured many of the finest views, has hastened the destruction of many fine old trees, especially the oaks, which, when crowded and starved by younger growth, yield to parasites and decay, and has increased the risk from fire. (Markham 1892:6–7)

Though regulations proscribed Native management, enforcement was still comparatively disorganized and intermittent under the management of the Commission. Native Americans still returned to the valley seasonally to undertake traditional burning practices, but these became increasingly clandestine and were carried out beyond the margins of those places frequented by visitors (Deur 2007; Gassaway 2005). In 1890, an act of Congress created Yosemite National Park, which was placed under the administration of federal troops. Under new regulations, fire and other traditional management methods were actively and strictly suppressed, which further marginalized long-standing Native practices (Rothman 2005:16–19; Taylor 2006:2).

In the first decades of federal management, many observers noted a range of dramatic changes to Yosemite Valley. The rapid expansion and increasing density of conifers; the loss of meadow areas and scenic vistas; an increase in shrubs and underbrush on the floors of the meadows; an increased threat and occurrence of wild fires and pathogens; and a reduction in the productivity and diversity of many culturally preferred plant species proliferated by anthropogenic means were all attributed to fire suppression policies (Deur 2007; Ernst 1949; Long et al. 2016:36–37). In 1894, Galen Clark wrote to the Yosemite Board of Commissioners, comparing the valley's conditions with its appearance forty years prior. Clark (1894:14) detailed the stark changes and attributed them to the management restrictions implemented by the Commission:

> My first visit to Yosemite was in the summer of 1855. At that time there was no undergrowth of young trees to obstruct clear open views in any part of the valley from one side of the Merced River across to the base of the opposite wall. The area of clear open meadow land with abundance of luxuriant native grasses and flowering plants, was at least four times as large as at the present time. The valley had then been exclusively under the care and management of the Indians, probably for many centuries. . . . Since Yosemite has been under the care of the State of California, it was for many years the policy of its managers to protect the valley as much as possible from the ravages of fires, and to preserve all the young trees from destruction. This constant vigilant care for the preservation of Yosemite has resulted in the whole valley being overrun with dense thickets of young forests, shrubbery and underbrush, and an accumulation of a vast amount of highly inflammable combustible material which in the event of accidental fires, are a fearful menace to the safety of property and the beauty of the landscape scenery. . . . Many of the former finest views in Yosemite are now so much obscured by the growth of trees that it is impossible for photographers to again reproduce their former finest work until the trees and underbrush are cut away.

By 1907, Galen Clark's growing apprehension regarding the dramatic changes in the valley was expressed in his "Yosemite Plea of 1907." His narrative describes the exacerbation of meadow encroachment following ceased Native management of the valley. He laments that "nearly all the open ground between the large scattering trees is now covered with a dense growth of young trees, which also extend out over hundreds of acres of the dryest portion of the meadow land" (Clark 1927:14).

In 1916, the National Park Service was established through the Organic Act. The act's expressed mandate was to "conserve the scenery and the natural and historic objects and the wild life therein and to provide for the enjoyment of the same in such manner and by such means as will leave them unimpaired for the enjoyment of future generations" (16 U.S.C. 1).

The restrictions on gathering were stressed again in the first iteration of NPS rules and regulations, published in the Federal Register in 1936. The rules dictated the preservation of public property, natural features and curiosities, stating that

> the destruction, injury, defacement, removal or disturbance in any way . . . of any tree, flower, [or] vegetation . . . is prohibited: *Provided*, [t]hat flowers may be gathered in small quantities when, in the judgement of the superintendent or custodian, their removal will not impair the beauty of the park or monument. (1 Fed. Reg. 672, 673 [June 27, 1936])

This conservation mandate further reinforced the perception of parklands as wilderness devoid of humans and their influence, and strengthened prohibitions against Native gathering and management (Schrack 2018:1–2)

By the latter part of the twentieth century, the debate over subsistence access was reflected in the 1983 Code of Federal Regulations (CFRs). Codifying long-standing agency policy, the CFRs imposed significant restrictions. The regulations permitted park superintendents to "designate certain fruits, berries, nuts, or unoccupied seashells that may be gathered by hand for personal use or consumption if it will not adversely affect park wildlife, the reproductive potential of a plant species, or otherwise adversely affect park resources" (United States Code of Federal Regulation 2016 [36 CFR 2.1]). Notably, the regulations specify that, with the exception of instances explicitly authorized by treaty or federal statute, "this section shall not be construed as authorizing the taking, use, or possession of fish, wildlife, or plants for ceremonial or religious purposes."

After the adoption of 36 CFR 2.1, there was significant internal disagreement within the NPS on the prohibition against tribal members gathering for religious and ceremonial purposes. This resulted in extensive and open noncompliance with the rule at several parks (PEER 2010). At Yosemite, in particular, the approach to tribal plant gathering has varied depending on park administrations. Some superintendents have supported plant gathering, and have not actively enforced prohibitions or have even issued passes to permit such gathering by tribal members; others have chosen to enforce prohibitions (Deur 2007:56). By the late twentieth to the early twenty-first century, Yosemite National Park was among a number of parks that established both official and unofficial ways in which tribal members could gather within the park. The park entered into a memorandum of understanding (MOU) with traditionally associated tribes and local park officials quietly endorsed gathering through non-enforcement of regulations, adopting a "don't ask, don't tell" approach (PEER 2010; Schrack 2018). The MOU was signed under the authority of individual superintendents, rather than at the behest of a regional or national NPS directive. The authority for these agreements was predicated, in part, on the authorities of the American Indian Religious Freedom Act (AIRFA), which protects the free expression of Native American religion (Schrack 2018:7).

Environmental groups that learned of these agreements argued that gathering was being authorized in ways that violated the CFRs. The Public Employees for Environmental Responsibility (PEER), an environmental watchdog group, reported that they had obtained documents revealing that, in 2009, the acting park superintendent had told tribal members that they could gather plants as they wished without filing reports or acquiring permits (Ruch 2010; Schrack 2018:10). Since the tribes were given verbal permission, they noted, it was "difficult to quantify the nature and extent of park noncompliance of the rules at 36 CFR 2.1 because much of that noncompliance has been undocumented" (PEER 2010:4). These groups also disputed the authority for the agreements based on AIRFA. PEER cites the Preamble to the Final Rule for 36 CFR Part 1 and 2, which specifies that

> the Service recognizes that the American Indians Religious Freedom Act directs the exercise of discretion to accommodate Native religious practices consistent with statutory management obligations. The NPS intends to provide reasonable access to and use of, park lands and park resources by Native Americans for religious and traditional activities. *However, the National Park Service is limited by law and regulation from authorizing the consumptive use of park resources.* (48 FR 30255; emphasis added by Ruch 2010)

In the 2010s, legal and political pressure from tribes increased while a growing number of studies demonstrated the anthropogenic origins of park vegetation. Nevertheless, park allowances for gathering continued to be considered illegal in the absence of formal changes to the CFRs. Under those circumstances, senior NPS officials feared the threat of political and legal action taken by environmental watchdog groups that objected to plant harvests on public lands (Deur and James 2020; PEER 2010). As a result, the NPS determined to reassess resource access policy and revise the CFRs addressing gathering, paving the way for 36 CFR 2.6, the Gathering of Certain Plants or Plant Parts by Federally Recognized Indian Tribes for Traditional Purposes.

REVISIONARY CRITIQUES, REVISIONARY POLICIES: PLANT GATHERING IN A NEW MILLENNIUM

In 2016, the NPS approved revised plant gathering regulations. The new regulation, 36 CFR 2.6, is entitled the "Gathering of Certain Plants or Plant Parts by Federally Recognized Indian Tribes for Traditional Purposes." The new regulations allow the NPS to negotiate and enter into agreements with federally recognized tribes for the gathering of plants or plant parts within areas of the National Park Service where those activities traditionally occurred. Gathering must take place for traditional purposes and must not result in a significant adverse impact on park resources or values. The regulations enable tribes and park managers to establish procedures for plant gathering and monitoring in accordance with a plant gathering agreement and permitting process (36 CFR 2.6; NPS 2017; Schrack 2018:1–2; Talken-Spaulding and Watkins 2018:58). The regulations also place a number of restrictions on who is permitted to gather and the methods they may use to do so. The new policy limits gathering to enrolled members of federally recognized tribes who are "traditionally associated with the specific park area" and specifies that "this traditional association must predate the establishment of the park" (36 CFR 2.6). The rules also state that "traditional gathering" may only be conducted using hand tools (36 CFR 2.6; Schrack 2018:14)

Before gathering may occur, the tribe must submit a written request to the park superintendent in order to create a gathering agreement (36 CFR 2.6). The tribe must provide information on a number of subjects including their traditional association with the park and the traditional purposes of their gathering activity; identification of tribal members that are designated to gather; the specific plants that may be gathered; and the size, quantities, seasons, and locations where the gathering and removal will take place (NPS 2017).

In order for the agreement to be approved, the NPS must then complete an environmental assessment (EA) in compliance with the National Environmental Policy Act of 1969 and make a Finding of No Significant Impact (36 CFR 2.6). Once the agreement is signed, the NPS will issue a permit for the activities outlined in the agreement and list the names of tribal members that the tribe has authorized to gather in the park (NPS 2017).

In many ways, one of the most significant contributions of the regulations was the recognition that Native American resource stewards were often responsible for creating the "natural" landscapes within parks. Native harvests enhanced, rather than damaged, the preexisting ecological integrity of such places. The regulatory language explicitly mentions traditional ecological knowledge and recognizes the enduring connections between plants and tribal communities. Published in full within the Federal Register, the regulation and its justification state, in part:

> Over the past 20 years, studies in ethnobotany and traditional plant management, along with consideration of traditional ecological knowledge in scientific symposia and scholarly gatherings, have increased greatly. Research findings have shown that traditional conservation of plant species includes gathering and management techniques as well as social and cultural rules for avoiding over-exploitation (Berkes 2012; Blackburn and Anderson 1993; Anderson 2005; Deur and Turner 2005). Traditional gathering is carried out in ways that ensure plant replacement and abundance by using specific harvest criteria and foraging and cultivation strategies. (Anderson 1993; Turner and Peacock 2005)
>
> Wild plant species used for food have been managed for thousands of years by native groups using specific gathering techniques to maximize both harvest and sustainability (McCarthy 1993; Farris 1993; Parlee and Berkes 2006), and the general management of landscapes and ecosystems by native peoples have been well documented (e.g., Hammett 2000; Nabhan 2000). (U.S. Federal Register, Vol. 81, No. 133 [July 12, 2016], 45025–26)

Though federal recognition of the role Native peoples played in the shaping of park lands and nurturing the species found within them is revolutionary compared to historical policies and attitudes, the new regulations have detractors among both the Native and environmentalist communities. Many of the issues that tribal members have with the regulations relate to the data that the NPS requires the tribes to share, including locations, methods, and plant quantities, as part of the gathering agreement. Tribes argue that this is culturally inappropriate and that disclosure of such information with people outside of the tribe goes against traditional practice. This is particularly the case in instances where knowledge is only passed to those with a specific right to possess it (Schrack 2018:17; Vasquez 2019:72). Tribes fear that the NPS will be unable to protect their traditional knowledge and keep it confidential and they have raised concerns that sensitive information might be shared with the public (Schrack 2018:17; Tirado 2015).

Many gatherers are hesitant to share information on quantities as it is considered a highly sensitive subject and there is an aversion to reducing sacred practices to quantifiable data (Schrack 2018:17; Vasquez 2019:34). Questions on this subject are often be considered intrusive and demeaning, in part due to the primacy granted western science over traditional ecological knowledge when the two are in conflict (Vasquez 2019:72). Tribal members traditionally associated with Yosemite describe the invasiveness of questions by park staff when they were trying to care for plant species; they were bombarded with questions on how they cut, why they cut, how much they cut (NPS 2016b). Additionally, tribes state that their relationship to the plants and the ritual practices associated with gathering them are sacred. They argue that it is wrong to place government officials as middlemen between them and the creator when undertaking these sacred practices (Tirado 2015).

Sharing locations, in particular, can be problematic and is highly contested by tribal members. Traditional practitioners tend to be secretive about gathering locations in order to protect them. There is a fear that sharing traditional knowledge and locations with outsiders opens the possibility that they will be abused and disrespected, either deliberately or unintentionally (Vasquez 2019:36–37). Tribal members describe instances in which they provided data on gathering locations to the government or other outsiders. In some cases, these locations were destroyed by people who were irresponsible and did not harvest sustainably. There is a fear that providing locations to the NPS about their preferred gathering spots is essentially "pointing an arrow" at them (NPS 2016c:4).

The requirement to identify designated gatherers is also problematic. Various tribal community members are endowed with different pieces of traditional knowledge and there are no single individuals that possess all of those pieces (Tirado 2015). Furthermore, gathering is commonly a social activity, undertaken by families or whole communities (NPS 2016b:5). Specifying that only particular individuals from a tribe are authorized to gather would thus exclude the knowledge of certain traditional practitioners and the social dimension of such cultural activities. The new policy also requires tribes to fund EAs, which causes an additional impediment to gathering for tribes with fewer financial resources (Schrack 2018; Vasquez 2019). Another contention, particularly as these regulations apply to Yosemite, is that the new rule only permits federally recognized tribes to make plant gathering agreements. Although Yosemite has seven traditionally associated tribes, two are not currently federally recognized. The rule, therefore, prevents tribal members whose ancestral lands are within the boundaries of the park from gathering within the legal framework (Vasquez 2019:44–45).

The new gathering regulations have also been opposed by environmental groups, the most vocal of which is PEER. Their opposition to the regulations is based largely on the grounds that they violate the Organic Act by disregarding the conservation mandate and encouraging consumptive use of resources. They also argue that only Congress, and not the NPS, possesses the authority to enact the changes (Ruch 2015; Schrack 2018). These views represent the sentiment of many individuals and organizations opposed to the resumption of Native American gathering rights within parks. They applied a "slippery slope" argument against tribal gathering rights, suggesting that restoring plant gathering rights to tribes might open opportunities for commercial plant harvests, wildlife harvests, and other more objectionable outcomes (Deur and James 2020).

In comments on the proposed rule in 2015, the executive director of PEER enumerates the reasons for the organization's opposition to the regulations in detail. The following represent some of the most pertinent comments:

- PEER seeks to learn which plants, in which parks, and in which ecosystems will Indian tribal plant destruction (by uprooting, digging, trimming, pruning, thinning) "conserve" the plants. We are unaware of plant communities whose natural processes of growth, succession, replenishment, and/or replacement would be advanced by human harvesting or removal.
- This notion that the "first peoples" have an unbroken connection or claim to the land reduces the last century of park preservation history to a footnote. . . . It was 119 years ago, in 1896, when the Supreme Court effectively ended the Bannock Shoshone hunting rights in Yellowstone National Park. Reversing so many years of history is neither easily done nor wise.
- Cultivated landscapes are especially inimical to the congressionally described purpose of designated wilderness. When Congress designates lands as wilderness it is to preserve "land retaining its primeval character and influence, without permanent improvements or human habitation, which is protected and managed so as to preserve its natural conditions." 16 U.S.C. § 1131(c). Man-made and artificially managed areas do not preserve a natural condition, even when the manipulation is by Indians. (For additional comments, see Ruch 2015.)

Many of these arguments contain an implicit foundation in nineteenth-century wilderness philosophies. As a result of such sentiments, Native American plant gathering rights remain legally contested by those who seek to impose contested Western notions of "wilderness" on the anthropogenic landscapes comprising many of the United States' national parks. Furthermore, the NPS faces potential litigation from environmental groups over their statutory authority to permit traditional gathering (Schrack 2018:24).

TOWARD A CONCLUSION

The same nineteenth-century ontologies that fostered the creation of the National Park Service are also implicit in the regulations that have restricted traditional management and gathering throughout the park system's history. The strict cessation of these methods crucial to Native American cultural life stemmed from the lack of recognition of the Native American role in creating the landscapes as they were when first encountered by Euro-Americans. The habitat mosaic so admired by early park proponents and environmentalists was a product of Yosemite Native peoples burning, pruning, and implementing other forms of management over the course of millennia (Nabhan 1995:94). While regulations excluding human intervention were intended to protect the spectacular vistas and species that were the reason for the parks' creation, they have instead resulted in their deterioration.

As a result of over a century of suppression of traditional management, biodiversity has decreased, species health has deteriorated, meadows have been encroached by conifers, scenic vistas have been obstructed, fuel loads have accumulated and increased the threat of fire, and traditional practices and culture have been negatively impacted (Ernst 1949; Long et al. 2016; Vasquez 2019). By contrast, Native American communities associated with Yosemite have stressed the caretaker responsibility toward plant species, which mandates that they must tend the plants in culturally appropriate ways, which includes gathering and using them. They assert that if the plants are not used, they decline in abundance and in quality (Deur 2007; NPS 2016b). The changing conditions in the valley appear to support this assertion.

Elders express their frustration. They state that they have been telling park employees that they needed to manage and gather for decades and that no one has listened to them because they did not have academic or professional qualifications that are sanctioned by the non-Native world. They blame the park's desire to "protect" for the decline in culturally and ecologically significant species (NPS 2016a). Their lament is consistent with assertions made by non-Native caretakers too, such as those of the Yosemite Commission in 1882: "In this one respect protection has worked destruction" (Briggs 1882:11). Only active human management—guided by tribal knowledge and administered within the context of modern NPS management—seems likely to restore these species to anything approaching their historical vitality and abundance.

Recent changes to the gathering regulations have made great progress in recognizing Native peoples' deep and lasting connection to the landscapes comprising the National Park system and their role in shaping those landscapes. This represents a significant step forward in repairing the degradation caused by severing the caretaker relationship between park-associated Native peoples and park ecosystems. While these regulations theoretically offer a way in which to bolster the reciprocal relationship between tribes and parklands, there are many inherent issues. For a park like Yosemite, it excludes two of the park's traditionally associated but non-federally recognized tribes, providing them with no legal manner in which to gather in their ancestral lands. Gathering agreements require that tribes share sensitive information with outsiders in a manner that runs counter to their traditions and with no guarantee that this information will be protected. The process also adds undue bureaucratic and financial burdens for which many tribes lack the resources. The necessity to designate gatherers also ignores the social and ritual realities of traditional gathering. In short, the method of gathering attempts to make traditional practices conform to a western framework in a way that is quantifiable, and yet, completely inimical to tribal values.

Challenges from environmental organizations reveal their intellectual roots in nineteenth-century ontologies that hold "wilderness" apart from human experience. Such positions lack awareness of the deeper historical context or sophistication of traditional indigenous caretaking. This still prevalent perception, and the threat of litigation, contribute to the difficulty of establishing a framework in which traditional management and gathering can be restored more fully and appropriately to recognize the reciprocal relationship between tribes and species within the park system.

Hope remains that parks may yet restore the vitality and quality of natural resources and landscapes that have been declining by reconnecting Native harvesters to the landscape. Furthermore, with greater access to their ancestral lands, tribes will succeed in protecting and transmitting their traditions, as well as the associated knowledge of plants, habitats, and places that sustained their ancestors—and were sustained by their ancestors—for generations to come.

REFERENCES CITED

Anderson, M. Kat. 1988. Southern Sierra Miwok Plant Resource Use and Management of the Yosemite Region: A Study of the Biological and Cultural Bases for Plant Gathering, Field Horticulture, and Anthropogenic Impacts on Sierra Vegetation. MS thesis, University of California, Berkeley.

———. 1990. Yosemite's Native Plants and the Southern Sierra Miwok. *Yosemite* 52(3):12–15.

———. 2002. An Ecological Critique. In *Forgotten Fires: Native Americans and the Transient Wilderness*, edited by M. K. Anderson, pp. 37–64. Norman, Ok: University of Oklahoma Press.

———. 2005. *Tending the Wild: Native American Knowledge and the Management of California's Natural Resources*. Berkeley: University of California Press.

Anderson, M. Kat, and Frank K. Lake. 2013. California Indian Ethnomycology and Associated Forest Management. *Journal of Ethnobiology* 33(1):33–85.

Anderson, M. Kat, and Jeffrey Rosenthal. 2015. An Ethnobiological Approach to Reconstructing Indigenous Fire Regimes in the Foothill Chaparral of the Western Sierra Nevada. *Journal of Ethnobiology* 35(1):4–36.

Ashburner, William. 1866. Letter from Secretary of the Yosemite Commission to Galen Clark re. Guidance as Guardian of the Yosemite Valley and Mariposa Big Tree Grove. 24 August 1866. Accession no. 29046, Roll #6, Papers of Galen Clark, Yosemite Research Library, National Park Service.

Barrett, Samuel A., and Edward W. Gifford. 1933. Miwok Material Culture: Indian Life of the Yosemite Region. *Bulletin of Milwaukee Public Museum* 2(4):117–376.

Baxley, Henry Willis. 1865. *What I Saw on the West Coast of South and North America, and at the Hawaiian Islands.* New York: D. Appleton & Co.

Beatty, M. E. 1935. Letter to Col. Thomson regarding Galen Clark's Letter to the Board of Commissioners, 1894 21 February 1935. Folder 68, Box 2, Craig Bates Collection, Yosemite Archives, El Portal, California.

Bibby, Brian. 1994. *An Ethnographic Evaluation of Yosemite Valley: The Native American Cultural Landscape.* Manuscript on file, Department of Anthropology, Yosemite National Park.

Boyd, Robert. 1999. *Indians, Fire and the Land in the Pacific Northwest.* Corvallis, OR: Oregon State University Press.

Briggs, M.C. 1882. Report of the Commissioners to Manage the Yosemite Valley and the Mariposa Big Tree Grove. In *Biennial Report of the Commissioners to Manage the Yosemite Valley and the Mariposa Big Tree Grove, so extended as to include All Transactions of the Commission from April 19, 1880, to December 18, 1882.* Sacramento: State Office, J.D. Young, Supt. State Printing.

Catton, Theodore. 1997. *Inhabited Wilderness: Indians, Eskimos, and National Parks in Alaska.* Albuquerque, NM: University of New Mexico Press.

Champion, Dale. 1986. Disease Threatens to Kill All of Yosemite's Evergreens. *San Francisco Chronicle* October 18.

Clark, Galen. 1894. Letter to the Hon. Board of Commissioners of the Yosemite Valley and Mariposa Big Trees Grove. Folder 68, Box 2, Craig Bates Collection, Yosemite Archives, El Portal, California.

———. 1904. *Indians of the Yosemite Valley and Vicinity: Their History, Customs, and Traditions.* Yosemite Valley: G. Clark.

———. 1927. A Yosemite Plea of 1907. *Yosemite Nature Notes* VI(2):13–15.

Deur, Douglas. 2007. *Yosemite National Park Traditional Use Study: Plant Use in Yosemite Valley and El Portal.* Pacific West Social Science Series No. 2007-001. Seattle, WA: USDI National Park Service.

Deur, Douglas, and Justine E. James, Jr. 2020. Cultivating the Imagined Wilderness: Contested Native American Plant Gathering Traditions in America's National Parks. In *Plants, People and Places: The Roles of Ethnobotany and Ethnoecology in Indigenous Peoples' Land Rights in Canada and Beyond,* edited by Nancy J. Turner, pp. 220–37. Montreal, QC: McGill-Queens University Press.

Ernst, Emil F. 1949. Vanishing Meadows in Yosemite Valley. *Yosemite Nature Notes* 28(5):34–40.

Gassaway, Linn. 2005. Hujpu-St: Spatial and Temporal Patterns of Anthropogenic Fire in Yosemite Valley. MA Thesis, San Francisco State University.

Goode, Ron W. 2014. Cultural Burn. Paper Presented to the Dinkey Collaborative, Dinkey Creek, California. https://water.ca.gov/LegacyFiles/waterplan/docs/tac/Cultural%20Burn%20(4).pdf (Accessed December 26, 2019).

Gibbens, Robert P., and Harold F. Heady. 1964. The Influence of Modern Man on the Vegetation of Yosemite Valley. California Agricultural Experiment Station, Manual 36. University of California, Division of Agricultural Sciences.

Haila, Yrjo. 1997. "Wilderness" and the Multiple Layers of Environmental Thought. *Environment and History* 3(2):129–147.

Kantor, Isaac. 2007. Ethnic Cleansing and America's Creation of National Parks. *Public Land & Resources Law Review* 28(41): 441–464.

Kuhn, Bill, and Brent Johnson. 2008. Status and Trends of Black Oaks (*Quercus kelloggii*) Populations and Recruitment in Yosemite Valley (a.k.a. Preserving Yosemite's Oaks). Final report prepared for the Yosemite Fund. National Park Service, Yosemite National Park, Yosemite, California. https://www.nps.gov/yose/learn/nature/upload/Status-Trends-Black-Oaks-2008.pdf (Accessed December 14, 2016).

Loendorf, Lawrence, and Peter Nabokov. 2004. *Restoring a Presence: American Indians and Yellowstone National Park*. Norman: University of Oklahoma Press.

Long, Jonathan W., M. Kat Anderson, Lenya Quinn-Davidson, Ron W. Goode, Frank K. Lake, and Carl N. Skinner. 2016. *Restoring California Black Oak Ecosystems to Promote Tribal Values and Wildlife. General Technical Report.* Albany, CA: U.S. Department of Agriculture, Forest Service, Pacific Southwest Research Station.

Mariposa Gazette. 1869. Town and County Matters. Volume 15, Number 8, August 20. https://cdnc.ucr.edu/. (Accessed July, 16 2019).

Markham, Henry H. 1892. Report of Yosemite Valley Commissioners. Biennial Report of the Commissioners to Manage the Yosemite Valley and the Mariposa Big Tree Grove for the Years 1891-92. Sacramento, CA: State Office, A.J. Johnston, Supt. State Printing.

Martin, Glen. 1996. Keepers of the Oaks. Discover Magazine, August. Craig Bates Collection (Box 2, Folder 68). Yosemite Archives, El Portal, California.

Muir, John. 1911. *My First Summer in the Sierra.* New York: Houghton Mifflin Company.

Nabhan, Gary Paul. 1995. Cultural Parallax in Viewing North American Habitats. In *Reinventing Nature? Responses to Postmodern Deconstruction,* edited by M. Soulé and G. Lease, pp. 87–101. Washington, DC: Island Press.

National Park Service (NPS). 2014. Notes Taken at Yosemite Forum - Kat Anderson Talk. December 9. Yosemite National Park, California. On file in the Anthropology Office, RMS, Yosemite National Park.

———. 2016a. Meeting to Discuss Black Oak Ethnographic Research Project, Meeting Minutes, March 17. Draft on file, Resources Management & Science Office, Yosemite National Park, El Portal, CA.

———. 2016b. Tribal Meeting and Site Visit to Discuss Black Oak Research Project, Meeting Minutes, October 18. Draft on file, Resources Management & Science Office, Yosemite National Park, El Portal, CA.

———. 2016c. Tribal Meeting and Site Visit to Discuss Black Oak Research Project, Meeting Minutes, October 19. Draft on file, Resources Management & Science Office, Yosemite National Park, El Portal, CA.

———. 2016d. Tribal Meeting and Site Visit to Discuss Black Oak Research Project, Meeting Minutes, October 24. Draft on file, Resources Management & Science Office, Yosemite National Park, El Portal, CA.

———. 2017. Tribal Leaders Guide to the National Park Service Plant Gathering Regulation. U.S. Department of the Interior, National Park Service, American

Indian Liaison Office. https://www.nps.gov/history/Tribes/Documents/Public_NPSPlantGathering_Guide_July2017.pdf (accessed July 5, 2019).

Ortiz, Beverly R. 1991. *It Will Live Forever: Traditional Yosemite Indian Acorn Preparation.* Berkeley, CA: Heyday Books.

People of Yosemite. n.d. Folder 1072, Box 22, Craig Bates Collection, Yosemite Archives, El Portal, California.

Public Employees for Environmental Responsibility (PEER). 2010. Native American Plant Gathering in the National Park System. https://perma.cc/9HHU-DEWN (Accessed July 6, 2019).

Pyne, Stephen J. 2015. *Between Two Fires: A Fire History of Contemporary America.* Tucson, AZ: University of Arizona Press.

Reynolds, Richard Dwan. 1959. Effect of Natural Fires and Aboriginal Burning upon the Forests of the Central Sierra Nevada. MS thesis, University of California-Berkeley.

Rothman, Hal K. 2005. *A Test of Adversity and Strength: Wildland Fire in the National Park System.* Washington, DC: National Park Service, U.S. Department of the Interior.

Ruch, Jeff. 2010. Letter from Jeff Ruch, Exec. Dir, PEER, to Mary Kendall, Acting Inspector Gen., Department of the Interior regarding noncompliance with plant gathering regulations, August 11. https://perma.cc/LH8K-NUW3 (Accessed July 6, 2019).

———. 2015. Letter from Jeff Ruch, to Executive Director, PEER, to Joe Watkins: Comments on NPS Proposed Rule for Tribal Gathering of Plants in Parks, April 20. https://perma.cc/8HWN-X3HB (accessed July 13, 2019).

Schrack, Andrew. 2018. The Shifting Landscape of Ancestral Lands: Tribal gathering of Traditional Plants in National Parks. *Arizona Journal of Environmental Law and Policy* 9(1):1–24.

Spence, Mark David. 1999. *Dispossessing the Wilderness: Indian Removal and the Making of National Parks*. Oxford, UK: Oxford University Press.

Stevens, Michelle. 1998. The Ethnobotany and Distribution of White Root (*Carex barbarae*). Folder 145, Box 3, Craig Bates Collection, Yosemite Archives, El Portal, California.

Stevens, Stan. 2014. *Indigenous Peoples, National Parks, and Protected Areas: A New Paradigm Linking Conservation, Culture, and Rights*. Tucson: University of Arizona Press.

Stewart, Omer C. 2002. *Forgotten Fires: Native Americans and the Transient Wilderness*. Norman: University of Oklahoma Press.

Stoy, William H. 1890. Letter to the honorable Secretary of the Interior. Biennial Report of the Commissioners to Manage the Yosemite Valley and the Mariposa Big Tree Grove for the Years 1889-90. *Reports of the Commissioners to Manage the Yosemite Valley and the Mariposa Big Tree Grove for the Years, Biennial Reports 1889-1904-1888*. Sacramento, CA: State Office.

Talken-Spaulding, Jennifer, and Joe Watkins. 2018. Applied Anthropology in the National Park Service's Second Century of Stewardship. *The George Wright Forum* 35(1):53–64.

Taylor, Alan H. 2006. Fire History of Yosemite Valley. Final Report for the Yosemite Fund through cooperative agreement 1443CA309701200 between the National Park Service and the Pennsylvania State University. On File, Yosemite RMS Library, El Portal, California.

Taylor, Mrs. H.J. (Rose Schuster). 1932. *The Last Survivor.* San Francisco, CA: Johnck & Seeger.

Tirado, Michelle. 2015. National Park Service Does Face-Plant with New Rules on Gathering Plants. *Indian Country Today,* August 20. https://newsmaven.io/indiancountrytoday/archive/national-park-service-does-face-plant-with-new-rule-on-gathering-plants-xYKGltAdPU6v1pYvDlBPrA/ (Accessed July 5, 2019).

Turek, Michael Francis, and Keller, Robert H. 1998. *American Indians and National Parks.* Tucson: University of Arizona Press.

United States Code of Federal Regulations 2016 36 CFR 2.6. Gathering of Certain Plants or Plant Parts by Federally Recognized Indian Tribes for Traditional Purposes. 36 CFR Part 2. https://www.govinfo.gov/content/pkg/FR-2016-07-12/pdf/2016-16434.pdf (Accessed July 5, 2019).

Vasquez, Irene A. 2019. Evaluation of Restoration Techniques and Management Practices of Tule Pertaining to Eco-Cultural Use. MS thesis. Humboldt State University.

West, Lorne. 1986. The Demise of Yosemite Valley's Evergreens. *Yosemite* 48(4):2.

Wickstrom, C. Kristina Roper. 1987. *Issues Concerning Native American Use of Fire: A Literature Review.* Publications in Anthropology No. 6. Yosemite National Park, CA: National Park Service, U.S. Department of the Interior.

Chapter 10

Nature's Belonging

Landscape, Conservation, and the Cultural Politics of Place in the Great Basin

Paul Berne Burow

"All this cutting for a hope. They are hoping to offer the bird better habitat." I stand looking across the open valley at a recent U.S. federal ecological restoration project with Thomas, an official with a nearby Paiute Nation, a Native American tribal nation whose ancestral lands include this valley.[1] Large stands of piñon pine (*Pinus monophylla*) trees lay on their sides, cut-over, and laid to waste under the hot Nevada sun. "They say these trees don't have any value," he continued. "They are no good for timber. But to us they are of great value. People don't care how we feel. Your heart drops when you see all the trees wiped out somewhere." The Paiute people have a long history of caring for these forests. They are a sacred space to the community—a site of hunting, collecting pine nuts and other plants, and family camps that are visited year after year. The landscape is thick with stories that mark the memories of generations. [2]

Although we stood on the ancestral territory of the Paiute, these lands are now almost entirely controlled by the U.S. federal government through the U.S. Forest Service and Bureau of Land Management.[3] Many in the Paiute community ignore the issue and resign themselves to the fate that federal land agencies will do whatever they want to do no matter what Indigenous people say. Consultation is a joke, they say, and the cutting of forests to restore habitat for sage grouse will continue.[4] Thomas shares concern about sage grouse and their well-being. But he does not always see their lives as inherently threatened by the presence of trees on the landscape. He holds the view that trees and birds are neighbors. Yet many federal land managers and ecological scientists hold the view that they are fundamentally incompatible. This view of the incommensurate nature of forest and steppe, the perceived opposition between shrub-dwelling birds and desert-dwelling trees is itself a culturally imbued way of seeing the landscape, something lost on many involved in sage grouse conservation efforts. Looking out at the clear-cut forest, Thomas laments, "they came into areas and cut down all the young trees. I mean that's like killing all the young children in the family."[5]

INTRODUCTION

The cultural politics of place poses questions about how bounded political communities are constituted in relation to space, place, and nature. It asks how politics comes to define landscapes through practices of governance and the institutions of environmental management, and how the movement of humans, plants, and animals across borders shapes claims to political belonging in particular places (Cattelino 2015; Kosek 2006; Moore 2005). I approach culture as a site of political struggle, and ethnography as a method for examining the situated practices that normalize and sustain social orders such that people and things come to be made into something belonging in some places and not belonging in others. Federal, state, and environmental groups' conservation projects that seek to restore ecosystems and protect endangered species are shaped by the politics of culture and place. These efforts contribute to the cultural displacement of human communities and result in collateral displacement of "non-target species," or plants and animals that get in the way. Peter Alagona describes the politics of place around endangered species protection as an "ongoing cultural conversation about who should have access to and control over lands and natural resources" (2013:11).

Indeed, the emergence of sage grouse as a target species for conservation efforts across the U.S. West is indicative of its status as a surrogate for political conflict over activities such as ranching, oil and gas drilling, and urban development on public lands.[6] Environmental groups see the sage grouse as a species with a broad distribution that holds the potential to remake the politics of land use if eventually listed as endangered. This led to a strategic effort to protect the bird that focuses on coalitions of public agencies, research institutions, private companies, and environmental organizations. Approaches labeled "collaborative conservation" also fit into this process as the mere prospect of an endangered species listing, and the top-down federal management that would ensue if it occurred, operates as a Sword of Damocles hanging over groups with a stake in Great Basin landscapes. This creates an incentive to cooperate, but it also displaces certain key issues while centering others as politics remakes the belonging of particular ecologies on landscapes. But given conflicting perceptions of what belongs on landscapes across human communities, such social phenomena are better described as *ecologies of belonging,* or configurations of social life imbued with power that include some people, plants and animals, and exclude others. Thus, the cultural politics of place references both representations of place, and the ways belonging becomes managed and materially instantiated on the land.

In the Nevada-California borderlands of the western Great Basin, landscape history is disjoined, with an emphasis on its pre-settlement state over its immediate past history (Cronon 1995; Spence 1999). Time is important to settler colonialism because it always casts indigeneity in the past tense, erasing the contemporary manifestations of settlement. This is relevant to conservation because ecosystems are commonly framed as "natural" based on how they differ from landscapes at the onset of colonial settlement. Most ecological restoration projects are predicated on returning lands to an imagined past that is static and knowable despite the value judgments and incomplete knowledge that infuse representations of historical landscapes. Indigenous peoples, though the target of genocidal policies and dispossession, never completely disappeared, and today are seeking redress for the harms as modern nations asserting sovereignty over lost lands and the exercise of unique political rights (Wilkinson 2006). This political context is something lost in settler society's racialization of Indigenous identity (Moreton-Robinson 2015). This temporal separation between before and after Euro-American settlement is an artifact of the colonial context of conservation work in the U.S. West. Settler colonialism is a structure of domination in which people (settlers) arrive from someplace else to lay claim to a new place, make a new home there, and displace extant inhabitants through dispossession and elimination (Veracini 2010). Settler colonialism is not an event, but an enduring structure that constantly reimagines and renews itself through the erasure of prior inhabitants and the continued substantiation of belonging for settlers through discourse, institutions, and the material transformation of lives and livelihoods. Patrick Wolfe, in his seminal article on settler colonialism, argues that "territoriality is settler colonialism's specific, irreducible element" and that its process "strives for the dissolution of native societies" (Wolfe 2006:388). Wolfe critically asserts that the settler-colonial situation forms an enduring structure rather than a passing event. The work of scholars in critical Indigenous studies and other disciplines carefully theorize these formations, but the nonhuman still remains an undertheorized facet of settler colonialism studies (Coulthard 2014; Simpson 2014). Important work in Indigenous political ecology demonstrates how the nonhuman world is implicated in relations of power in settler society (Carroll 2015; Middleton Manning 2015). This chapter extends this work by critically examining landscape conservation as a site of cultural and political struggle predicated on very different ontologies of the nonhuman across groups (Burow, Brock, and Dove 2018).

Building on Wolfe's observation, I argue here that settler colonialism *is also a multi-species project.* Taking a *more than human* frame offers a way to expand and deepen our understanding of domination to include the entities that co-produce human worlds despite a settler metaphysics that seeks to separate and objectify. I begin by highlighting the idea of conservation as *death-work*. For this, I draw from Kristina Lyon's "contrasting logics of life and death" (2016:59) in Colombian ecologies remade by militarism. Similarly, Kali Rubaii's description of counterterrorism tactics targeting ecologies by "changing the rhythm of life and the shape of landscapes" (2018:348) illustrates the parallels between the occupation of Iraq and settler-colonial militarism on landscapes in the United States.[7] Settler-colonial violence is foundational to environmental management. Nature is objectified such that it is amenable to control. Settler-colonial natures are produced through two orders of denial: elision and erasure. This is the double amnesia of settler-colonial visions of landscapes. First, any evidence of prior inhabitation is marked off as part of "pre-history" with little or no relationship to present Indigenous communities, and second, no continuity is established between historical phenomena and contemporary conditions. Lands taken in 1850 are still dispossessed lands today, raising the question of the endurance of dispossession and how settler society attempts to justify the sustained erasure of Indigenous political claims given the ultimate, though devastating, failure of this genocidal effort (Madley 2016). Furthermore, the past is used to regulate cultural authenticity, forcing contemporary claims into a framework of history to be accorded recognition.

This "slot" of cultural authenticity denies Indigenous nations a claim to the shaping of modernity and the right to political and cultural self-determination (Barker 2011; Li 2000). The temporal rupture that divides an Indigenous past from an Indigenous present is fundamental to the human sciences in the Great Basin and decouples contemporary politics from historical processes (Blackhawk 2006). This is how landscapes are made that erase Indigenous political claims to territory and belonging. It also precludes the nonhuman from having its own politics and claims to rightfully belong. The cultural politics of place in settler societies is premised on the erasure of Indigenous peoples' emplacement, along with nonhuman kin that cannot be turned into resources for exploitation. But more importantly, it is a displacement of ecologies of belonging that link people to their world, for example, the Paiute, and their links to pine nut forests, sage grouse, and the practices of caring for the land.[8] I follow this analysis with a discussion of the ways landscape change is understood and represented through photography to create canonical ideas about what landscapes *ought* to look like and the implications of this for Indigenous politics and the nonhuman.

ON LANDSCAPES AND CONSERVATION

The sage grouse is a ground-dwelling bird that lives in sagebrush steppe across much of the western United States. Its population and habitat have dwindled in size over the past century owing to the rapid development of the region (Connelly and Braun 1997). The sage grouse is a threatened species under review by the U.S. Fish & Wildlife Service for listing through the Endangered Species Act. In the western Great Basin, home to a genetically distinct subpopulation of sage grouse, government agencies, environmental organizations, scientists, ranchers, and Indigenous nations are caught up in an effort to keep the sage grouse off the endangered species list through a model of "collaborative conservation." This region, called the "bi-state" because it straddles the Nevada-California border south of Reno, is cited by federal government officials and environmental organizations as one of the success stories of collaborative, landscape-scale conservation.[9]

This "collaborative" model purports to be the answer to the kinds of intense political conflict involved in previous endangered species listings such as the spotted owl in the Pacific Northwest. The case of the spotted owl lingers in the minds of many given how conservation became associated with the radical remaking of rural political economies, even as the region was facing changes well underway given the growth of global timber markets (Prudham 2005). The conflict over the spotted owl listing as an endangered species created a stark political divide between rural, natural resource-dependent communities, and urban environmentalists that persists today as a cautionary tale about the politics of endangered species conservation (Yaffee 1994).

In Nevada and eastern California, one of the greatest threats to sage grouse is argued to be invasive species, with piñon and juniper trees foremost among the suggested culprits. The scourge of "conifer encroachment" has given rise to forest clearance projects, usually labeled as ecological restoration by federal government agencies and some environmental groups. These projects seek to return the landscape to its purportedly natural state as steppe shrublands without trees. Conifer encroachment is an ecological theory about widespread expansion of woodlands into erstwhile shrub and grasslands, and the increase in woodland density in already established stands (Jacobs 2011; Shaw, Steed, and DeBlander 2005). But a skeptical land manager in the region noted, "There is no pan-basin pattern of encroachment."[10] The historical context for the piñon-juniper forests is an essential, if ignored, part of this story. It was not just piñon and juniper that faced widespread removal from the 1950s to the 1980s, sagebrush itself was also maligned for its expansion into precolonial settlement grasslands (Sayre 2017). The scientific literature always refers to "piñon-juniper woodland" as the category of vegetation type consisting of dominant or codominant piñon and/or juniper trees. I use the term "pine nut forest" or "piñon forest" to apply to piñon-juniper as a cultural category. The heterogeneity of Great Basin landscapes makes either categorical approach necessarily limiting.[11] The "conifer expansion" thesis that holds sway among range managers today suggests that piñon-juniper woodlands have infilled to create much denser stands and expanded to "encroach" on former sagebrush steppe and grasslands over the past 150 years. The reason this change occurred, according to proponents of this view, is the exclusion of fire from the landscape. Their logic is that regular fires would burn through woodlands and prevent them from growing on fine-grained soils of the lowlands.

Critics, on the other hand, argue that fire never played an important role in shaping the distribution and stand dynamics of piñon-juniper woodlands because the fuel load was never sufficient to support widespread fires in these areas. However, anthropogenic fire was certainly used by Indigenous peoples of the region for a long time. Piñon and juniper are not fire-adapted trees. They have thin bark and low crowns and thus cannot withstand even low-intensity burning. Furthermore, proponents of the encroachment thesis argue that piñon-juniper only grows on rocky, coarse-grained soils where water infiltrates easily and gives an advantage to trees with deeper root systems. The trees gradually outcompete shrubs, grasses, and forbs. As the forest increases in density, the understory disappears. This perspective reinforces an already well-established successional view of plant community dynamics. However, the reality is quite varied. Stands of piñon-juniper are of various densities, from places with a few trees per acre and dominant shrub communities, to dense piñon-juniper forests with no shrub or grass community underneath.

Whereas these kinds of techno-scientific arguments are the core of debates among federal agencies, scientists, and environmental organizations, many other members of local communities, some settler communities, and some Indigenous communities draw upon modes of knowledge that come from multigenerational histories of being close to the land. For example, both mining and ranching fomented widespread clearing of trees, but these practices were not substantiated with an argument about invasion. Trees were removed to improve the production of cattle forage on public lands. But with the rise of environmental legislation such as the National Environmental Policy Act and the Federal Land Policy and Management Act, federal agencies have shifted toward an "objective" and "science-based" management approach. This land-use history illustrates the deeply imbedded cultural values that shape perspectives on piñon trees (Lanner 1981).

In addition to optimizing forage production for cattle, land managers also cited the presence of piñon forests as a degrading influence on watersheds. Soil erosion also came to be connected with forest management. During the mid-twentieth century, federal land managers argued that dense woodlands created the conditions for severe erosion, which necessitated conifer removal to restore an understory that could hold the soil in place. In recent years, range managers justified conifer removal on the basis of unnatural infill of woodlands and expansion into erstwhile shrublands and grasslands. These changes in the rationale for removing piñon and juniper forests suggest very different understandings of landscape dynamics but are subtended by a common valuation of the landscape—or rather the devaluation of piñon trees because they cannot be easily commodified. Conifer encroachment is often treated as a universal condition, and treatments are often conducted through uniform appraisals of vegetation dynamics across the region. A "one size fits all" approach is evident in federal agency environmental assessments that are identical from one project to the next despite the variation of site locations. This leads to the main thrust of critics' cautions that site-specific ecological assessments, including site visits, are critical to projects and should be considered. Some of the latest research, critical of the conventional wisdom about conifer encroachment, argues that the overall distribution of piñon-juniper woodland is negatively impacted by large-scale mortality events that have occurred since the 1980s (Flake and Weisberg 2019). Areas of massive die-back in New Mexico and Arizona in past decades suggest greater trepidation is warranted in the Great Basin given climate change (Kosek 2006; McDowell et al. 2016).

The key point, however, is that the situation varies greatly from place to place. The other central issue is reestablishment of forests as opposed to expansion. Range managers often fail to account for forest history, including the way that vast areas of woodland were deforested during the mining boom of the late nineteenth century (Lanner and Frazier 2011). Thus, many areas where conifers are supposedly expanding are actually experiencing the reestablishment of stands previously removed. This can hardly be called "expansion" in the sense of being in a place where the trees should not belong. But the broader point is that different people have ideas about what defines the belonging of piñon trees. For land managers, belonging is judged through two layers: first, whether a species is "native" and second whether its place on its native range can be inferred as proper based on a prototypical habitat. Piñon trees are in their proper place when situated on rocky ground rather than deep soils. So when a tree appears on deep soils, it is often labeled as invasive.

What is "natural?" The ecological baseline that is widely used to establish what is "natural" and "unnatural" is the onset of Euro-American settlement in the mid-nineteenth century. A plant is native if it existed in a particular place before settlement. Yet this kind of ecological baseline is inherently problematic given the dynamic and often social changes on landscapes that fail to represent any steady, natural state. To say that a tree belongs in one place, but not another, is a statement about what the world *ought* to look like.

As one Paiute interlocutor said to me, "These trees aren't invading—they are doing what they are designed to do." This view of belonging suggests that life itself, something living and growing in a particular place, is evidence of a plant being in its proper location. Such an argument precludes large-scale projects to remove native species such as piñon trees, because there is no such thing as invasion unless it came from elsewhere.

Putatively objective descriptions of the world, such as labeling piñon trees as "weedy native species" obscure foundational normative claims when associated with a scientific discourse. This association imbues them with the authority of science when they are perhaps better adjudicated as questions of value and morality. A weed is simply plant matter out of place. It does not represent an enduring natural state, but the projection of human values on something. Furthermore, the strength of the discourse on invading trees is reinforced by the reliance of researchers at government agencies and academic institutions on funding from the same agencies promoting these ideas in the first place. Projects that seek to test ideas about conifer expansion are unlikely to receive support from land managers who need scientific studies to support their arguments for a science-based management paradigm. In effect, a self-reinforcing circle is created where land management practices shape the kind of research that is funded to argue for the same policies applied in the first place. But only certain kinds of knowledge count. The empirical, science-based knowledge of local communities, including Indigenous peoples and multigenerational ranching families, cannot be accommodated by agencies that need scientists with particular credentials and research practices to produce reports and peer-reviewed studies. Despite the federal agencies stated desire to include "traditional ecological knowledge" (TEK) in management, federal agencies have done no more than pay lip service to the term without indicating the way TEK would be included. This poses its own problems as studies demonstrate the power relations involved in projects of knowledge integration (Nadasdy 2003).

Sage grouse live in open sagebrush steppe, not mixed sagebrush-conifer savanna, according to ecological science research being produced about the bird by the U.S. Geological Survey (Coates et al. 2017). But this operates on the presumption that habitat is an object that can be untethered from its relations and moved around seamlessly, like any other commodity. Wildlife management, as a practice, depends upon interchangeable units of a species that alienates the subject from its relations in place. Largely unsuccessful efforts at translocation, something widely criticized by Paiute people, demonstrates the animal-as-commodity paradigm in wildlife management where an animal can be displaced from its home and be expected to survive in a completely new location that is unfamiliar. Only an ontology that objectifies animals as units to be counted and optimized for representation as data in abstract population models enables this kind of management practice. While it may be true that sage grouse are more likely to be preyed upon when trees are present, this does not mean a landscape with trees is not habitat. Translocation data shows that birds frequent areas with trees, though at a far lower rate than open steppe. The latest rationale for cutting pine nut forests is the protection of habitat as a kind of ideal-typified set of environmental conditions conducive to living. Trees are viewed as anathema to livability for sage grouse, and therefore trees are targeted for removal. But this depends upon a nature-culture divide that sees human development as separate from natural changes in ecosystems. This is not lost on many land managers. It would be a mistake to suggest they are unaware of the impacts that expanding urban development and resource extractive industries have upon sage grouse populations. The relatively ahistorical assessment of sage grouse, and the boundary work that sets extractive and urban development beyond the purview of land managers, works to instantiate a nature-culture divide that fails to address anything beyond "conifer encroachment." An ecologist with a career of work in the region commented on the long-term management trends, how much of the work on conifer expansion is "not grounded in science" as forests are highly dynamic, expanding and contracting as climate conditions change. And this is hardly a new phenomenon in the region and it does not risk species survival. Rhetoric about conifer expansion also demonstrates that federal management agencies want to make peace with ranchers and ranchers want fewer trees, which they think affect forage for cattle. This is a policy serving social goals, not putatively scientific ones.

Sage grouse do respond to the location of trees, but forests' impacts on overall sage grouse population trends are arguably very low on the list of impacting factors relative to urbanization, grazing, conversion of shrublands to cheatgrass monocultures, resource extraction, and large-scale changes in climate. Sage grouse might not be doing well even with conifer removal, although there is little evidence to assess the results of these removal projects. It is easy to report metrics on cutting trees, but the projects also focus on only one point in the sage grouse lifecycle. Taking trees out does not make instant habitat. Rather than approach the piñon forest as a kind of logical machine, which is what scientists often see in these ecosystems, I am interested in the knots of collaboration among humans and the other-than-human that make these forests the center of vibrant lifeways. These forests grow out of the ruins of capitalist exploitation, reestablishing in areas cleared of trees during the nineteenth-century mining boom and post-war clearing for cattle production. This is the "third nature" Anna Tsing writes about when discussing lively communities that survive capitalist ruin and create novel ecologies (Tsing 2015). When scientists speak of "encroachment," perhaps it could be better framed as resurgence; trees are reestablishing themselves in spaces where they were previously cut down. In some places, trees grow into new environments. In others, they die back as spaces become inhospitable. The overall picture is a rhythmic growing and shrinking as regimes of disturbance—human, climatic, and otherwise—prod these forests into change. Can we imagine land managers as trying to stop history when they move in to cut a section of forest down? After all, forest growth is—like Thomas says—what trees are meant to do. To call this "unnatural" misses the anthropogenic history of landscapes.

While this may appear at first glance to be a straightforward technical and scientific project of environmental management, as many federal agencies and environmental groups argue, I frame these management practices as a cultural and political conflict over the meanings attached to landscapes as instantiated in material practices, such as wildlife conservation, and representational forms, such as landscape photography.

SURPLUS LANDSCAPES AND SPECIES OF CAPITAL

The production of place in Great Basin forests and rangelands references both a material landscape marked by surplus nature and a representational field constituted through imaginaries that rework value around species of capital. Surplus nature captures the way that nature is enrolled in processes of accumulation. While resource extraction such as mining and ranching offers a clear example of accumulation of capital through nature, landscape conservation, including endangered species protection, is another example (Smith 2008; Sayre 2003). Social difference figures centrally in the construction of the sagebrush steppe as an iconic national landscape in need of saving by eliding the meaning and productive values of these spaces for Indigenous communities and multigenerational ranching families.[12] As settler society-driven production of nature sorts out landscapes based upon their value and capacity to sustain the extraction of profit, landscape conservation becomes another form of adjudicating value, with instrumental effects on material livelihoods and livability of landscapes for human and nonhuman beings alike. Central to this is conservation as death-work, that is the biopolitical project of managing populations through the ability to determine whether to sustain or end life based on the perceived needs of the population.[13] In order to save the sage grouse, federal agencies execute projects to kill plants (piñon and juniper trees) and animals (ravens and crows), in service of saving sage grouse. The material remaking of landscapes is premised on the prerogative of land managers to make some spaces livable for certain species through the killing of others. This only becomes possible when these techniques are naturalized as part of system of rational, scientific environmental management that produces new forms of value that sustain the production of profit and maintenance of state control over landscapes. Landscape conservation is predicated on the scaling up of management actions. It means coordinating efforts across scale to produce commensurate effects across a large area. But it also relies on interchangeability in order to work. The spatial abstraction of landscapes as units of habitat or vegetation type is a necessary process to create a gridded landscape amenable to capitalist production.

What kind of space and place is a landscape? David Harvey writes, "space is neither absolute, relative or relational in itself, but it can become one or all simultaneously depending on the circumstances. The problem of the proper conceptualization of space is resolved through human practice with respect to it" (Harvey 2009:13). To the extent that we can ground various modes of producing nature in practices such as ranching, wildlife ecology, and landscape conservation, we can find a way to spatialize it. Paying attention to human practice is then the "only strategy that really works is to keep the tension moving dialectically across all positions in the matrix. This is what allows us better to understand how relational meanings (such as value) are internalized in material things, events and practices (such as concrete labour processes) constructed in absolute space and time" (Harvey 2006:292).

The kinds of practice prevalent on a landscape shift with political-economic changes. Neil Smith's description of "seesaw movement of capital" illustrates how underdevelopment is produced in some spaces and, with time, create the conditions for a high rate of profit (Smith 2008:197). Sagebrush rangelands are characterized by a low rate of return from the raising of livestock through ranching practices (Sayre 2017). The highly heterogeneous distribution of forage resources for livestock means a lower carrying capacity. Ranching is a marginal enterprise for all but the largest operations, and most ranching families engage in the work because of a cultural connection to the land. Although rangelands in this region are overwhelming owned by the federal government, the rights to graze an allotment are held as leases for the use of public lands in cattle production with lease prices set artificially below market rates. This public subsidy for ranching was historically important for sustaining the underdevelopment of the region after an era of heavy mining and livestock grazing that were abandoned as resource availability (and thus profitability) declined. With the rise of environmentalism and environmental laws such as the Endangered Species Act since the 1970s, these landscapes are now being revalued through endangered species and leisure economies driven by urban tourism in rural landscapes. Attention to the production of nature and its links to the cultural politics of nature demonstrates how the material transformation of landscapes highlights the ways that seemingly "out of the way" regions are implicated in transnational economic processes and the circulation of discourses that shape social conditions on the ground (West 2006:36).

This also reflects the qualities of single-asset landscapes. Sagebrush steppe and piñon-juniper are only seen as valuable for cattle forage by ranchers. With endangered species, it is no different. The social category of "endangered species" just replaces one form of capital with another. The symbolic and material capital of sage grouse is just another single-asset mode of valuing the landscape. All of the money oriented around sage grouse study and management—knowing them, controlling them, preventively trying to regulate their life and reproductive cycle—is just a different regime of assigning and regulating value. The conditions of possibility for this single-asset landscape is creating optimized conditions to produce life such that it can be saved.

In the case of sage grouse, the conditions of life are its habitat, which is reduced to an ideal construction of the conditions that maximize its reproduction. This is imagined by land managers as sagebrush steppe with the absence of any trees. Thus, habitat itself becomes materialized on the ground as an object alienated from relations beyond what sustains sage grouse—a mode of commodification that highlights the role of the state in processes of capital formation, regulation, and flow. Markets emerge out of these management regimes, for example, the market for sage grouse habitat that lets someone destroy something in order to enhance the object of production.

In other cases, habitat itself circulates as a commodity. When mining projects destroy land for mineral production, they are required to mitigate the impacts by creating habitat somewhere else. This is often accomplished by cutting piñon trees to make sage grouse habitat in another location. This practice of creating habitat in one place to compensate for its loss in another is called "habitat mitigation banking." But the creation that negates the destruction is premised on the disposability and interchangeability of life as a distinct form. There is no recognition of entanglement in this mode of life. In other words, units of habitat stand in relation to one species and not the clusters of relationships that sustain many species in a given place.

To "conserve" a landscape just for sage grouse is to sever lives from the ecologies that sustain them. Although I focus on piñon pine in this chapter, Paiute people relate to many different plants and animals on the landscape, so it is never only about one species, though piñon trees hold particular cultural import, but the sets of relationships that sustain an ecosystem of plants. Habitat represents the negation of these relations by reducing it to a dyadic relation of a species to a particular type of space in place.

Mining and urban development encroach on sage grouse habitat as much as anything else. Projects to "restore habitat" in piñon forests is a project to replace a landscape of myriad relations to a single one through making refuge for an endangered species and not the many forms of life that also share that place. This culturally informed model of nature assumes that species can be dislocated and replicated. It assumes no necessary locality for being able to survive. It is abstracted such that it can be quantified and moved anywhere. This is a settler-colonial idea—to privilege one form of life, such as endangered species, and move it somewhere else such that it should come to dominate that new place. This form of extractive capitalism suggests that life, or a species, can be anywhere at any time—it assumes an ubiquity of time and space. The living landscape is change over time through difference. A flat thing on a map is amenable to being moved, much like the map's pixel that shifts color, but life is not so easily disentangled.

The bi-state conservation collaborative indexes larger tensions around the politics of place. Placemaking is conventionally approached as something phenomenological that emerges from a human subject. The materialist emphasis of biological ecology where relations are treated as mechanistic chains of causality is in contrast with non-materialist and phenomenological approaches where human placemaking is premised on the experience and perception of the subject. However, the materiality of human placemaking is evident in Indigenous practices of caring for forests through fires and trimming trees, as well as in federal government projects of eradicating species seen as out of place.

The phenomenal world of the nonhuman is also evident in the way sage grouse confound ideal-type models of habitat, living in trees even though scientists think they should not and returning home when they are forcibly relocated by ecologists for a translocation project. When ecologists view telemetry data that shows aberration in patterns of habitation, they dismiss it as abnormal behavior. Translocation projects that remove sage grouse from their nests to relocate them to areas depleted of animals often return to their home. The abysmal success rate of these translocation efforts, where a majority of relocated birds die, shows the acute stress on the birds of being displaced from a home environment. This speaks to the importance of place as an environment sage grouse actively seek to inhabit, even when habitation is disrupted by the exigencies of wildlife management. Paiute people criticize these wildlife management practices for their disrespect toward the animal and the violence of dislocation. This objectification of sage grouse bears an uncanny resemblance to the violent and dehumanizing practices of settler-colonial dispossession where Paiute communities were forcibly relocated from their homelands. The impact of this displacement on community well-being and cultural revitalization is profound, yet still inscrutable to many in settler society that lack the depth of place attachments in Indigenous communities.

Collaborative conservation for federal agency coordinators of the bi-state effort relies on the voluntary participation of government agencies, nonprofit organizations, ranching operations, Indigenous nations, and members of the public. Meetings are mostly open to the public, and records are publicly available on the internet. This represents an uncommon amount of openness relative to contentious policy issues that are adjudicated through fixed public comment processes and behind closed doors. Yet collaborators also rely on subtle mechanisms that enforce boundaries around the objective of management and the entities with the resources to commit staff time to participation. Although many of the collaborative landscape planning efforts purport to be inclusive and representative of many stakeholders, my research shows that they heavily over-represent government agencies, scientists, and environmental organizations. Few ranchers appear at these meetings and even fewer tribal government officials. The claim of inclusivity is true in the sense anyone can join and participate. But those with differing views choose not to participate because there is no process for democratic decision making. Meetings represent only the existence of public forum, not actual influence.[14] The space is not set up to adjudicate different cultural values. When Thomas stands up to speak to the group and relays the sacredness of the piñon pine, members of the audience are keen to allow him to speak, but rarely incorporate his suggestions because they represent incommensurate understandings of proper social relations with plants and animals.

Julia, a Forest Service official, said that at first, sage grouse was the single masthead of sagebrush steppe conservation efforts. This was often to the chagrin of land managers who saw the larger ecosystem and all of its plants and animals as important. But this is how the endangered species legislation is designed. Endangered species become the hook that brings in agency resources. Julia saw a divergence between the cases of the spotted owl and the sage grouse. Spotted owl conservation took the form of a pitched battle between different interests. Its listing decision made management top-down with the U.S. Fish & Wildlife Service having to approve all actions. This effort around sage grouse conservation is a collaborative effort, according to Julia, and uses partnerships to take a more flexible approach that brings together different interests. The objective of collaboration is to avoid the top-down model that listing brings as the U.S. Fish & Wildlife Service takes over central control of management.

Through endangered species protection, sage grouse become invested with symbolic capital as bureaucratic agencies reframe their management projects to fit how this one species will benefit to bring in resources that sustain the objectives of government agencies and conservation nonprofit organizations. This is mixed with the bureaucratic capital of agency investments in endangered species and habitat restoration that sustain their operations and realize their ability to control and remake ecologies of life that create place on federally controlled lands. Much of the debate on how a landscape *ought* to appear is based on historical evidence about sagebrush steppe and pine nut forests. One of the most common sources of evidence for landscape change, including the ostensible invasion of sagebrush steppe by piñon forests, is through photography, which plays an important role in shaping landscape imaginaries in settler-colonial nation-states.

LANDSCAPE IMAGINARIES AND THE SETTLER PASTORAL

Nevada is littered with the ruins of boom-and-bust production. During the nineteenth century, it was a major mining area, and also saw open-range grazing until the forage ecosystem collapsed. Although largely abandoned for decades, these landscapes were revalued by new communities that emerged due to sunbelt population shifts that brought people who desired recreation opportunities and the aesthetic qualities of the landscape. This goes along with the recent conservation campaigns that seek to remake sagebrush steppe into a charismatic landscape through newly marked species such as sage grouse.

The settler pastoral is a naturalized landscape that secures space for settlers from perceived "before" of Indigenous homelands and the "after" of latter-day migrants. It does so on the grounds of productivity, and the production of things of value, such as cows on rangeland or endangered sage grouse on sagebrush steppe, through capitalist relations. It also instantiates forms of belonging that make some things natural to the landscape and other things unnatural. One way this is manifested is in discursive practices that rematerialize the expectations of landscapes through landscape photography in the desert southwest of the United States. (figures 10.1 and 10.2)

Expectations about landscapes are made and reproduced through images. One common tool for marking landscapes as degraded is through repeat photography, or rephotography. This is the practice of taking a photo series of the same subject. It is often described as "before and after" or "then and now" photographs. Key in its methodology is the taking of photographs of the same place, from the same location over a period of time. The practice ranges from the informal—often done without regard for season, frame, or lens—to the putatively "scientific" with precise measurements taken to produce a standard of replicability. The photograph's reliance on the simulation of human visual perception in place, is still fundamentally partial.[15] In some cases, historic photographs are replicated. In others, rephotography is intended from the beginning. It can function as a form of landscape surveillance for expansive spaces where sites may only be visited once every five or ten years. For example, repeat photography of melting glaciers is a common

Figure 10.1 Repeat Photograph of Deadhorse Meadow in California's White Mountains from c. 1925. Photograph courtesy of Deep Springs College Archives.

Figure 10.2 Repeat Photograph of Deadhorse Meadow in California's White Mountains from 2015. Photograph by Daniel W. Pritchett.

visual tool to show the impact of climate change. Climate change itself can only be made visual through its effects—its material character is implicit. Unlike texts or maps, the visual "before and after" of disappearance conjures an effective response and the specter of loss due to climate change. This is the re-materialization of a generalized form (planetary change) in a specific context (the loss of a particular glacier).

As discussed above, one of the most prevalent discourses in the ecology of arid and semi-arid ecosystems is "woody plant encroachment" or the movement or intensification of woody plants in erstwhile grasslands, shrublands, and savannas. "Woody plant encroachment" is viewed as degrading to grass and shrub landscapes and is due to multiple factors, including especially grazing by livestock, invasion by non-native species, and changes in the fire regime due to fire suppression policies. In the Great Basin, pine nut forests (piñon-juniper woodlands in the taxonomy of the ecological sciences) are, according to most scientists and land managers, invading shrublands. This is seen as undesirable for livestock (loss of forage) and for targeted conservation species such as sage grouse (trees enable predation by birds). But there is still a need for an indisputably "objective" ways of explaining ecological dynamics so that the "problem" of invading trees can be matched to the solution, albeit one already being practiced for many decades, the cutting of forests to maximize forage production while avoiding urban development, oil/gas drilling and mining impacts. Moving from the scale of the plot, the lowest common denominator in range science research to the scale of management intervention (landscape) required certain tools.

Photographs allow a scaling up of the unit of analysis that carries with it, via methodology, a process that enables arguments about homogeneous ecological change across landscapes, making the field of intervention the scale of the landscape. This scale jumping in the image mirrors the scale of landscape conservation, which seeks to impact places on a large geographic scale. The landscape caught in repeat captures a sensorium of experience in space and time through the sense of the photograph as "objective reality" enframed by the caption, which is critical to the experience. Rephotography clears the way for imagined geographies of a "natural landscape." The physics of optics is reproduced through the prosthetic eye (camera) into a machine for abstraction. In the Great Basin, these photo dyads are commonly used in the grey literature, including government reports and some peer-reviewed scientific papers, as a form of empirical evidence demonstrating the invasion of conifers into erstwhile shrublands.

Landscape rephotography creates powerful imaginaries. But more important than the practice, the equipment, the camera, or even the photos themselves is what Christopher Pinney reminds us is central: the human eye, "trapped ineluctably in an enfleshed body" repeatedly becoming "the original camera" (Pinney 2008). Landscape rephotography is commonly cited by land managers to substantiate claims about environmental change, especially "conifer encroachment." Unpacking the way that photography is a form of discourse used to tell certain stories, while obscuring others, shows how landscape imaginaries shape current management practices such as piñon forest removal.

CONCLUSION: PLACE AND CULTURAL POLITICS

Gillian Rose (1994:46) asks how cultural practices give rise to representations of place that link structural social inequality and ideology. Cultural politics refers to the ways subjects, identities, and production are co-constituted and mobilized as grounds for contesting social difference. The cultural politics of place examines the material and discursive constitution of locations. Cultures of scientific knowledge production, settler state bureaucracies, and environmental organizations find common ground where invasive forests and threatened birds make their homes or place in the world. Scientific management reifies the material conditions of existence but does so by separating human from nonhuman, and disregarding the ways scientific projects are responsive to bureaucratic agendas and nature-culture dualisms that set human landscapes outside of the purview of ecological study. Wildlife conservation, operating through the paradigm of scientific and managerial control of nature, depends on the separation of nature from culture. Human problems mired in politics such as extractive industries and urban development are commonly set outside the boundaries of land managers' ecological models, and made to stand as social problems outside the control of public land managers rather than social problems that are intertwined with environmental problems. In this case, larger human forces, including climate change, resource extraction, urban development, and tourism are remaking landscapes. Despite all of the efforts to protect sage grouse, their population numbers continue to decline in the region, perhaps owing to processes much larger than can be changed by projects to cut piñon trees or poison birds that prey on sage grouse. Given the planetary scope of human transformation, it is important now more than ever to consider these realms as part of the same structure.

"Collaborative conservation" pushes group interests to converge onto threats that do not undermine group members' institutional power. It bounds group interests by excluding alternative approaches or understandings of environmental change. Oil and gas development, livestock grazing, energy infrastructure, roads, power lines, urban development, and off-road vehicle use are all significant factors impacting sage grouse that get deprioritized from the scope of federal management endeavors. Instead, land managers and environmental groups converge around the least politically contentious threat: seemingly "weedy" trees.[16] The conditions of possibility for invasiveness—trees being in a place they are perceived to not belong—are created when sage grouse are pushed out of valley areas due to development. Great Basin landscapes are remade through images of ecological change that "enframe" certain understandings of the meaning of environmental change for multispecies livability. Endangered species protection, with its focus on single species and movable habitat, is a mode of producing nature in the same way as mining and ranching. Species of capital ultimately index the myriad forms of commodification that permeate landscapes even as what is valued changes across time and space.

NOTES

1. The particular name of this Indigenous government is omitted to protect the confidentiality of those who spoke with me. I use pseudonyms for all named interlocutors.

2. The author is appreciative of Paiute colleagues and community members in the western Great Basin for their insight into landscapes as sites of culture and politics. Additional thanks are due to Kali Rubaii, Paige West, K. Sivaramakrishnan, Yale's Environmental Anthropology Collective, and the editors of this volume, who offered helpful feedback along the way. Final thanks is due for the photographs that appear in this chapter, courtesy of Daniel W. Pritchett and Deep Springs College.

3. The U.S. Forest Service is part of the U.S. Department of Agriculture and the Bureau of Land Management is part of the U.S. Department of the Interior. Nevada has the highest percentage of land owned and managed by the federal government (80 percent) of any state in the country. The Bureau of Land Management, in the Department of the Interior, manages the greatest proportion of these lands (84 percent of public lands in the state). This is followed by the U.S. Forest Service, in the U.S. Department of Agriculture, which manages forested uplands in the higher mountain ranges (10 percent of public lands in the state).

4. Consultation is part of the government-to-government relationship between Tribal Nations and the U.S. federal government. It is enshrined in federal statute and generally involves sending a certified letter to the tribal chairperson or other designated official. The perfunctory approach to consultation is a source of great frustration to tribal governments that seek meaningful engagement, including regular face-to-face meetings and a willingness to substantively address concerns rather than giving mere notification of a preordained outcome.

5. Preserving pine nut trees for their cultural value, according to federal agencies, depends upon their age. The oldest trees are supposed to be avoided in cutting projects because they meet the criteria as a historic or pre-historic object in the language of "cultural resources management." Yet by removing all of the young trees, there is no future forest for subsequent generations, as Thomas notes. This illustrates the

way time functions in settler-colonial conservation contexts by denying Indigenous communities and landscapes the capacity for change without losing their authenticity. The perceived unnaturalness of change becomes the basis for denying political rights and justifying projects of displacement.

6. Urban development does not occur directly on public lands but is enabled by land transfers that effectively privatize erstwhile public lands. This is common with the Bureau of Land Management lands in Nevada, with Las Vegas being the prime example.

7. I reference two phenomena when describing militarism on the U.S. landscapes: the very direct use of desert lands as "wastelands" (in regions like the Great Basin) for military weapons storage, testing, and disposal. And second, I reference environmental management practices used by federal agencies that are militarized in their use of surplus war equipment, military style and organization, and deployment of large-scale, systematic violence against life on landscapes in the name of ecological restoration.

8. Although this article highlights Paiute relations with pine nut trees and sage grouse, there are many different plants and animals that are important. This focus on certain charismatic or keystone species is itself an artifact of Euro-American paradigms of knowing nature.

9. I use the term "environmental organizations" advisedly to reference a group of land conservation, endangered species advocacy, and recreational groups that are not tied to Indigenous communities. In fact, most of these organizations have had little or no contact with Paiute Nations in the region, though this lack of recognition and engagement is slowly beginning to change.

10. There is widespread skepticism about "conifer encroachment" among federal agency staff, but it is still a minority opinion. Skeptics are hesitant to contradict the orthodoxy, however, because of the professional risks it poses to influence in decision-making and advancement in these agencies.

11. It is important to note that scientific conventions in naming ecosystem types are themselves cultural products as much as the naming practices of Paiute communities. Piñon-juniper woodlands are often colloquially referred to as "PJ" by land managers and scientists across the region despite the fact that many woodlands occur as pure stands of piñon or juniper trees. Yet most Indigenous people from the Great Basin say pine nut tree or piñon, if not using the respective Indigenous language term for the plant.

12. Paiute people are also involved in ranching, as both ranch owners and workers, so these are not mutually exclusive groups of people. Though the vast majority of ranchers in the region are Euro-American.

13. For this theoretical framing, I draw upon Foucault (2010) and Agamben (1998) who both theorized the ways that life became the object of state control. Although conventionally applied to the human, these analytical frameworks are also helpful for understanding how the nonhuman can be subject to the same regimes of control.

14. This parallels the earlier discussion of consultation in government-to-government relations between Tribal Nations and the U.S. federal government where there

is no obligation for the latter to address or respond to the concerns of the former, despite statutorily vague language about "meaningfulness." In practice, many agency employees are sympathetic to the interests of Tribal Nations but fail to engage more meaningfully given the institutional inertia of large state bureaucracies.

15. An analogous example is police violence against predominantly young, African-American men in the United States that is increasingly challenged by cell phone videos of police encounters. A commonly implemented solution is the introduction of police body cameras where were purported to instill better behavior and a chronicle of visual evidence. Yet these videos do not offer a complete chronicle of encounter because they are inherently partial, having a perspective of the event, but rarely providing a definitive account.

16. Federal agencies are also limited in their ability to influence some of these activities, such as the preferential treatment for mining enshrined in the General Mining Act of 1872. Statutory obligations can constrict the possible options. Additionally, many key habitats for sage grouse, such as wet meadows, are held as private property.

REFERENCES CITED

Agamben, Giorgio. 1998. *Homo Sacer: Sovereign Power and Bare Life*. Stanford, CA: Stanford University Press.

Alagona, Peter. 2013. *After the Grizzly: Endangered Species and the Politics of Place in California*. Berkeley, CA: University of California Press.

Barker, Joanne. 2011. *Native Acts: Law, Recognition, and Cultural Authenticity*. Durham, NC: Duke University Press.

Blackhawk, Ned. 2006. *Violence Over the Land: Indians and Empires in the Early American West*. Cambridge, MA: Harvard University Press.

Burow, Paul, Samara Brock, and Michael Dove. 2018. Unsettling the Land: Indigeneity, Ontology, and Hybridity in Settler Colonialism. *Environment and Society: Advances in Research* 9:61–78.

Carroll, Clint. 2015. *Roots of Our Renewal: Ethnobotany and Cherokee Environmental Governance*. Minneapolis, MN: University of Minnesota Press.

Cattelino, Jessica. 2015. The Cultural Politics of Water in the Everglades and Beyond. *HAU: Journal of Ethnographic Theory* 5(3):235–50.

Coates, Peter, Brian Prochazka, Mark Ricca, K. Ben Gustafson, Pilar Ziegler, and Michael L. Casazza. 2017. Pinyon and Juniper Encroachment into Sagebrush Ecosystems Impacts Distribution and Survival of Greater Sage-Grouse. *Rangeland Ecology and Management* 70(1):25–38.

Connelly, John, and Clait Braun. 1997. Long-Term Changes in Sage Grouse Centrocercus Urophasianus Populations in Western North America. *Wildlife Biology* 3(1):229–34.

Coulthard, Glen. 2014. *Red Skin, White Masks: Rejecting the Colonial Politics of Recognition*. Minneapolis, MN: University of Minnesota Press.

Cronon, William. 1995. The Trouble with Wilderness; or, Getting Back to the Wrong Nature. In *Uncommon Ground: Rethinking the Human Place in Nature*, edited by William Cronon, pp. 69–90. New York: W.W. Norton & Company.

Flake, Samuel, and Peter Weisberg. 2019. Fine-scale Stand Structure Mediates Drought-induced Tree Mortality in Pinyon–Juniper Woodlands. *Ecological Applications* 29(2):e01831.

Foucault, Michel. 2010. *The Birth of Biopolitics: Lectures at the Collége de France, 1978-1979.* Michel Senellart, ed. Graham Burchell, tran. New York: Palgrave Macmillan.

Harvey, David. 2006. Space as a Keyword. In *David Harvey: A Critical Reader*, edited by Noel Castree and Derek Gregory, pp. 270–93. London: Blackwell.

———. 2009. *Social Justice and the City*. Athens, GA: University of Georgia Press.

Jacobs, Brian. 2011. Spatial Patterns and Ecological Drivers of Historic Pinyon Juniper Woodland Expansion in the American Southwest. *Ecography* 34:1085–95.

Kosek, Jake. 2006. *Understories: The Political Life of Forests in Northern New Mexico*. Durham, NC: Duke University Press.

Lanner, Ronald. 1981. *The Piñon Pine: A Natural and Cultural History*. Reno, NV: University of Nevada Press.

Lanner, Ronald, and Penny Frazier. 2011. The Historical Stability of Nevada's Pinyon-Juniper Forest. *Phytologia* 93(3):360–87.

Li, Tania. 2000. Articulating Indigenous Identity in Indonesia: Resource Politics and the Tribal Slot. *Comparative Studies in Society and History* 42(1):149–79.

Lyons, Kristina. 2016. Decomposition as Life Politics: Soils, Selva, and Small Farmers under the Gun of the U.S.-Colombian War on Drugs. *Cultural Anthropology* 31(1):56–81.

Madley, Benjamin. 2016. *An American Genocide: The United States and the California Indian Catastrophe, 1846–1873*. New Haven, CT: Yale University Press.

McDowell, N.G., A. P. Williams, W. T. Pockman, T. Dickman, S. Sevanto, J. Pangle, J. Limousin, D. Plaut, S. Mackay, J. Ogee, C. Domec, D. Allen, A. Fisher, X. Jiang, J. D. Muss, D. D. Breshears, A. Rauscher, and C. Koven. 2016. Multi-Scale Predictions of Massive Conifer Mortality Due to Chronic Temperature Rise. *Nature Climate Change* 6:295–99.

Middleton Manning, Beth Rose. 2015. Jahát Jatítotòdom: Toward an Indigenous Political Ecology. In *The International Handbook of Political Ecology*, edited by Raymond Bryant, pp. 561–76. Northampton, MA: Edward Elgar Publishing.

Moore, Donald. 2005. *Suffering for Territory: Race, Place, and Power in Zimbabwe*. Durham, NC: Duke University Press.

Moreton-Robinson, Aileen. 2015. *The White Possessive: Property, Power, and Indigenous Sovereignty*. Minneapolis, MN: University of Minnesota Press.

Nadasdy, Paul. 2003. *Hunters and Bureaucrats: Power, Knowledge, and Aboriginal-State Relations in the Southwest Yukon*. Vancouver, BC: University of British Columbia Press.

Pinney, Christopher. 2008. The Prosthetic Eye: Photography as Cure and Poison. *Journal of the Royal Anthropological Institute* 14:S33–S46.

Prudham, W. Scott. 2005. *Knock on Wood: Nature as Commodity in Douglas-Fir Country*. New York: Routledge.

Rose, Gillian. 1994. The Cultural Politics of Place: Local Representation and Oppositional Discourse in Two Films. *Transactions of the Institute of British Geographers* 19(1):46–60.

Rubaii, Kali Jessica. 2018. Counterinsurgency and the Ethical Life of Material Things in Iraq's Anbar Province. Ph.D. Dissertation, University of California, Santa Cruz.

Sayre, Nathan. 2003. *Ranching, Endangered Species, and Urbanization in the Southwest: Species of Capital*. Tucson, AZ: University of Arizona Press.

Sayre, Nathan. 2017. *The Politics of Scale: A History of Rangeland Science*. Chicago, IL: University of Chicago Press.

Shaw, John, Brytten Steed, and Larry DeBlander. 2005. Forest Inventory and Analysis (FIA) Annual Inventory Answers the Question: What Is Happening to Pinyon-Juniper Woodlands? *Journal of Forestry* 103(6):280–85.

Simpson, Audra. 2014. *Theorizing Native Studies*. Andrea Smith, ed. Durham, NC: Duke University Press.

Smith, Neil. 2008. *Uneven Development: Nature, Capital and the Production of Space*. 3rd edition. Athens, GA: University of Georgia Press.

Spence, Mark David. 1999. *Dispossessing the Wilderness: Indian Removal and the Making of the National Parks*. Oxford, UK: Oxford University Press.

Tsing, Anna. 2015. *The Mushroom at the End of the World: On the Possibility of Life in Capitalist Ruins*. Princeton, NJ: Princeton University Press.

Veracini, Lorenzo. 2010. *Settler Colonialism: A Theoretical Overview*. New York: Palgrave Macmillan.

West, Paige. 2006. *Conservation Is Our Government Now: The Politics of Ecology in Papua New Guinea*. Durham, NC: Duke University Press.

Wilkinson, Charles. 2006. *Blood Struggle: The Rise of Modern Indian Nations*. New York: W.W. Norton & Company.

Wolfe, Patrick. 2006. Settler Colonialism and the Elimination of the Native. *Journal of Genocide Research* 8(4):387–409.

Yaffee, Steven. 1994. *The Wisdom of the Spotted Owl*. Washington, DC: Island Press.

Index

Note: *Italic* page numbers refer to figures and page numbers followed by "n" denote endnotes.

Abbey, Edward, 84
Agamben, Giorgio, 194n13
AIRFA. *See* American Indian Religious Freedom Act (AIRFA)
Alagona, Peter, 176
American bison, 134. *See also* wild bison; Yellowstone bison
American Indian Religious Freedom Act (AIRFA), 163
American Prairie Reserve (APR), 145, 146n8
American West ties, 4, 37
Anaya, Rudolfo, 91
Anderson, Benedict, 17
Anderson, M. Kat, 153
Anglos, 83; potential converts, 87; as target subject of enchantment, 86–89
Animal and Plant Health Inspection Service (APHIS), 139, 142, 143
Animas River, 104–6, 108, 113
anthropogenic burning, 155–56
anthropogenic fire, 180
anti-federal movements, 124–27
anti-public lands Utah delegation, 63
Antiquities Act (1906), 11
Archeological Resources Protection Act, 119
Ashburner, W., 159
Assimilative Crimes Act, 122
Atlas uranium mill, 110–11
atomic bomb, 104
Atomic Energy Commission, 104, 105, 108
Austin, J. L., 22

Babbitt, Bruce, 23
Bartrum, Ian, 43, 44, 49
Basso, Keith H., 12–14, 18, 63, 64
Baxley, Willis, 155–56
Bears Ears National Monument, 7, 24, 111
BFC. *See* Buffalo Field Campaign (BFC)
Blackfeet Territory in Montana, 143
BLM. *See* Bureau of Land Management (BLM)
BLM law enforcement: advent of, 119–21; catch-22 of, 121–22
Blomley, Nicholas, 22
Blumm, Michael C., 44, 49

Bon, Lauren, 72, 74
Brenden, John, 141
Briggs, M. C., 160
Brown, F. Lee, 14
brucellosis, 135, 137, 139–43, 145
Buffalo Field Campaign (BFC), 137–40
buffalo nation restoration, 142–44
Bullock, Steve, 136, 141
Bundy, Ammon, 41, 53
Bundy, Cliven, 35, 36, 40–41, 44–46, 50, 52, 53, 118, 120
Bundy Ranch Standoff, 120, 122, 124, 125
Bundy War, 49; mapping revitalization onto, 51–53
Bunkerville, 40–41
Bureau of Indian Affairs, 116
Bureau of Land Management (BLM), 3–6, 8, 24, 36, 39–42, 51, 53, 60, 115, 116, 118, 120, 123–28, 142, 175, 193n3, 194n6

Caffey, David L., 81
California State Water Resources Control Board, 72
caretaker responsibility, 158, 168
Casey, Edgar S., 52, 63
Castillo, Edward, 4
Catron County, New Mexico, 127, 138–42
cattle grazing, with federal government, 42–45
cattle industry, 37–38, 44, 143
cattle ranchers, 35, 38, 135, 148. *See also* ranchers
cattle ranching, 38, 50. *See also* ranching
Cedar City, 41–42, 47
Cedar City Livestock and Heritage Festival, 47
chile, 81; cultivars of, 93; New Mexico cuisine, 95; red and green, 92–95; unripe, 93–94
Chimayo Chile Project, 93, 94
Church of Jesus Christ of Latter-day Saints (LDS), 45–47, 52
Citizens for Balanced Use, 143
Civil Rights Act, 122
Civil War, 19, 21
Clark, Galen, 159, 161
Clean Water Act (CWA), 68
climate change, 181, 191–92
Clinton (President), 23
Cliven Bundy Ranch, Bunkerville, 36
Cold War, 104, 111
collaborative conservation, 176, 179, 187–88, 192
colonialism, 85; contemporary, 83, 86; settler, 4, 27, 177, 178
Colorado Plateau, 104, 107, 109
conflict: over access, 35; over public lands, 12; performatives of collaboration and, 21–25; Wildlife Conflict Resolution Program, 144
conifer encroachment, 179, 181, 183, 192, 194n10
conifer expansion, 180, 182, 183
conservation: cattle ranching and, 50; landscapes and, 179–84
conservationists, 20, 73, 117, 141, 153
conservation protections, on western public lands, 11
Constitutionalist Sheriffs, 125
contemporary colonialism, 83, 86
County Supremacy Movement, 122, 124
Crespi, Juan, 69
cultural authenticity, 178
culturalized space, 12, 52, 63
cultural politics: place and, 176, 192–93; of race and ethnicity, 88
CWA. *See* Clean Water Act (CWA)

Denver-based Radioactive Chemical Company, 103
Department of Interior (DOI), 117, 119
Department of Justice (DOJ), 62
Designated Surveillance Area, 140
difference, 49, 85; social, 184, 192; social-political reality of, 89

Disposal of Excess Federal Lands Act (2017), 123
drilling, 6, 7, 22, 176, 191
Durango mill, 105, 107, 109
Dust Bowl tragedy, 39

Earthjustice, 140, 143
ecologies of belonging, 177, 178
Eisenhower, Dwight D., 102
enchantment: of active engagement, 81–84; Anglos as target subject of, 86–89; of consuming place, 90–92; presence, and absence, 84–86
encroachment, 45, 155, 183; conifer, 179, 181, 183, 192, 194n10; federal regulatory, 45; meadow, 161; of sheep ranching, 38; woody plant, 191
endangered species, 176, 179, 184–88, 193
Endangered Species Act (1973), 23, 127, 179, 185
Energy Fuels, 111–12
environmental assessment (EA), 119, 143, 164, 166
Environmental Impact Statements, 119
environmental injustice, 107
environmentalist, 20, 26, 68, 71, 74, 152
environmental organizations, 176, 179, 180, 188, 192, 194n9; groups, 163, 176
Environmental Protection Agency, 109
Experimental Breeder Reactor I (EBR-I), 101, 102, 110, 113
exploitation, 74; capitalist, 183; of resources, 5, 16, 73, 178
extraction: of hard-rock minerals, 6; resource, 6, 184, 192; of uranium, 6; in western United States, 6
extractive capitalism, 187

Fairfax, Sally K., 20, 21
farmland, 43
federal agencies, 17, 38, 104, 116, 121, 123, 124, 180–82, 184, 187, 193, 194n7, 195n16
Federal Emergency Management Agency, 71
federal funding, Los Angeles River, 68
Federal Land Enforcement Training Center (FLETC), 121
Federal Land Policy and Management Act (FLPMA), 23, 39, 118–20, 127, 180
federal law enforcement, 115, 128; *versus* local law enforcement, 122–23; partnership with local law enforcement, 124
federal law enforcement agents, 116
fence lines, 65n1; Myers Valley property, 61–63
Ferguson, Harvey, 85
Fiesta, 87–90, 95
Finicum, LaVoy, 36, 41, 42
FLETC. *See* Federal Land Enforcement Training Center (FLETC)
Flood Federal Control Act (1936), 70
FLPMA. *See* Federal Land Policy and Management Act (FLPMA)
FoLAR. *See* Friends of the Los Angeles River (FoLAR)
Ford, Richard T., 22
Forest Service, 24, 117, 118
Fort Belknap Reservation, 143
Fort Peck Reservation, 143, 145
Freedom of Information Act, 111
Friends of the Los Angeles River (FoLAR), 71, 76

Gallatin Wildlife Association, 144
Garcetti, Eric, 75
Gardiner Basin, 136, 137, 140
General Mining Act (1872), 195n16
Gilbert, Fabiola Cabeza de Baca, 95
Gold Butte, 40–41
Grand Staircase-Escalante National Monument, 7, 126
grazing, 116–18, 120, 141, 189; use of public lands for, 44

grazing fees, 38, 40–43
Great Basin landscapes, 176–81, 184, 191
Great Depression, 38–39, 59–60, 104
Greater Yellowstone Area, 135, 143
green chile, 92–95

habitat mitigation banking, 186
Hammond, Dwight, 41
Hammond, Steven, 41
Harkin, Michael E., 50
harvesting, 26, 156, 157, 158; commercial and recreational, 15; selective, 157; sustainable, 143
Hatch, 94
heritage, 47–49
Hispanic New Mexicans, 89–90
Hispanics, 83, 87
Hispano Catholicism, 93
Homestead Act (1862), 44
homesteading, 38, 39
Hoover, Herbert, 38–39
Hueper, W. C., 108
human-nonhuman boundary, 27
hunting, of bison, 135–37
Hyperion Water Reclamation Plant, 79n2

IBMP. *See* Interagency Bison Management Plan (IBMP)
Idaho Falls, 101, 102, 110, 113
Idaho National Laboratories, 101
identity, 47–49, 84–85, 88, 92; cultures and, 90; racial, 90
Indigenous communities, Indigenous Peoples, 85, 177, 178, 180, 182, 184; political ecology, 177
industrial uses, public lands, 16, 24
inequality: social-political reality of, 89; structural, 40, 192
Ingram, Helen, 14, 22
Interagency Bison Management Plan (IBMP), 26, 136–37, 143
International Agency on Atomic Energy, 111
InterTribal Bison Cooperative (ITBC), 142, 143

Jackson, Lisa, 77
Jacobs, Comfrey, 138
Jeffrey City, 101, 112

Kerr-McGee uranium mill, 107
Kosek, Jake, 14

LA County Flood Control District, 70
LA-Glendale Water Reclamation Plant, 79n2
Lakota, 134, 142, 143, 157; Lakota Ghost Dance, 54; Sioux, 54
land-claim narrative, 52
Land Management Police Training (LMPT), 121
Land of Enchantment, 82, 83, 94
landscape conservation, 177, 184, 185, 191
landscape imaginaries, 189–92, *190*
landscape rephotography, 191–92
landscapes, 176; anthropogenic, 158–59; and conservation, 179–84; expectations about, 189; Great Basin landscapes, 176–81, 184, 191; park, 5–6; place as, 82; public land–dominated, 35; rural, 185; settler-colonial, 69–70; settler-colonial visions of, 178; Sierra-Nevada landscape, 152; single-asset, 186; surplus landscapes, 184–89
language of rights, 13
law enforcement, 115; anti-federal law enforcement legislation, 125; BLM law enforcement, 119–22; federal, 115, 128. *See also* federal law enforcement; local, 115, 122. *See also* local law enforcement
Lazarus, Richard J., 24
Leopold, A. Starker, 134
Leopold Report, 134, 138, 141, 144, 145, 146n2
Leshy, John D., 14

livelihood, 35, 37, 40, 45, 51, 52, 54, 117, 139, 140, 177, 184
LMPT. *See* Land Management Police Training (LMPT)
Local Enforcement for Local Lands Act (2017), 123
local-federal struggle, history of, 116–19
local law enforcement, 115, 122; *versus* federal law enforcement, 122–23; partnership with federal law enforcement, 124; to patrol public lands, 128
Looking Horse, Avrol, 143
Los Angeles River, 67–68; challenges, 78–79; place of (and for) nature, 75–78; significance and history of, 69–71; water resource, 71–75
low-carbon-emitting electricity source, 102
lung cancer, 108, 109

Malheur National Wildlife Refuge, 36, 41, 42, 46, 53, 120
management framework plan (MFP), 118
Manhattan Project, 104
"manifest destiny," 4
McFarlane, Todd, 42
McGee, William J., 73
Mease, Mike, 137
Merrill, Karen R., 37, 38, 40
Mesa Verde National Park, 105
Metabolic Studio, 71–72, 74
MFP. *See* management framework plan (MFP)
mining, 6, 184, 186; uranium, 111; and urban development encroach, 186–87
Mining Act (1872), 6
Montana Department of Livestock, 135, 137
Montana Farm Bureau Federation, 140
Monticello Mill, 110
Mountain Crow Chief Plenty Coups, 142
Muir, John, 77, 152
Museum of New Mexico, 86
Myers Valley property, 59–60, 63; fence lines, property boundaries, and physical barriers, 61–63; private ranching and the federal government, 60–61

Nadasdy, Paul, 14
National Environmental Policy Act (NEPA), 23, 39, 119, 164, 180
National Forest Management Act (1976), 23
National Monument: Bears Ears National Monument, 24, 111; creation of, 16; Grand Staircase-Escalante National Monument, 126
national myths, 19
National Park Service (NPS), 3, 5, 19–20, 24, 26, 27nn2, 3, 116, 135, 162; creation of, 167; environmental assessment, 164; iteration of rules and regulations, 162; potential litigation, 167; regional/national directive, 163; revised plant gathering regulations, 164; traditional knowledge protection, 165
National Park system, 11, 19, 20, 168
National Resources Defense Council, 144
National Wildlife Federation, 144
Native Americans, 90, 151, 160, 168; cultural life, 167; diets, 155; gathering rights, 166; groups, 136; population, 83; resource stewards, 164; tribal nation, 175
Native North Americans, 7, 8, 16, 18, 21–23, 27; governmental entities, 23; modernity, 15; rights, 7, 15, 18, 19, 23, 165; self-determination, 23, 178; sovereign land claims, 12, 15, 16, 153, 170, 177; tribes, 26
nativism, 51
natural resource, 62, 73, 155; vitality and quality of, 169

Navajo Nation, 101, 107, 109, 110
Nay Book, 45–47
NEPA. *See* National Environmental Policy Act (NEPA)
Nesper, Larry, 14
Nevada: anti-federal government organizations and militias, 40–41; boom-and-bust production, 189; federal government, 193n3; nuclear tests, 113; public lands, 125; threats to sage grouse, 179
Nevada-California borderlands, 177
Nevada nuclear tests, 113
Nevada Test Site, 101
Newmark, William, 138
New Mexico, 81; culture, 83; enchantment, 81–86. *See also* enchantment; narrative, 82; natural environment, 82; red chile and green chile, 92–96; U.S. nuclear project in, 88
New Mexico Native North Americans, 82–83, 85
North American Free Trade Agreement, 51
nostalgic imagined past, 47–49
NPS. *See* National Park Service (NPS)
nuclear bomb test, 106, 113
nuclear energy, 102
nuclear fission chain reaction, 101
nuclear plant, 103, 111, 112
nuclear power, 101–3, 114; public perception of, 110
Nuclear West, 103, 114
Nutex Company, 103
Nye County, Nevada, 126–27
Nye County Ordinance, 127

Obama (President), 11, 16, 23
occupations, 35, 36, 44, 50
Olmsted-Bartholomew design, 76
Organic Act, 117, 133, 162, 166
Owyhee County, Idaho, 126

Paiute Indian Tribe of Utah, 8
Paiute Indian Tribe of Utah Restoration Act (1980), 7
Paiute Nation, 175, 178, 182, 186, 187, 193n2, 194n9
Palo Verde nuclear plant, 103
park landscapes, 5–6
Partner Organizations (POs), 121
Payne, Ryan, 36, 41
PEER. *See* Public Employees for Environmental Responsibility (PEER)
performatives, 18, 22; of collaboration and conflict, 21–25
physical barriers, Myers Valley property, 61–63
Pinchot, Gifford, 73
pine nut forests, 178, 180, 183, 189, 191
piñon-juniper woodland, 179–81, 194n11
Pioneer Day, 47
place: and cultural politics, 176, 192–93; enchantment of consuming, 90–92; as landscape, 82; of (and for) nature, Los Angeles River, 75–78; production in Great Basin forests and rangelands, 184; in rural Utah, 63–64
place-based activities, 18
place-based identity, 26
placemaking, 13, 76, 187
plant gathering, 164–67
Portola, Gaspar de, 69
predator eradication, 134, 135
Preemption Act (1841), 44
private land, 60, 65n1; *versus* public land, 12, 23, 59, 63
property, 22, 59, 60; Myers Valley, 59–63; notion of, 24; ownership of, 40; private, 44, 71, 73, 137, 140, 145; public, 38
Public Employees for Environmental Responsibility (PEER), 163, 166, 167

public lands: boundaries of, 13, 16; clashes for, 3, 8; dimension of, 21; hegemonic histories about, 14; leasing, 25; legitimate interest in, 19; notion of, 15; and private lands boundaries, 12; recreational uses and industrial uses, 16; variety of categorizations, 15
public lands agencies, 5, 13, 42, 43, 59, 62
public-private land tensions, 59
Pueblo Revolt, 87

race, 86, 88, 89
racial identity, 90
radium, 103, 110
ranchers, 26, 35, 38, 62, 105, 139, 141, 186, 188; coalition of, 135; and federal government, tensions between, 36; LDS, 46; militia, 36; private, 60; resentment, 141; western cattle ranchers, 35–36
ranching, 14, 35, 139, 184, 185; culture, 6; environmental impact, 54n2; in rural Utah, 63–64; in Western U.S. Federal policy, 59
range war, 36; mapping revitalization onto Bundy War, 51–53; as revitalization movement, 49–53; and sagebrush rebellions, 37–40; under siege on ecological margins, 50–51
range warriors, 35, 43, 45, 46, 54
Reagan, Ronald, 12, 39
Reconstruction Finance Corporation (RFC), 104
recreational space, 78, 79
recreational uses, public lands, 16
Recycled Water Advisory Group, 74
red chile, 92–95
reservation system, 4
resource extraction, 6, 184, 192
resources: cultural resources management, 193n5; economic, 5; exploitation of, 5, 16, 73, 178; Native Americans resource stewards, 164; natural, 62, 73, 155; renewable, "beneficial use" of, 45; shared public natural resources, 12; traditional resource management, 155; water, 71–75
revisionary policies, plant gathering, 164–67
revitalization movement, 35, 49–50; mapping onto range war/Bundy War, 51–53; under siege on ecological margins, 50–51
Rio Grande Valley, 91, 93–95
river management, 71
Roosevelt Arch, 133, 138
Roosevelt, Theodore, 73, 116

sagebrush rangelands, 185
sagebrush rebellions, 19, 21, 23, 119; range wars and, 37–40
sagebrush steppe, 179, 180, 182, 184, 186, 188, 189
sage grouse, 175, 176, 178, 179, 182–84, 186–89, 191–93, 194n8; emergence of, 176; population and habitat, 179
Santa Fe, 88, 89, 95; Fiesta, 87–90, 95; Holy Faith, 87; indigenous chiles, 94; languages on, 84
Sarat, Austin, 21
selective harvesting, 157
senses of place, 11; exploring, 14; grounded in, 18–21; integral part of configuring places, 21; Los Angeles River, 68; and public lands, 12; shared senses of place, 17, 20, 25; short-term and long-term practices, 13; social senses of place, 18; social sensibilities, 13
settler colonialism, 4, 27, 177, 178
settler-colonial landscape, 69–70
settler-colonial violence, 178
settler government agencies, 26
settler pastoral, 189–92, *190*
settlers, 3, 4, 44, 47, 177, 189

settler society, 19, 24; social imaginary, 16
settler state sovereign land claims, 16
sheep camp, 48, 55n8, 65n2
Sheriff Supremacy Movement, 125
Shoshone-Bannock case, 4–5
Sierra Forest Reserve, 117
Sierra-Nevada landscape, 152
Skousen, W. Cleon, 46, 55n7
Smith, Joseph, 45, 46
Smith, Neil, 185
social-political reality, of difference and inequality, 89
soil erosion, 180–81
Southern Paiute, 7, 8
Southern Ute Indian Reservation, 105
space, 63, 186, 188; conceptualization of, 185; culturalized, 12, 52, 63; recreational, 78, 79
Spanish colonization, 83
Spanish Empire, 83, 90
species, of capital, 184–89
Spence, Mark David, 14, 19, 133–34
Standing Rock Sioux Nation, 11
standoffs, 35, 36, 44, 50
Stationary Low Power Reactor Number One (SL-I), 114
Stephens Creek Capture Facility, 137, 138
Stevens, Stan, 22
stormwater, 68, 70, 71, 73, 74, 78, 79
Stormwater Capture Master Plan, 74
Sundry Civil Bill (1897), 118
surplus landscapes, 184–89

Taylor Grazing Act (1934), 37, 39, 44
techno-scientific arguments, 180
TEK. *See* traditional ecological knowledge (TEK)
territorial lands, 15, 16
thorium, 107, 109, 110
Thornton, Thomas F., 14, 18, 22, 24
Thunder, Rosalie Little, 137, 138
Timber Culture Act (1873), 116
time immemorial, 15, 18
tourism, 82, 95, 96, 185, 192
Toxic Substances and Diseases Registry, 104
traditional ecological knowledge (TEK), 182
traditional ecological practices: Euro-American settlement, 159; *Mariposa Gazette,* 159–60; memorandum of understanding, 163; National Park Service, 162; park creation, surveillance, and displacement of, 158–63; park-imposed land-use regulations, 159
traditional management, 153–55, 158, 159, 161, 167–69
translocation project, 187
Trump, Donald, 7, 11, 12, 16, 20, 41, 72, 112
Tsing, Anna, 183

Udall, Stewart, 134
United Nuclear Corporation, 109
United States, 11; creation of national parks, 151; European habitation in, 82; myths of, 16
United States Forest Service (USFS), 3, 5, 6, 8, 24, 36, 38, 39, 43, 60–63, 115, 116, 120, 123, 127, 142, 175, 193n3
United States-Mexican War, 87
Unlawful Enclosures Act (1885), 38
uranium, 102, 103, 105, 107; extraction of, 6; mining and milling operations, 110, 111
Uranium Watch, 110, 111
urban development, 186–87, 192, 194n6
U.S. Constitution, 122, 129; Article 4 of, 46; Article 10 of, 43; God, the Nay Book and, 45–47; "property clause" of, 44
U.S. Environmental Protection Agency (EPA), 67
U.S. federal ecological restoration project, 175

U.S. federal government, 16, 175, 193n4, 194n14; Myers Valley property, 60–61
U.S. federal public domain lands, 15, 20
U.S. Fish and Wildlife Service (USFWS), 3, 5, 24, 116, 179, 188
USFS. *See* United States Forest Service (USFS)
USFWS. *See* U.S. Fish and Wildlife Service (USFWS)
U.S. Public Health Service, 105–7
U.S. uranium industry, 111, 112
U.S. Vanadium Corporation, 104
Utah, 55n11; Bears Ears National Monument in, 24; Cedar City, 41–42; criminal trespass case in, 121; nuclear plant in, 111; Paiute Indian Tribe of Utah, 8; Western Freedom Festival, 7
Utah Transfer of Public Lands Act (2012), 55n11

Vanadium Corporation of America, 105, 106, 108

Wallace, Anthony F. C., 49, 51, 55n9
wastewater recycling, 74, 79n2
Wastewater Treatment Plant, 75
water extraction, 78, 79
water management, 73, 74
Water Reclamation Plant, 79n2
western anti-government extremist groups, 125
Western Freedom Festival, 7, 47–49
"Western Legends Heritage and Music Festival," 6
western public lands, 8, 23, 43, 115, 122, 128; conservation protections on, 11; establishment of, 118
Western Rangelands Property Rights workshop, 42
western United States: extraction in, 6; public land–dominated landscape, 35; public land in, 3
Western U.S. Federal policy, 59
White Mesa Mill, 110–12
wild bison, 135; food source, 142; migration, 140; *See also* Yellowstone bison
wilderness, 152, 153, 169; historical impacts of, 154; Western fiction of, 153–54; Western notions of, 167
Wilderness Act (1964), 23, 154
Wilderness Study Area (WSA), 120, 124
Wildlife Conflict Resolution Program, 144
wildlife conservation, 184, 192
wildlife management, 140, 182, 187
Wildlife Refuge, 41
Wise-Use Movements, 122, 124
Wolfe, Patrick, 177, 178
woody plant encroachment, 191
World Wildlife Fund, 145
Wylie, Heather, 76

Ydarte, Maria Lebrado (Totuya), 153
Yellowstone bison, 136, 140, 144, 146n1. *See also* wild bison
Yellowstone National Park, 5, 20, 26, 133, 134, 138, 140, 142, 145, 146; hunting inside of, 135; management practices, 135; number of bison in, 139; ongoing culling program, 144–45; predator eradication, 135
Yosemite Grant Act, 159
Yosemite National Park, 20, 151, 160–62
Yosemite Park Commission, 159, 168
Yosemite Valley, 153–54, 161; anthropogenic landscape, 158–59; traditional ecological management in, 154–58
Yosemite Valley Native North American tribes, 151–152

About the Editors

Kathleen M. Sullivan, PhD, is a professor in the Department of Anthropology at California State University Los Angeles. She has published in *PoLAR: Political and Legal Anthropology Review* and *Studies in Law, Politics, and Society*. Her research examines democratic and bureaucratic governance pertaining to coastal zones, oceans, public lands, wild capture, and aquaculture fisheries, including the roles of oceans law, science, media, and big data. Her ethnographic field research focuses on the west coast of North America (the United States and British Columbia), and southern Chile.

James H. McDonald holds a PhD in anthropology from Arizona State University, and most recently served as provost at the University of Montevallo, Alabama's public liberal arts university. Previously, he was the dean of Humanities and Social Sciences at Southern Utah University and worked in a variety of administrative positions from department chair to associate vice provost at the University of Texas at San Antonio. He is an applied cultural anthropologist with thirty years of fieldwork experience in rural Mexico and the Maya Western Highlands of Guatemala. Much of his research centers on problems concerning rural development, inequality, globalization, power, governance dynamics, and the anthropology of higher education.

About the Contributors

Rochelle Bloom is a research associate with the Department of Anthropology at Portland State University. With an advanced degree in cultural heritage, she collaborates in ethnographic and ethnohistorical research focusing on the U.S. national parks. She has been stationed at Yosemite National Park, providing on-site research support to park staff, PSU researchers, and park-associated Native American tribes.

Paul Berne Burow is a PhD student in the School of the Environment and Department of Anthropology at Yale University. Paul's research interests include the political ecology of forests and rangelands, the cultural politics of nature and belonging, and the history of conservation and settler colonialism in western North America. He has spent more than a decade working with Indigenous and other rural communities in California and Nevada on issues of environmental justice and sustainable rural prosperity.

Douglas Deur, PhD, is a research faculty in the Department of Anthropology, Portland State University and Adjunct Professor in Environmental Studies, University of Victoria, British Columbia. He specializes in Indigenous North American ethnoecology, the meaning and contestation of sacred sites, and Indigenous communities' enduring attachments to landscapes and resources in parks and other public lands. For over two decades, he has been the primary third-party researcher assisting Native American tribes and the U.S. National Park Service in documenting Indigenous peoples' past and current connections to lands and resources in Western national parks.

David Knowlton, PhD, is a professor of anthropology at Utah Valley University. Although much of his work is in the Andes, Knowlton maintains an intellectual interest in the American West, where he both grew up and lives. He was the bilingual director at Human Pursuits, which organized bilingual reading and discussion groups on Latino (including especially New Mexican) and Latin American literature in six western states. While there, he also wrote many overviews and study guides. Knowlton publishes in Cuzco Eats about food, culture, and land. He is the author of pieces on Latinos in Kansas, Colorado, and Utah. Most recently, Knowlton presented on fiestas in Cusco as well as on conservatism and place among Mormons at the Society for the Scientific Study of Religion. He is also the author of "Lamanites, Apologetics, and Tensions in Mormon Anthropology," in Blair Van Dyke and Loyd Erickson, eds, *Perspectives on Mormon Theology: Apologetics* (2017) and "Global standards vs. local practices: LDS and drinking in rural Bolivia" in John Charles Duffy and David Howlett, eds *Mormonism: The Basics* (2016).

Sayd Randle, PhD, is an S.V. Ciriacy-Wantrup postdoctoral fellow in the Department of Geography at the University of California Berkeley. Trained as an ethnographer and a political ecologist, her research interests include environmental change, infrastructure, urban development, and water management. She received her PhD from Yale University's combined degree program in anthropology and environment studies in 2018 and previously held a postdoctoral appointment with the University of Southern California's Society of Fellows in the Humanities.

Jacqueline J. Russell has been the business manager for the College of Humanities and Social Sciences at Southern Utah University since 2015. Prior to moving to Cedar City, she worked for the National Park Service and served ten years in the United States Army; six years as an active-duty officer in the Adjutant General Corps; and four years as an enlisted member in the Corps of Engineers. During that time, Jacqueline had the opportunity to take on several leadership roles and to deploy on a fifteen-month combat tour to Iraq. Jacqueline completed her BA in Philosophy, Politics, and Law from Binghamton University in 2004, her Masters of Business Administration with a Human Resources concentration from Texas A&M-Central Texas in 2012, and is currently a doctoral candidate in Organizational Change and Leadership at the University of Southern California. She is a project management professional (PMP) and a Lean Six Sigma Black Belt (LSSBB). Her interests include women's and veterans' initiatives, human resource development, and continuous improvement.

Bruce R. Tebbs was born the sixth child and first son to a mathematics professor and rancher in the high mountain desert of Southern Utah. His father was excited to have a son work with him on the ranch and began taking Bruce with him into the mountains in his infancy. As he matured through adolescence, Bruce was given the responsibility of living on the mountain, irrigating the pastureland, and caring for the livestock during the summers. Bruce is the fourth generation to manage the ranch, which includes private property, BLM, and Forest Service permits in Garfield, Iron, and Beaver counties. Bruce holds a master's degree in Business Administration and has spent the past sixteen years working for Southern Utah University, managing the academic budget. He continues his family tradition of ranching with his four children, who love going to the ranch with him.

Jonathan P. Thompson has been an environmental journalist focusing on the American West since he signed on as a reporter and photographer at the Silverton Standard and the Miner newspaper in 1996. He has written for *High Country News* since 2006, and his work has appeared in numerous publications. He is the author of *River of Lost Souls: The Science, Politics, and Greed Behind the Gold King Mine Disaster* (2018) and the upcoming novel *Behind the Slickrock Curtain* (2020). He currently splits his time between Colorado and Bulgaria with his wife Wendy and daughters Lydia and Elena.

Scott Turner, PhD, is a professor of political science at the University of Montevallo in central Alabama, where he teaches courses on American government, international relations, and political theory. He taught at the University of Nairobi on a Fulbright scholarship in 2002–2003. His research interests include global civil society, human rights, national parks, and public lands.

www.ingramcontent.com/pod-product-compliance
Ingram Content Group UK Ltd.
Pitfield, Milton Keynes, MK11 3LW, UK
UKHW041842031026
15587UKWH00002B/962

9 781793 637062